LITERARY MASTERPIECES

ISSN 1526-1522

LITERARY MASTERPIECES

Volume **9**

The Woman Warrior and China Men

Deborah L. Madsen
South Bank University - London

A MANLY, INC. BOOK

Detroit
New York
San Francisco
London
Boston
Woodbridge, CT

THE WOMAN WARRIOR AND CHINA MEN

Matthew J. Bruccoli and Richard Layman, *Editorial Directors*

While every effort has been made to ensure the reliability of the information presented in this publication, The Gale Group does not guarantee the accuracy of the data contained herein. Gale accepts no payment for listing; and inclusion of any organization, agency, institution, publication, service, or individual does not imply endorsement of the editors or publisher. Errors brought to the attention of the publisher and verified to the satisfaction of the publisher will be corrected in future editions.

This publication is a creative work fully protected by all applicable copyright laws, as well as by misappropriation, trade secret, unfair competition, and other applicable laws. The authors and editors of this work have added value to the underlying factual material herein through one or more of the following: unique and original selection, coordination, expression, arrangement, and classification of the information.

All rights reserved including the right of reproduction in whole or in part in any form. All rights to this publication will be vigorously defended.

Copyright ©2001

The Gale Group

27500 Drake Road

Farmington Hills, MI 48331

ISBN 0-7876-5129-X

ISSN 1526-1522

Printed in the United States of America

10 9 8 7 6 5 4 3 2 1

ADVISORY BOARD

Matthew J. Bruccoli
    Jefferies Professor of English
    University of South Carolina

Denis Donoghue
    Henry James Professor of English and American Letters
    New York University

George Garrett
    Henry Hoyns Professor of Creative Writing
    University of Virginia

Trudier Harris
    J. Carlyle Sitterson Professor of English
    University of North Carolina at Chapel Hill

Hugh Kenner
    Franklin Professor and Callaway Professor
    University of Georgia

Alvin Kernan
    Senior Advisor in the Humanities
    The Andrew W. Mellon Foundation

Richard Layman
    Vice President
    Bruccoli Clark Layman

R.W.B. Lewis
    Neil Grey Professor, Emeritus
    Yale University

Harrison Meserole
    Distinguished Professor of English, Emeritus
    Texas A & M University

TABLE OF CONTENTS

A Note to the Reader
    George Garrett ix

Acknowledgments xi

THE WOMAN WARRIOR AND CHINA MEN

ABOUT THE WOMAN WARRIOR AND CHINA MEN 1

    Plot Summary 1

    Information about Maxine Hong Kingston 18

    People of The Woman Warrior 21

    People of China Men 24

    Themes, Images, Allusions, and Metaphors 27

THE EVOLUTION OF THE WOMAN WARRIOR AND CHINA MEN 37

THEMES IN THE WOMAN WARRIOR AND CHINA MEN 47

    Summary of Themes 47

    Autobiographical Themes 49

    The Author's Era 54

    Events of the Day 58

    Representations in Other Literature 61

CRITICAL RESPONSE TO THE WOMAN WARRIOR AND CHINA MEN 69

    Critical Summary 69

    Critical Survey 75

    Critical Selections 78

Approaches of the Critics 96

The Woman Warrior *and* China Men *Critically Analyzed* 98

THE WOMAN WARRIOR AND *CHINA MEN* IN HISTORY................ **107**

Public Response 107

Historical Reflections 109

The Woman Warrior *and* China Men *through Time* 120

ADAPTATIONS OF *THE WOMAN WARRIOR* **122**

THE WOMAN WARRIOR AND *CHINA MEN* AS STUDIED **126**

RESOURCES FOR STUDY OF *THE WOMAN WARRIOR* AND *CHINA MEN* ... **143**

Study Questions 145

Glossary of Terms in
The Woman Warrior *and* China Men 149

Unfamiliar Words or Terms in
The Woman Warrior *and* China Men 151

Historical Events, People, and Places in
The Woman Warrior *and* China Men 155

Selected Bibliography 157

MASTER INDEX... **163**

A NOTE TO THE READER

Think of it this way: you are about to embark on a journey. This book is, among other things, designed to be at once a reservation and a round-trip ticket. The purpose of the journey, the goal and destination, is for you to experience, as fully and as deeply as you can, a masterpiece of literature. Reading a great work is not a passive experience. It will be demanding and, as you will see, well rewarded.

by George Garrett, Henry Hoyns Professor of Creative Writing, the University of Virginia

What is a masterpiece? The answer is easy if you are dealing with the great works of antiquity—for example, the *Iliad* and *Odyssey* of Homer, the tragedies of Aeschylus, Sophocles, and Euripides—works that have endured for millenia and even outlasted their original language. Closer in time there are the accepted monuments of our languages and culture, such as the plays of Shakespeare, the *Divine Comedy* of Dante, and the comedies of Molière. But here and now we are dealing with work that is nearer to us in time, that speaks to and about persons, places, and things that we either know at first hand or at least know about. These works are accepted by critical consensus (and tested in the marketplace and in the classroom) as among the most original and influential works of their times. It remains for you to experience their power and originality.

There is much to be gained from close and careful study of a great book. You will always find much more than you expected to, than you are looking for. Whether we know it and admit it or not, we are one and all constantly being changed and shaped by what we read. One definition of a literary masterpiece is that it is a great work that can touch us most deeply. It can be, is, if you are wide awake and fully engaged, a profound experience. Lighthearted or deadly serious, it is about things that matter to us. The Gale Study Guides are intended to help you to enjoy and to enlarge your understanding of literature. By an intense focus, these Guides enhance the values you discover in reading enduring works. Discovery is always an important part of the process. With guidance you will see how personal discoveries can be made and, equally important, can be shared with others studying the same book. Our literary culture is, ideally, a community. This book is meant to serve as your introduction to that community.

From the earliest days of our history (until the here and now), readers have looked for pleasure and meaning in whatever they read. The two are inextricable in literature. Without pleasure and enjoyment, there can be no permanent meaning. Without value and significance, there is no real pleasure. Ideally, the close study of literary masterpieces—comedy or tragedy, past and present—will increase our pleasure and our sense of understanding not only of the individual work in and of itself but also of ourselves and the world we inhabit.

There is hard work involved. What you have labored to master you will value more highly. And reading is never exclusively a passive experience. You have to bring the whole of yourself to the experience. It becomes not a monologue, but a dialogue between you and the author. What you gain from the experience depends, in large part, on what you bring and can give back. But, as great voices have told us since the dawn of literature, it is well worth all the effort, indeed worth any effort.

We learn how powerful words can be. The language of great voices speaking to us across time and space, yet close as a whisper, matters enormously. Sooner or later, our buildings will crumble; our most intricate and elegant machines will cough and die and become rusty junk; and our grand monuments and memorials will lose all their magic and meaning. But we know that our words, our language, will last longer than we do, speaking of and for us, over centuries and millenia. Listening to great voices, reading their words and stories in the enduring works of literature, we are given a reward of inestimable value. We earn a share in their immortality.

You will meet some memorable characters, good and bad, and you are going to participate in unforgettable events. You will go to many places, among them the Africa of Chinua Achebe, the England of Virginia Woolf, the China of Maxine Hong Kingston. You can visit 1920s Paris with Ernest Hemingway, the magical Latin America of Gabriel García Márquez, the Mississippi of William Faulkner, the dark side of San Francisco with Dashiell Hammett. Gale Study Guides are good maps to the literary territory. Envision the journey as a kind of quest or pilgrimage, not without difficulty, that can change your understanding of life.

ACKNOWLEDGMENTS

This book was produced by Manly, Inc. R. Bland Lawson is the series editor and Teresa D. Tynes is the in-house editor.

Production manager is Philip B. Dematteis.

Copyediting supervisor is Phyllis A. Avant. The copyediting staff includes Brenda Carol Blanton, Allen E. Friend Jr., Melissa D. Hinton, William Tobias Mathes, Nancy E. Smith, and Elizabeth Jo Ann Sumner.

The index was prepared by Alex Snead.

Layout and graphics series team leader is Karla Corley Brown. She was assisted by Zoe R. Cook and Janet E. Hill, graphics supervisor.

Permissions editor is Jeff Miller.

Photography supervisor is Paul Talbot. Photography editors are Charles Mims and Scott Nemzek. Digital photographic copy work was performed by Joseph M. Bruccoli.

Systems manager is Marie L. Parker.

Typesetting supervisor is Kathleen M. Flanagan. The typesetting staff includes Patricia M. Flanagan, Mark J. McEwan, Pamela D. Norton, and Alison Smith.

Following is a list of the copyright holders who have granted us permission to reproduce material in this volume of Gale Study Guides to Great Literature. Every effort has been made to trace copyright, but if omissions have been made, please let us know.

COPYRIGHTED MATERIAL IN *Literary Masterpieces, Vol. 9: The Woman Warrior* **and** *China Men,* **WAS REPRODUCED FROM THE FOLLOWING SOURCES:**

Bergland, Betty Ann. "Representing Ethnicity in Autobiography." *Yearbook of English Studies,* 24 (1994): 83–84.

Chin, Frank. "The Most Popular Book in China." In his *The Chinaman Pacific and Frisco R. R. Co.: Eight Stories*. Minneapolis: Coffee House Press, 1988. Reprinted in *Maxine Hong Kingston's The Woman Warrior: A Casebook*, edited by Sau-Ling Cynthia Wong. New York & Oxford: Oxford University Press, 1999.

Islas, Arturo, and Marilyn Yalom. "Interview with Maxine Hong Kingston." In *Conversations with Maxine Hong Kingston*, edited by Paul Skenazy and Tera Martin. Jackson: University Press of Mississippi, 1998.

Juhasz, Suzanne. "Maxine Hong Kingston: Narrative Technique and Female Identity." In *Contemporary American Women Writers*, edited by Catherine Rainwater and William J. Scheick. Lexington: University Press of Kentucky, 1985.

Kingston, Maxine Hong. "Cultural Mis-readings by American Reviewers." In *Asian and Western Writers in Dialogue*, edited by Guy Amirthanayagam. London: Macmillan, 1982.

Kubota, Gary. "Maxine Hong Kingston: Something Comes from Outside Onto the Paper." In *Conversations with Maxine Hong Kingston*.

Li, David Leiwei. "*China Men*: Maxine Hong Kingston and the American Canon." *American Literary History*, 2 (Fall 1990): 482–483.

Lim, Shirley Geok-lin. "Immigration and Diaspora." In *An Interethnic Companion to Asian American Literature*, edited by King-Kok Cheung. New York & Cambridge: Cambridge University Press, 1997.

Lim. "Twelve Asian American Writers: In Search of Self-Definition." In *Redefining American Literary History*, edited by A. LaVonne Brown Ruoff and Jerry W. Ward. New York: Modern Language Association, 1990.

Miller, Elise. "Kingston's *The Woman Warrior:* The Object of Autobiographical Relations." In *Compromise Formations: Current Directions in Psychoanalytic Criticism*, edited by Vera J. Camden. Kent, Ohio & London: Kent State University Press, 1989.

Nishime, LeiLani. "Engendering Genre: Gender and Nationalism in *China Men* and *The Woman Warrior*." *MELUS*, 20, no. 1 (1995): 67–69.

Rabine, Leslie W. "No Lost Paradise: Social Gender and Symbolic Gender in the Writings of Maxine Hong Kingston." *Signs*, 12 (Spring 1987): 477–479.

Rabinowitz, Paula. "Eccentric Memories: A Conversation with Maxine Hong Kingston." *Michigan Quarterly Review*, 26 (1987): 177–179.

Smith, Sidonie. "Filiality and Woman's Autobiographical Storytelling." In her *A Poetics of Women's Autobiography: Marginality and the Fictions of Self-representation*. Bloomington & Indianapolis: Indiana University Press, 1987.

Thompson, Phyllis Hoge. "This is the Story I Heard: A Conversation with Maxine Hong Kingston." *Biography*, 6, no. 1 (1983): 4.

Wang, Veronica. "Reality and Fantasy: The Chinese-American Woman's Quest for Identity." *MELUS*, 12, no. 3 (1985): 23–24.

Wong, Sau-ling Cynthia. "Necessity and Extravagance in Maxine Hong Kingston's *The Woman Warrior*: Art and the Ethnic Experience," *MELUS*, 15 (Spring 1988): 3–5, 7, 23.

Yuan Yuan. "The Semiotics of China Narratives in the Con/texts of Kingston and Tan." *Critique: Studies in Contemporary Fiction*, 40 (Spring 1999): 292.

Zackodnik, Teresa C. "Photography and the Status of Truth in Maxine Hong Kingston's *China Men*." *MELUS*, 22, no. 3 (1997): 55.

PHOTOGRAPHS AND ILLUSTRATIONS APPEARING IN *Literary Masterpieces, Vol. 9: The Woman Warrior* **and** *China Men,* **WERE REPRODUCED FROM THE FOLLOWING SOURCES:**

Chinese American boy writing Chinese characters, 1952. Balch Institute Library/Holy Redeemer Chinese Catholic Church Photographs.

Chinese Americans rallying in New York City, 1992. © Corkey Lee.

Chinese men in a U.S. laundry. National Archives, Mid-Atlantic Region.

Chinese men working for the Southern Pacific Railroad near Sacramento, California, 1877. Library of Congress.

Chinese railroad worker in the Sierra Nevada Mountains, 1897. The Bettmann Archive.

Friedan, Betty, 1993. Photograph by Joyce Ravid.

Galley proof page from *China Men* with Kingston's corrections. The Bancroft Library, University of California, Berkeley.

Kingston, Maxine Hong. Anthony Barboza.

Kingston, Maxine Hong, at the opening of the Berkeley Repertory Theatre production of *The Woman Warrior,* 18 May 1994. © 1994 Lia Chang Gallery.

Kingston, Maxine Hong, in 1993. Photograph by Jane Scheer/ University of California, Berkeley.

Kingston, Maxine Hong, as a young woman. Photograph by Karen Huie.

Map of northern California showing Stockton.

National Organization of Women members protesting at the White House.

Parade in New York City's Chinatown during World War II. Chinatown History Museum, New York.

Passengers arriving at Angel Island, California, 1924. California Department of Parks and Recreation.

Slave girl in Chinatown, San Francisco, circa 1895–1906. Arnold Genthe Collection.

Sun Yat-sen, 1910. National Archives.

Tan, Amy. © Robert Foothorap.

ABOUT *THE WOMAN WARRIOR* AND *CHINA MEN*

The Woman Warrior: A Memoir of a Girlhood Among Ghosts and *China Men* were originally written as a single long work. *The Woman Warrior*, published in 1976 by Alfred A. Knopf, was the first book by Maxine Hong Kingston who, at that time, was an unknown Chinese American writer working as a high-school teacher in Hawaii. *The Woman Warrior* received popular and critical acclaim. Kingston followed this success in 1980 with the publication of *China Men*.

PLOT SUMMARY

Kingston's major formal achievement in *The Woman Warrior* is to create a narrative that is at once coherent as a single entity and also comprises five distinct stories: "No Name Woman," "White Tigers," "Shaman," "At the Western Palace," and "A Song for a Barbarian Reed Pipe." The connecting thread is the idea of femininity. Each story presents the adolescent narrator with a female role model from which to learn as she seeks her own way to live as a woman in modern America. In the first story, "No Name Woman," she learns of her father's sister, the aunt she never knew existed, and her aunt's terrible fate. Her aunt's shame and subsequent suicide characterize her as a victim of the misogyny Kingston finds in so many stories and memories of the China her parents left behind. The following story, however, tells of the legendary Chinese warrior woman, Fa Mu Lan. In "White Tigers" Kingston begins her speculation about how she might translate Fa Mu Lan's acts of courage into modern American terms. Her indomitable mother, Brave Orchid (Ying Lan), is the protagonist of the next story, "Shaman." Here, Brave Orchid's achievements in both China and America offer a potential model of the modern warrior woman. In contrast, "At the Western Palace" tells of Brave Orchid's sister, Moon Orchid, who cannot survive the move from Chinese to American culture. Moon Orchid's story reveals the dangers that her daughter faces as a Chinese American woman destined to live a

Maxine Hong Kingston in 1993

"hyphenated" existence as a woman who is Chinese by nature but American by nurture. In the final story, "A Song for a Barbarian Reed Pipe," the legendary Chinese poet T'sai Yen provides the narrator with an example of a woman who lived and translated between two cultures. In T'sai Yen's story she perceives the possibility that as an artist she may be able to bridge the difference between her Chinese and American worlds and through her writing come figuratively to conquer the obstacles that face her both as an Asian and as an American. The stories are self-contained but also are united by a common authorial voice. Only "At the Western Palace" is told by a third-person narrator; all the other stories are related by the first-person narrator. Throughout the book she recalls her childhood experiences and the Chinese legends and histories her mother has told her. Consequently, the stories are united also by the presence of Brave Orchid, who is the dominant influence upon her daughter's early life.

KINGSTON ON *CHINA MEN*

"What I am doing is putting many kinds of stories and people right next to one another, as they are in real life. Each character is viewed from the vantage point of the others.

I have a father character who comes up in various guises throughout the book. He is really only one character, but I call him different things, like 'the legal father,' 'the illegal father,' 'the father from China' and 'the American father.' In the course of the book, I have him coming into this country five different ways. I'm very proud of that."

Maxine Hong Kingston

From Timothy Pfaff, "Talk with Mrs. Kingston," in *Conversations with Maxine Hong Kingston*, edited by Paul Skenazy and Tera Martin (Jackson: University Press of Mississippi, 1998), pp. 16–17.

The narrative begins with Brave Orchid's insistence that her daughter keep silent about the well-kept family secret she is going to reveal to her. The young narrator then learns that in China her father had a sister about whom the family never speaks. The family, because of the shame she brought upon them, disowned this No-Name Woman. Brave Orchid then tells about the time, in 1924, when their village in China celebrated many hurried weddings. These "hurry-up weddings,"[1] as Brave Orchid calls them, were designed to ensure that each young man who was about to leave to find work in America would leave behind in the village a wife to whom he would send money and to whom he would be sure to return. Brave Orchid recalls that some years after her husband left the village, she noticed that her sister-in-law was developing the protruding stomach of a pregnant woman. At first Brave Orchid does not believe this situation is possible because a pregnancy so long after her husband's departure could only mean that her sister-in-law had committed adultery. The family did not discuss this woman's condition, but it had not gone unnoticed by the other villagers. On the night the baby was due to be born, masked villagers raided the family's house, slaughtering the livestock, spoiling the food stocks, tearing clothes, and destroying the furnishings. Later that night the baby was born in the pigsty, and in the morning Brave Orchid found both mother and infant drowned in the family well. Brave Orchid tells this story to her adolescent daughter as a warning that she should not bring shame upon her family by repeating her aunt's fate.

The narrator observes that while she was growing up her mother told stories in order to ensure the survival of her family. She identifies Brave Orchid as belonging to the generation of immigrants, and she herself as one of the first American-born generation, whose task was to relate the cultural world of their immigrant parents to the physical world of America in which they lived. The generational gap between parents and children is emphasized when the children cannot distinguish what is real in their parents' stories from ritual, legend, exaggeration, and fiction. She also wonders to what extent her family is typical of Chinese families, or even representative of Chinese American families. She does not know how to ask her parents about this matter, just as she cannot discuss the aunt about whom she is forbidden to speak. So she speculates about No Name Woman. She uses what she knows about the China of her parents and then creates versions of what might have been her aunt's history. Remembering that women in China did not choose their partners, she assumes that her aunt did not act out of her own romantic motives but was commanded by some man to become his lover. She wonders how the two might have encountered each other; she wonders whether her aunt was raped; she wonders whether the man organized the raid against her aunt. Upon reflection, she thinks it odd that her aunt should be living with her own parents and not with the family of her husband, as was the custom. She then considers that her aunt may have been disgraced in other, still unspoken ways that caused her husband's family to send her back to her own parents in disgrace. The recollection that her aunt was the only daughter in a family of boys, all of whom left for America, suggests to her the possibility that her aunt was not the repository of tradition that her family expected but a sojourner like her brothers, an explorer of social rather than geographical boundaries. In this view, the No Name Woman deliberately crossed the invisible boundary between conventional and unacceptable feminine behavior. Perhaps she was a romantic who fell in love with another man after her husband left for America; perhaps she paid an inappropriate amount of attention to her appearance in order to lure this man. She compares her own attempts to make herself attractive by resisting her mother's ideals of Chinese femininity and re-creating herself as "American-feminine" (11). She speculates that her aunt's privileged position as the beloved only daughter may have fueled in her a dangerous belief in her own individuality. This sense of herself as an individual may have motivated the aunt's actions and those of her fellow villagers: "The villagers punished her for acting as if she could have a private life, secret and apart from them" (13).

The narrator is bothered by thoughts of Brave Orchid's role in the punishment of her aunt. She wonders whether her mother was among the masked crowd who raided the house. Certainly, Brave Orchid helps to ensure that the dispossession of her aunt, the silence that greets her history, is sustained into the youngest generation of the family. The narrative begins with the breaking of this silence. The narrator confesses that for twenty years she has cooperated in the punishment of her aunt by maintaining the family's silence. In this story, however, she begins to correct the injustice she believes has been done, though she is aware that her aunt's presence in the narrative may not necessarily be benevolent. She reflects at the close of this first chapter, "I am telling on her, and she was a spite suicide, drowning herself in the drinking water. The Chinese are always very frightened of the drowned one, whose weeping ghost, wet hair hanging and skin bloated, waits silently by the water to pull down a substitute" (16).

The idea of the warrior woman, who is strong and capable of avenging injustices committed against their families and villagers, is introduced in the following chapter, "White Tigers." She has begun her narrative by avenging the injustice done to her aunt; now she turns her attention to the idea of a woman who is able to avenge wrong. She remembers her mother's stories of heroic swordswomen and the images of female combatants in Chinese movies. She remembers, "When we Chinese girls listened to the adults talking-story, we learned that we failed if we grew up to be but wives or slaves. We could be heroines, swordswomen. Even if she had to rage across all China, a swordswoman got even with anybody who hurt her family" (19). In the dreams this image inspired, she would confuse her mother's voice with that of the warrior women, and the distinction between dream and reality would become indistinct. Thus, she comes to learn the power of her mother's storytelling, which enabled her to imagine herself in the role of the woman warrior.

In the story "White Tigers," the narrator adopts the role of Fa Mu Lan, the mythical woman warrior, and from that perspective tells of her years of training. The young girl, only seven years old, leaves her family to be tutored by an old man and woman. They teach her the skills she will need to learn if she is to become a warrior and avenge the wrongs done to her people. Fa Mu Lan must learn the physical and mental discipline that will allow her complete control of her body and her mind. She learns to endure hunger, silence, and immobility, and she learns metaphysical discipline as well: "I learned to make my mind large, as the universe is large, so that there is room for paradoxes" (29). Part of Fa Mu Lan's training is her periodic exposure to the injustices she will fight. The old couple allows her on special occasions to look into a gourd of water that opens a window to the lives of her family. She sees her parents and her villagers; she witnesses her symbolic marriage as her parents betroth her in order to give her a line of descent that will ensure her eventual return home; she watches as "fat men sat on naked little girls. I watched powerful men count their money, and starving men count theirs" (30). Most disturbing of all to Fa Mu Lan is the scene she witnesses as an army of horsemen sent by the local baron arrives in the village to conscript her father and takes her new husband and brothers instead. Though her impulse is to intervene immediately in these events, she is held back by the warning that her training is not yet complete. Fa Mu Lan will have completed her education only when she can "point at the sky and make a sword appear, a silver bolt in the sunlight, and control its slashing with my mind" (33).

Fa Mu Lan decides to leave to rejoin her family when she has seen in the magical gourd the baron's messenger come to fetch her father for the baron's army. The woman warrior knows that she must assume men's clothes and armor and take her father's place. Before she leaves to join the army, however, her parents carve into her back the wrongs and injustices suffered by her family and the village: "'Wherever you go, whatever happens to you, people will know our sacrifice,' my mother said. 'And you'll never forget either.' She meant that even if I got killed, the people could use my dead body for a weapon" (34). Fa Mu Lan's submission to this agonizing procedure demonstrates what the narrator calls "perfect filiality" (45). The narrator finds she cannot emulate this complete submission to the authority of her parents. When the evil baron, along with his followers, have been destroyed, Fa Mu Lan returns to her village and kneels at the feet of her husband's family: "'Now my public duties are finished,' I said, 'I will stay with you, doing farmwork and housework, and giving you more sons'" (45).

The maturing narrator objects to the traditional feminine role and the devaluation of women that accompanies it. She feels that her own achievements, in her life in America, are ignored by her parents. Unsure of an American equivalent to the martial victories of Fa Mu Lan, she excels at school, hoping that her straight A's will impress her parents with her worth. She feels compelled to impress her parents in order to persuade them that she is not one of the useless girls of the traditional Chinese sayings that the neighbors repeat. She quotes the maxims about the worthlessness of girls that are repeated around her: "Feeding girls is feeding cowbirds" and "There's no profit in raising girls. Better to raise geese than girls" (46). These sayings breed in her mind the terrifying possibility that, should her family eventually return to China, she will be sold along with all the other unwanted girls. Consequently, she determines to commit some heroic act that will compel her parents to value her. The reason girls are not esteemed like boys is that in China, girls were betrothed at an early age and, once they were married, they belonged solely to their husband's family. So she reflects, "It was said, 'There is an outward tendency in females,' which meant that I was getting straight A's for the good of my future husband's family, not my own" (47). Her response is to transform herself into a girl no one will want to marry. She cultivates poor housekeeping skills, refusing to cook and breaking the dishes as she washes them: "'Bad girl,' my mother yelled, and sometimes that made me gloat rather than cry. Isn't a bad girl almost a boy?" (47).

As she grows up, the protagonist does not lose her determination to live independently and to support herself. At the same time she is not without some envy of the women who are looked after and supported by their husbands. She comments, "Even now China wraps double binds around my feet" (48). China has given her the gender model of the submissive and dependent woman but also the desire to live as a warrior woman. She finds that she must battle not only the misogyny of traditional Chinese culture but also the racism she encounters in her everyday life in California. Private injustices, as well as racism and sexism, stir up the avenging rage she has acquired from Fa Mu Lan's example: "It's not just the stupid racists that I have to do something about, but the tyrants who for whatever reason deny my family food and work" (49). Perhaps she should seek to restore the family's estate in China, which was confiscated by the communists, and the laundry business in New York, out of which her father was cheated. She is confused about events in communist China, particularly when her family members who remain there are not counted among the poor but are executed like the corrupt baron in Fa Mu Lan's story. She goes on to recall that none of the fighting and killing she has seen was glorious. The recollection of high-school fights and the spectacle of "dead slum people," from which her mother tried to shield her children, reminds her that she must become a swordswoman in another way besides physical combat. The words carved into Fa Mu

Dust jacket for Kingston's first book, published in 1976, a hybrid form of autobiography that combines reality and myth

Lan's flesh provide the crucial clue: words are what the swordswoman and she have in common: "The reporting is the vengeance—not the beheading, not the gutting, but the words" (53), she realizes.

The next chapter, "Shaman," tells of her mother's experiences in China and of her immigration to the United States, where she is reunited with her husband. The story begins with her comparison of various family photographs—pictures of her mother as a graduate of the To Keung School of Midwifery, in which Brave Orchid looks stern and unsmiling in the Chinese fashion; and ones of her father as a recent immigrant, smiling at the camera in the Western style, with his friends in New York. Her father sent back to China photographs along with money to support his wife and their two children, born before his departure. After the deaths of their two children, and the prolonged absence of her husband, however, Brave Orchid has no one upon whom to spend the money. She decides to use the money for her own education and become a doctor. Brave Orchid travels to the college in Canton where, for the first time, she knows the luxury of privacy and a space of her own. Here, Brave Orchid enjoys a life free of the servitude that was the condition of her life before, one typical of a Chinese woman's life at that time. Here also, Brave Orchid's extraordinary strength of character emerges. She studies night and day, but always in secret, because she is older than the other students and must appear wiser. The respect she inspires in her fellow students increases when Brave Orchid exorcises the ghost that has been haunting one of the rooms of the college. Not only does she dare sleep in the haunted room but also, after her first confrontation with the ghost, she leads all the students as they banish the ghost from their lives. The narrator interprets this strength of character as representative of Brave Orchid's "dragon" quality: "She could make herself not weak. During danger she fanned out her dragon claws and riffled her red sequin scales and unfolded her coiling green stripes" (67).

Brave Orchid's return to her village after graduation is greeted by her family as a triumphant return: "She had gone away ordinary and come back miraculous, like the ancient magicians who came down from the mountains" (76). This description is clearly reminiscent of the warrior woman who trained in the mountains and returned in triumph to her village, having banished the forces of evil. Like Fa Mu Lan, Brave Orchid is feted by the villagers in a manner usually reserved for men. Also like Fa Mu Lan, Brave Orchid participates in the devaluation of women, despite her own transcendence of gender prejudice. Fa Mu Lan devalues her own achievements as a woman. She ends her triumphant military career by returning to her husband's family. She kneels before her parents-in-law and promises them that she will now live as a dutiful wife and daughter: "I will stay with you, doing farmwork and housework, and giving you more sons" (45). Among the things Brave Orchid buys to celebrate her new status as a doctor is a slave girl.

She is both appalled and fascinated by the image of her mother as the owner of a slave because she herself fears the same fate—to be returned to China and sold as a slave. She has a morbid curiosity about her mother's participation in other misogynistic practices, such as female infanticide. In response to her questions, however, her mother tells nightmarish stories of dead and deformed babies, ghosts, and monsters, which leave her confused. She attempts to divide her life into Chinese and American compartments and to keep the monstrous Chinese images she inherits from her mother for "the language of impossible stories" (87). The ghosts of Brave Orchid's Chinese stories are transformed after her immigration to the United States into the foreign ghosts that haunt her everyday life: "Taxi Ghosts, Bus Ghosts, Police Ghosts, Fire Ghosts, Meter Reader Ghosts, Tree Trimming Ghosts, Five-and-Dime Ghosts" (97). No longer a respected village doctor, Brave Orchid labors hard at the laundry, working day and night, as well as undertaking factory work and fruit picking to earn extra money to send to her extended family, her aunts and uncles, who remain in China. Through all this misfortune, she teaches her daughter to triumph over adversity with strength and courage, as she acknowledges: "I am really a Dragon, as she is a Dragon, both of us born in dragon years" (109).

The next story, "At the Western Palace," presents the narrator with the character of a woman unfit to survive in the harsh cultural environment of the United States. Whereas Brave Orchid's courage and determination enabled her to triumph in China and America, her sister Moon Orchid is a delicate and fragile woman who is accustomed to being looked after and has no resources for independent living. Brave Orchid comes to recognize that Moon Orchid is a woman of "the lovely useless type" (128), a quality inherited by Moon Orchid's daughter, who accompanies Brave Orchid to the airport to await her mother's arrival from Hong Kong. Even as she waits at the airport, Brave Orchid concentrates upon keeping her sister's airplane aloft by sheer force of will. When the two sisters are finally reunited, the narrator observes, "Moon Orchid, who never understood the gravity of things, started smiling and laughing, pointing at Brave Orchid" (118). This impractical attitude continues to frustrate Brave Orchid as she tries to persuade her sister to claim her traditional rights as first wife over the husband she has not seen for more than thirty years and his American second wife: "'Claim your rights. Those are *your* children. He's got two sons. *You* have two sons. You take them away from her. You become their mother,'" Brave Orchid tells her sister (125).

Moon Orchid fails to adapt to the demands of life in America in a myriad of ways, small and large, as the narrator details. So the humiliation of her eventual confrontation with her husband, who tells her that with her daughter she has come to seem to him "people in a book I had read a long time ago" (154), only emphasizes the sense of alienation that has been developing since Moon Orchid left the comforting familiarity of Hong Kong. With this sense of alienation she develops a paranoid delusion that Mexicans are out to get her. Eventually, and despite all Brave Orchid's attempts to bring her sister back to sanity, Moon Orchid retreats into complete madness, from which she never emerges.

"At the Western Palace" is the only story in *The Woman Warrior* to be told by a third-person narrator. This point of view creates the impression that the story is told objectively, without the subjective interpretations and embellishments of the earlier stories. The reliability of this story, however, is put into question at the beginning of "A Song for a Barbarian Reed Pipe," the final story, which undermines the preceding narrative by telling another version of the same events. The story begins,

"What my brother actually said was . . ." (163). Her brother, who drove the two women to Los Angeles for the meeting with Moon Orchid's estranged husband, witnessed few of the events and remembered even fewer details of the story. She then reveals that in fact she heard the story from her sister, to whom her brother told it. So the entire story of "At the Western Palace" is reduced from history to invention. The themes of storytelling and its opposite—silence—are stressed in this final chapter. The narrator describes the difficulty in speaking that she experienced as a child and how her mother cut her frenum, the piece of skin anchoring the tongue to the lower jaw, in order to help her to speak. The requirement of speaking English at school caused her to become silent, just as it did her sister and other Chinese girls. They were not dumb, however, when attending Chinese school in the evenings. Silence, for these girls, was then a consequence of cultural confusions.

The narrator describes the various demands placed upon the voices of the children of immigrant parents. She is required to translate words that have little cultural meaning to her. An example of this problem is her mother's insistence that she collect "reparation candy" from the druggist whose delivery boy mistakenly brought medicine to the laundry, thus cursing the family. She must get from him something sweet to dispel the bitter curse he has brought upon them. The young protagonist cannot explain to the druggist what her mother requires and why, so she allows him to think she is simply begging for candy, even though this situation embarrasses her. She observes that the cultural differences also extend to the timbre of girls' voices: Chinese women have "strong and bossy" (172) voices while American women have softer, more feminine ones. Members of the Chinese immigrant community use words to mislead the American authorities about their histories, to obscure the circumstances of their immigration, and to protect themselves against what they perceive to be racist laws. So children become confused about the history of the older generation, just as they are confused about the Chinese rituals that their parents do not explain. She complains about all the things her parents refuse to discuss: "If we had to depend upon being told, we'd have no religion, no babies, no menstruation (sex, of course, unspeakable), no death" (185). The complex powers of language reduce her to a state of confusion.

The self-consciousness the heroine develops about her voice makes her angry, but she directs the rage outward toward a Chinese girl whose own silence represents everything she fears and hates about herself. Finally, she corners the girl and tries physically to beat her into talking; she fails, and after this episode she is confined to bed for eighteen

KINGSTON ON THE RELATIONSHIP BETWEEN *THE WOMAN WARRIOR* AND *CHINA MEN*

"A lot of *China Men* I was writing simultaneously with *The Woman Warrior*. I saw this as a big novel about men and women, and going from ancient feudal times up to the Vietnam War and past that. The books seemed to fall into place as two separate books because the power in *The Woman Warrior* has so much to do with a feminist vision and feminist anger, and so it became a coherent work without the men's stories. The men's stories were sort of undercutting the women's stories, so it fell into two books, and I think that reflects the history of Chinese American people, where the women were excluded from immigrating to the United States, where men set out on these great journeys."

Maxine Hong Kingston

From Kay Bonetti, "An Interview with Maxine Hong Kingston," in *Conversations with Maxine Hong Kingston*, edited by Paul Skenazy and Tera Martin (Jackson: University Press of Mississippi, 1998), pp. 35-36.

months, suffering from a mystery illness. As she grows up, she learns that "talking and not talking made the difference between sanity and insanity" (186). She notices that every Chinese family appears to have a mentally unstable woman who requires care. She fears that she will prove to be the madwoman in her family. Her fear causes her to collect hundreds of grievances that she finally reveals in an uncontrollable outburst to her mother. Brave Orchid, however, refuses to take her daughter seriously, accusing her instead of an inability to distinguish reality from fiction.

The Woman Warrior ends with fiction, a story that the narrator shares with her mother: "The beginning is hers, the ending is mine" (206). The story illustrates the power of literature to sustain the human spirit against the vagaries of life. She begins with the story of her grandmother, who would insist that the entire household accompany her to the theater, despite the activity of bandits in the area. Consequently, when bandits raided the theater and left the family unharmed, this episode was "proof to my grandmother that our family was immune to harm as long as they went to plays" (207). The moral of the story is a demonstration of the practical value of talk-story. She follows this family story with the legend of T'sai Yen, a poet who was taken hostage by barbarians and kept among them for twelve years. She is sustained by the songs she would sing of her loneliness and longing for her own people. Upon her return, these songs were played upon Chinese instruments, but the expression of common emotions "translated well" (209), as the narrator comments. Similarly, Brave Orchid's talk-story united her memories of her own people with her experiences among the "barbarians" of her new home, and her daughter's stories also empower her to reconcile the Chinese and American dimensions of her experience.

Like *The Woman Warrior, China Men* is organized into distinct but related sections: "The Father from China," "The Great Grandfather of the Sandalwood Mountains," "The Grandfather of the Sierra Nevada Mountains," "The Making of More Americans," "The American Father," and "The Brother in Vietnam." Unlike *The Woman Warrior,* each of these sections ends with one or two short stories that are based upon traditional Chinese myth. The overall structure of the narrative is therefore based upon the juxtaposition of historical with mythic stories. *China Men* begins with two short vignettes: "On Discovery" and "On Fathers." "On Discovery" tells of the experience of a man named Tang Ao who visits the Land of Women. Before he can be presented to the queen he must be prepared. The women mutilate his body in ritual ways: his feet are broken and bound, his body hair is removed, and his ears are pierced. Most of all, his spirit is broken by the pain and humiliation he has to endure. This story offers an image of the mutilation of women's bodies in traditional Chinese culture, which is made more disturbing by Kingston's reversal of gender roles. Tang Ao initially set out to find the Gold Mountain, the name given to America by Chinese travelers. At the end of the story the reader learns that the Land of Women was rumored to be in North America. By creating an analogy between the two places, Kingston suggests the disempowerment and emasculation experienced by Chinese immigrants to America. Thus, the short vignette introduces the two primary themes of the narrative: the misogyny of male-dominated Chinese culture and the emasculation of Chinese male emigrants as a consequence of widespread anti-Asian prejudice in America. In *China Men,* Kingston develops a complex analysis of the relations between sexism and racism.

"On Fathers" describes an incident, recalled by the young narrator, when she and her sisters and brothers mistake a stranger for their father, whom they were expecting to return home. Later, when their own father appears, the narrator realizes that the stranger's clothes had confused her. This incident suggests the narrator's anxiety that she does not really know her father. In the following chapter, "The Father from China," the narrator tries to remember all that she knows about her father. The first part of the chapter is told in the second person, as she addresses her father. What she recalls most vividly are the times when her father would vent his anger by shouting obscenities about women. She hopes that these outbursts are merely common sayings and not personal attacks aimed at individual women. She remembers her fear when her father would awaken the house with his wordless screams, she recalls his protracted, mysterious silences, and she observes his complete rejection of China: "No stories. No past. No China. . . . You only look and talk Chinese."[2] Because he will not explain his behavior, his daughter must speculate about his motives, challenging her father to correct her mistakes: "I'll tell you what I suppose from your silences and few words, and you can tell me that I'm mistaken. You'll just have to speak up with the real story if I've got you wrong" (15).

The author begins her narration of her father's life with his early years in China. His mother's delight with this baby, who shows auspicious signs of a born scholar, is contrasted with his father's disappointment in having another son rather than the daughter for whom he longs. Ah Goong envies a family in the village who has recently had a daughter and is saddened by the poor treatment she receives. Only baby boys are welcomed with a party, new clothes, and toys. He hatches a plan to exchange his son for this baby girl, unaware that the family would have sold him the girl if only he had asked. When his wife, Ah Po, realizes that her husband has swapped the babies, she is enraged that he should be swindled into "trading a son for a slave" (21). The young narrator wonders what effect this situation, the experience of being exchanged for a worthless girl, has had upon her father. His brothers tease and shun him because of his love of studying and, at the age of fourteen, he departs the village to take the Imperial Examinations. He succeeds well enough to be awarded the post of village schoolteacher but he is unhappy in his profession, becoming increasingly frustrated by his pupils' resistance to learning and their misbehavior. Finally, he determines to accompany his male relatives who are planning to travel to America, the Gold Mountain, to seek their fortunes. Before leaving, the single men are married to ensure they will return to their wives and families in China. The narrator's father marries Brave Orchid, with whom he has two children, before setting out to make his fortune. The narrator speculates upon the possible methods by which her father may have entered the United States, for he never told the story himself. After arriving in New York, he joins with two other friends to operate a laundry. His wife then writes from China the news that their two children have died. He instructs her to obtain a degree and tells her that when she has graduated he will send for her to join him in America. After fifteen years apart, he is reunited with his wife but her presence alters the working arrangement at the laundry. Shortly after, the two partners draw up deeds of the business that exclude him from his rightful share. In disgust, he leaves New York for California to start a new life again.

This chapter is followed by the mythical story titled "The Ghostmate." In this story a young man is returning from the Imperial Examinations when he is caught in a terrible storm and is offered shelter in the house of a beautiful woman. His stay is prolonged until he forgets all about his family, but he finds that people flee from him in terror. The house is revealed then to be but the grave marker of a noble woman who is long since dead. The moral of the story is observed by the narrator, "Fancy lovers never last" (81). This vignette encapsulates the fears of the families left behind by the men who traveled to America and who feared they would become ghosts in the memory of their men far away.

In the next chapter, "The Great Grandfather of the Sandalwood Mountains," the narrator considers what she knows of her relatives who remain in China and, indeed, what she knows of life in postrevolutionary China. She admits, "I want to talk to Cantonese, who have always been revolutionaries, nonconformists, people with fabulous imaginations, people who invented the Gold Mountain. I want to discern what it is that makes people go West and turn into Americans" (87). The story of her great-grandfather Bak Goong follows. In her narration she seeks to find some answers to these questions she puts to herself. Bak Goong, she learns, was recruited by an agent of the Royal Hawaiian Agricultural Society to work in the Hawaiian sugar industry. The agent's fine promises contrast with the harsh reality of Bak Goong's sea voyage and the working conditions on the sugar plantation. He finds that he has been recruited as cheap indentured labor to clear wilderness and establish the plantation. He has to endure extremes of heat, thirst, and an enforced code of silence that proves too much for him. Bak Goong devises ways to circumvent the rule that laborers may not speak while they are working, and the chapter ends with the defiant "shout party" (118) he organizes for the workers. Two mythical stories are juxtaposed with Bak Goong's story: "On Mortality" and "On Mortality Again." The first of these concerns the character Tu Tzu-chun, who works for a Taoist monk under an obligation to keep silent. One day he cannot repress a gasp and his outburst spoils the elixir of immortality prepared by the monk for the human race. The second story, "On Mortality Again," tells a similar story of the attempt to bring immortality to humanity, but in this story the Polynesian trickster god, Maui, makes the attempt.

Bak Goong's story of life in the Hawaiian sugarcane fields complements the story of Ah Goong as he works on the building of the railroad in California. His story, "The Grandfather of the Sierra Nevada Mountains," is also characterized by the experience of extremes: extremes of weather, fear, and human brutality. Death was an ever-present possibility as the workers dug and dynamited their way through the mountains: "They lost count of the number dead; there is no record of how many died building the railroad. Or maybe it was demons doing the counting and chinamen not worth counting" (138). The inequality between Chinese and white workers motivates the Chinese to strike for improvements in their working conditions and pay equal with that of whites. Their slogan is "Eight hours a day good for white man, all the same good for China Man" (141). The strike wins only a compromise, not real equality. As soon as the railroad is completed, the Chinese know that rather than celebrate with the other workers they must move on because the "Driving Out had begun" (145). Ah Goong moves from place to place for fear of lynching until finally he returns to his family in China. The laws that institutionalized the racial prejudice from which Ah Goong fled are set out chronologically in the chapter that follows, which is simply titled "The Laws." As Kingston explains, these laws represented a concerted effort to prevent the establishment of a permanent Chinese community in the United States. The forcible exclusion of the Chinese who traveled to Alaska to work in gold mining is described in "Alaska China Men."

"The Making of More Americans" tells of the protagonist's "grandfathers," a term loosely applied to all older male ancestors. She recalls how the ghost of Say Goong haunted his brother, Sahm Goong, until he was ordered home: "Go back to China. Go now. To China" (170). One of Sahm Goong's grandsons is haunted by his mother, whose begging letters from China he ignores. She does not respond to direct orders as Say Goong's ghost had done. Only after her son has traveled to China to make reparation by performing all the necessary rituals at her grave can he return to his life in America. The narrator describes in great detail the funeral of her great-uncle Kau Goong and asks her parents about the significance of the rituals that are performed. Her parents do not understand the distinction between Chinese and American cultures that is implicit in her question. They answer, "We treat Kau Goong and any other grandfathers who may be in that cemetery like any American dead" (189). She reflects that although she might not want to hear stories like these, she has a duty to her family and her community to hear and remember them.

This chapter ends with two short stories. The first, "The Wild Man of the Green Swamp," tells of a Chinese man found living in a swamp in Florida because he has nowhere else to go: he refuses to return to China but cannot live in the United States either. The second, "The Adventures of Lo Bun Sun," is her mother's version of the Robinson Crusoe story. She tells how Lo Bun Sun survives shipwreck, frees a captive from the cannibals who are about to eat him, and, with Sing Kay Ng, enjoys a series of adventures before returning to China.

The next chapter, "The American Father," compares her father's official life, which is recorded in various documents, with her knowledge of his life. She reasons that, if he was born in San Francisco in 1903 as his documents indicate, then either his mother "gave birth at a distance" or else "the men of those days had the power to have babies" (237). She knows, however, that in reality he was born and was married in China, not America. She resumes the story of her parent's life with their departure from New York and arrival in Stockton, California. She tells of her father's work as the manager of a gambling house and his subsequent depression when the gambling house closed. Only when he takes over the laundry does his "liveliness" (254) return. Juxtaposed with this chapter is the story of Ch'ü Yüan, or Ch'ü P'ing, titled "The Li Sao: An Elegy." Ch'ü Yüan is banished from the Chou Kingdom for giving the emperor unpopular advice and travels around the kingdom, unable to find a single person who is not corrupt. Eventually, he drowns himself and only then, once he is gone, do the people realize the value of the incorruptible man they have lost.

The final chapter is called "The Brother in Vietnam" and begins with her early consciousness of war in relation to the Japanese invasion of China and, later, the Korean War. Her father and uncles left China at an age when they would have been subject to conscription, and she observes that many men left China in order to escape the threat of serving in the military: "The Gold Mountain does not make war, is not invaded, and has no draft. The government does not capture men and boys and send them to war" (269). Her brother, however, must choose between moving to Canada to escape conscription or enlisting to fight in the Vietnam War. He chooses to enlist in the navy, reasoning that "he would be a Pacifist in the Navy rather than in jail, no more or less guilty than the ordinary stay-at-home citizen of the war economy" (285). She tells of his experience as a communications expert before returning home, triumphant in the knowledge that he has survived and not killed anyone.

China Men concludes with the story of "The Hundred-Year-Old Man" and the narrator's suggestion, in "On Listening," that because so many versions of the Gold Mountain legend exist, a single narrative of the Chinese experience in America is impossible.

KINGSTON ON THE LO BUN SUN EPISODE IN *CHINA MEN*

"I'd heard the Robinson Crusoe story first as a Chinese talk-story. The Defoe novel had become Lo Bun Sun. When I retold it, for some reason, Friday's father became a major figure. China Men is a story about a search for my father, or all of us searching for our fathers—and Friday found his father. There's wonderful, loving, physical touching between the two of them. To show these two black men having been apart and coming together is a healing thing for all of us, to look at the Defoe story not as man on an isolated island but man finding man, hugging him and touching him."

Maxine Hong Kingston

From Jody Hoy, "To Be Able to See the Tao," in *Conversations with Maxine Hong Kingston,* edited by Paul Skenazy and Tera Martin (Jackson: University Press of Mississippi, 1998), p. 56.

INFORMATION ABOUT MAXINE HONG KINGSTON

Clear parallels exist between Kingston's life and her literary works; most obviously in the autobiographical elements of *The Woman Warrior* (which is subtitled a memoir) and *China Men*. Family history, cultural mythology, and factual history provide the materials for these books. The settings she uses are the village in China described in her mother's stories and the city of Stockton in which Kingston grew up. In an interview with Paul Skenazy, Kingston explained that an important part of her determination to be a writer grew out of an need to understand Stockton and how she related to the place that formed her. She explained, "I always came back to Stockton because that's where my parents are and my roots and my brothers and sisters, and my Chinatown."[3]

Maxine Hong Kingston was born on 27 October 1940 in Stockton, California, the eldest daughter of immigrants from southern China. Her parents came from the village of Sun Woi, near Canton. In China her father, Tom Hong, had trained as a scholar for the Imperial Examinations and was awarded the post of schoolteacher. Her mother, Brave Orchid, studied medicine and, for a time, was the village doctor. Her father immigrated to the United States in 1924 and her mother followed in 1939. Upon his arrival in New York, Tom Hong established a laundry business with two friends. Fifteen years later he sent for his wife to join him. Shortly after Brave Orchid was reunited with her husband, he found that he had been cheated of his proper share of the laundry business, and so he moved his family from New York City to Stockton, California. In Stockton, he found work as the manager of a gambling house. His job was to prepare the premises for business each day and to take the real owner's place when the police raided and arrested staff and clientele. When the gambling house closed, Tom fell into a depression that lifted only when he bought and began operating the New Port laundry on El Dorado Street. The laundry was an important part of the family's life and everyone, including the children, shared the hard work. Here Kingston listened to her parents and the other relatives and neighbors who would come by and "talk-story" as they recalled Chinese myths, fables, and history. In *The Woman Warrior* and *China Men* Kingston makes reference to the Stockton in which she grew up. In *The Woman Warrior*, for example, she refers to the time when "urban renewal tore down my parents' laundry and paved over our slum for a parking lot" (48). In fact, Stockton's contemporary Chinatown was built to replace the neighborhood that was destroyed for freeway construction. The Chinatown in which Kingston grew up was situated in the vicinity of Lafayette Street, adjacent to the modern Chinatown. In *China Men* the narrator provides a guided tour of the landmarks of Stockton's old Chinatown, as the narrative follows Kau Goong's funeral procession past the places he used to frequent: the Hong's house, the laundry, the Chinese Benevolent Association, and the Chinese school.

Kingston represents in her writing an honest picture of the tough neighborhood of Stockton in which her family lived. She has no interest in creating a false, exotic image of Stockton's Chinatown. In *The Woman Warrior* she tells how her sister once barricaded herself in the house to escape a violent drunk, who was banging on the doors and windows. She also recalls that her mother "locked her children in the house so we couldn't look at dead slum people" (51). In addition to the school she attended each day, Kingston and her siblings also attended Chinese school. In Stockton, the Chung Wah Chinese School, once located at 131 East Church Street, offered Chinese American children instruction in how to write and speak Chinese. These classes were held every evening and on Sunday mornings. In *The Woman Warrior,* Kingston compares the American school with the Chinese School, highlighting such differences as the verbal abilities of children who would not speak English at the American school but would speak Chinese at Chinese School.

Throughout her childhood and upbringing Kingston was influenced by two sets of cultural factors: the Chinese values, beliefs, and experiences of her immigrant parents, and the American culture in which she lived her life day to day. The experience of cross-cultural identity has shaped Kingston's subsequent work, along with her understanding of the position of women in Chinese culture, and her awareness of American racism. Kingston describes her upbringing as the direct origin of her feminist commitment: "Growing up as a kid, I don't see how I could not have been a feminist. In Chinese culture, people always talk about how girls are bad."[4] Kingston recalls that she has spent a lot of her life angry and that this anger arises from the unequal treatment of women in sexist societies. She remembers her anger when her mother first told her the story of her father's sister, the woman who became the No Name Woman in *The Woman Warrior:* "I was so mad at my mother for telling me a cruel tale for the joy of the telling."[5] In *The Woman Warrior* Kingston expresses this anger by transforming it into an avenging rage for justice for all the women who have been victimized by misogynistic attitudes and practices.

Kingston breaks the silence that has sustained sexist Chinese traditions that oppress and disempower women through practices such as female infanticide, infant betrothal, female slavery, concubi-

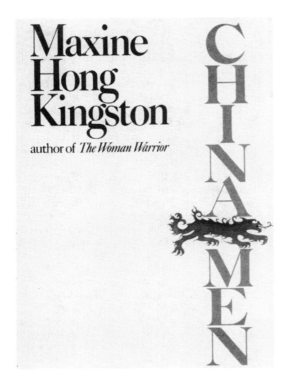

Dust jacket for Kingston's second book of memoirs, published in 1980, which tells the stories of her male relatives

nage, and prostitution. In *The Woman Warrior* one of her bitter memories is of her father telling her how "Chinese smeared bad daughters-in-law with honey and tied them naked on top of ant nests. . . . A husband may kill a wife who disobeys him. Confucius said that" (193). The effect upon the young heroine of the antifeminine attitude that characterizes the community in which she grew up is to make her feel ashamed of being a woman. In *The Woman Warrior* she remembers walking down the street in Stockton with her parents and younger sister and feeling her parents' embarrassment when friends commented upon the lack of sons in the family. A motif that is repeated throughout the narrative is Kingston's outrage at the degrading proverbs that were repeated around her as a child such as "When you raise girls, you're raising children for strangers," and "There's no profit in raising girls. Better to raise geese than girls" (46). Not the child but the older, more mature narrator realizes that in a male-dominated culture, language itself articulates the assumption of feminine inferiority and the reality of female powerlessness. Again in *The Woman Warrior* she observes, "There is a Chinese word for the female I—which is 'slave'. Break the women with their own tongues!" (47).

Kingston's attitude toward the Communist Revolution in China and its aftermath is affected by her awareness of what political change might mean for the women who have suffered acutely under the emperor's regime. The Communists at least promised to "put an end to prostitution by giving women what they wanted: a job and a room of their own" (61). Her mother was able to benefit from political change—she gained an education and a profession. Attitudes, however, had not changed so much; Brave Orchid was able to purchase a slave girl to act as her assistant. So while Brave Orchid's life improved, the situation of girls deemed worthless by their families and condemned to a life of slavery had not changed.

The theme of cross-cultural experience, and the peculiar pressures this duality brings to bear upon individuals, is prominent in both *The Woman* Warrior and *China Men*. The young narrator represented in both narratives describes herself as caught between the conflicting demands of the old China her parents have left behind, which no longer exists except in the memory of the immigrant community, and the demands of modern American society in which she must make her own future. Kingston represents her desire to win approval on the terms of both cultures, even when this goal is impossible because the demands contradict each other. Her voice must be soft and whispering if she is to be "American feminine," but a strong and bossy voice is characteristic of the Chinese women she knows. Thus, Kingston is caught between the two cultures. She admits her understanding of Chinese culture is limited, particularly because her parents leave so much unspoken and unexplained. In *The Woman Warrior* she wonders, "How can Chinese keep any traditions at all? They don't even make you pay attention, slipping in a ceremony and clearing the table before the children notice specialness. The adults get mad, evasive, and shut you up if you ask" (185). Kingston also admits that she fails to understand much of American culture. She belongs to both cultures and to neither, and her work emerges out of this ambivalence.

PEOPLE OF *THE WOMAN WARRIOR*

THE NARRATOR: Four of the five stories that comprise *The Woman Warrior* are recounted by the young narrator, who, while not identical with Maxine Hong Kingston, shares many aspects of Kingston's early life and experience. She grows up in Stockton, California, in the 1940s and 1950s, the daughter of immigrant Chinese parents who run a downtown laundry. The narrative tells primarily of her adolescent years, though she mentions her life after graduation from college. She is attempting to navigate a way through the conflicting demands made upon her by the contemporary American society in which she lives, on the one hand, and the traditional Chinese culture that her parents left behind when they immigrated to the United States, on the other. She is the eldest of six children—three girls and three boys—and she fears for the future of her younger sisters, as well as herself, in view of the antifemale attitudes expressed by her parents and others of the immigrant Chinese community. She is also engaged with the political values of her time. She has a strong feminist commitment and is outraged by stories about misogynistic Chinese practices and the negative sayings about women. She is also committed to the values of the Civil Rights movement and the passive noncooperation with the agents of racial discrimination. The figure of the warrior woman inspires her to oppose the forces of sexism and racism, to transcend the cultural divide within which she is caught, and to forge a powerful sense of personal identity from elements of her dual heritage.

NO NAME WOMAN: The narrator's aunt, whose story opens the narrative, is her father's sister. Kingston refers to her aunt as "No Name Woman" to indicate the punishment inflicted on her even after her death—her family obliterated her from their history and her name is never spoken again. In the narrative the protagonist seeks to avenge the injustice done to her aunt by telling her story and restoring her historical reality.

BRAVE ORCHID: The narrator's mother, whose life story Kingston recounts in the section of *The Woman Warrior* titled "Shaman," is Brave Orchid. After the death of the two children born in China, and at her husband's request, Brave Orchid entered college where she studied medicine. When she traveled to America in 1939 to join her husband, she found that her studies in China did not qualify her to practice medicine and so she had to take up menial work: fruit picking, working in canneries, and laboring hard in the family's laundry. She is a woman of great courage, determination, and spirit; she is also practical and tireless. She is able to exorcize the ghost that haunted the medical college and she is able to deal with the metaphorical "ghosts," the people of the foreign American culture in which she must live. Even as an old lady, Brave Orchid refuses to retire from work, just as she is unable to stop herself from trying to shape the lives of those around her. In important respects, *The Woman Warrior* is about Kingston's struggle to understand her mother and the nature of the influence Brave Orchid has had upon her daughter.

FATHER: The narrator's father, Tom Hong, is a relatively minor character in *The Woman Warrior*; his story is told in detail in *China Men*. Moon Orchid describes him as embodying "the ideal in masculine beauty, the thin scholar with the hollow cheeks and the long fingers" (119). He emigrated from China to the United States in 1924 with a group of male relatives, according to Brave Orchid earlier in the "No Name Woman" chapter. He sent money back to his wife and family in China, and instructed his wife to use the money to obtain an education. Once her studies were complete, she could join him in America. Fifteen years after his departure, his wife joined him in New York, where he operated a laundry with a group of friends. Shortly after her arrival, they left New York and moved to Stockton, California. At first, he worked as the manager of a gambling house—at one point the narrator stops just short of telling an American teacher what her father's occupation is—and then he operated a laundry in Stockton. The narrator expresses a greater anxiety about her mother's attitude toward girls, in terms of female slavery and forced marriages, than she does about her father.

MOON ORCHID: The narrator's aunt and Brave Orchid's sister, Moon Orchid is featured in the section of *The Woman Warrior* titled "At the Western Palace." Brave Orchid arranges for her sister to travel to the United States in order to confront the husband who has never sent for her to join him. Moon Orchid's husband has assimilated to life in America, marrying a Chinese American second wife and practicing medicine as a highly paid neurosurgeon in Los Angeles. He has forgotten about Moon Orchid, though he pays for their daughter to be educated and for Moon Orchid herself to live a life of relative luxury in Hong Kong. The confrontation with her estranged husband and his rejection of her unbalances her mind, and she subsequently dies in an insane asylum.

SISTER: The narrator's younger sister remains unnamed in *The Woman Warrior*; she calls her "my almost-twin" (190). This sister is referred to as the daughter with whom she is unfavorably compared. The immigrant Chinese men, invited into the house by Brave Orchid, express interest in marrying her, not the narrator, although she is older and should be married first. She seeks to protect her sister against their mother's traditional attitudes toward daughters and how they should live their lives. She consults her when she wonders just how "normal" is the fantasy world, or "free movies" (190) as she terms them, in which she takes refuge. Her youngest sister is mentioned only in connection with her middle sister, when Brave Orchid responds to her accusation that her sisters need protection from their mother by accusing her daughter of endangering both her sisters; she warns, "You're always leading them off somewhere. I've had to call the police twice because of you" (203).

FA MU LAN (THE WOMAN WARRIOR): The legendary warrior woman, a kind of Chinese Joan of Arc, Fa Mu Lan disguised herself as a man in order to lead an army against the enemies of her family and her village. The figure of Fa Mu Lan appears in traditional Chinese stories, operas, and ballads. In the late 1990s the Walt Disney Company produced an animated feature motion picture, titled *Mulan,* based upon her story. Kingston recounts her version of the legend of Fa Mu Lan in the section of *The Woman Warrior* titled "White Tigers."

TS'AI YEN: The Chinese poet Ts'ai Yen in 195 A.D. was captured by the Southern Hsiung-nu and held captive by them for twelve years. Kingston recounts her version of Ts'ai Yen's story in the section of *The Woman Warrior* titled "Eighteen Stanzas for a Barbarian Reed Pipe." Like the young protagonist and her mother, Brave Orchid, Ts'ai Yen is caught between two cultures: the Chinese culture from which she has been abducted and the barbarian culture in which she is imprisoned. She is a captive soldier and as such she fights alongside her barbarian captors. Ts'ai Yen is married to the chieftain who captured her and bears him two children, "barbarian" children who do not speak Chinese and with whom she cannot communicate. Eventually, she is ransomed and returned to China.

SILENT GIRL: In the section of the narrative titled "Eighteen Stanzas for a Barbarian Reed Pipe" the narrator tells of her difficult search for a voice. She is unable to speak at the American school; she is so self-conscious and so aware of all that her parents have told her not to divulge to her American teachers that she is unable to speak except in hesitant whispers. During this time she meets another Chinese American girl who is just like her. The girl maintains a silence that she finds impenetrable—yet she is compelled to break the girl's silence—as if by making her speak, she will somehow overcome her own inability to speak freely. This situation leads to an ugly episode where she attempts to force the girl to speak by bullying her: cornering her and then hitting and taunting her until she cries, but still the girl refuses to speak. She notes that as she grows up, this girl is protected by her family; she remains unmarried and continues to live with her parents and sister, who take care of her as if she remained a child.

PEOPLE OF *CHINA MEN*

BABA: The narrator's father is referred to as BaBa and BiBi in the early part of the narrative. He is the youngest of four boys born in China. Destined by his family to be a scholar, Baba is prepared by the family to take the Imperial Examinations and he participates in the last of these examinations. On the basis of his performance, he is appointed village schoolteacher, a disappointing outcome for him, but he is unable to retake the examinations because the system has been abandoned. In 1924, after a frustrating and unsuccessful career as a teacher, he leaves his wife and two young children to travel with his male relatives to America, the Gold Mountain.

AH PO: The narrator's paternal grandmother is BaBa's mother Ah Po. She represents the values of traditional Chinese culture. Her feet are bound and she can barely walk without assistance. She objects violently to her husband's plan to exchange his youngest son, BaBa, for the daughter he wants so badly, accusing him of swapping a son for a slave. The character of Ah Po offers an interesting comparison with her daughter-in-law, Brave Orchid. Both women express antifeminine views and refer to women as powerless slaves; yet these women represent the dominant forces in their own households.

AH GOONG: The narrator's paternal grandfather, Ah Goong, is the husband of Ah Po. Maxine refers to him as the grandfather who was bayoneted by the Japanese. As a young man he traveled to the Gold Mountain, where he worked on the building of the Central Pacific Railroad. In his old age he becomes the father of four boys, although he desperately wants a girl. In his desperation, he attempts an exchange of his baby son for the baby daughter of his village neighbors. The narrator speculates whether this experience of being swapped for an inferior girl is one of the reasons why her father expresses antifeminine sentiments.

SAY GOONG: The narrator's fourth grandfather, Say Goong, is Ah Goong's youngest brother. With his brother Sahm Goong, he farms a market garden in Stockton and home-delivers fresh produce. After his death, he returns silently to haunt his brother until Sahm Goong utters the words that banish him from the world of the living.

KAU GOONG: Ah Po's brother and the narrator's overbearing great uncle, Kau Goong is the former riverboat pirate who helps at the laundry. She remembers him for his sheer physical size and for the clear distinction he makes between boys, who think of him as a generous old man, and girls, who recall only his scoldings and insults.

BAK GOONG: The narrator's great-grandfather who traveled to Hawaii, the Sandalwood Mountains, where he worked as an indentured laborer on sugar plantations.

BAK SOOK GOONG: Another of the narrator's great-grandfathers is Bak Sook Goong. While working on the sugar plantations in Hawaii, he met Bak Goong. When Bak Sook Goong returned to China, he took with him a Hawaiian woman to be his third wife. This woman subsequently bore him a son, the father of the black Chinese cousin who writes to the narrator asking for money with which to buy a bicycle.

DAI BAK: The narrator's "Big Uncle," Dai Bak, is BaBa's oldest brother.

SAHM BAK: "Third Uncle" is BaBa's third brother, Sahm Bak. As a small child he feels that his place as the baby in the family has been usurped by BaBa. The family tells the story of how at the baby's one-month birthday party, Sahm Bak took the opportunity to jump and bounce upon the sleeping baby's stomach. Sahm Bak's grandson, Sao Elder Brother or Mad Sao, is haunted by his mother after he ignores her requests for help and allows her to die of starvation in postrevolutionary China.

NGEE BAK: BaBa's second brother is Ngee Bak.

INCORRUPTIBLE BRIDGE: Pure Bridge is the narrator's eldest brother; Han Bridge is her second brother; and Bright Bridge, or Incorruptible Bridge, or Severe Bridge, is her youngest brother. Her youngest brother enlists in the navy during the war in Vietnam.

WOODROW, ROOSEVELT, AND WORLDSTER: The three friends with whom BaBa, known by the American name Ed, establishes a laundry business in New York, Woodrow, Roosevelt, and Worldster eventually cheat BaBa out of his share of the business.

CH'Ü YÜAN: Also known as Ch'u P'ing or Kwut Ngin, Ch'ü Yüan is a legendary poet and philosopher. As a minister to the king, he refuses to give the advice the king wants to hear. Instead, he expresses his genuine view, an unpopular opinion for which he is banished. In despair, he kills himself. Once he is gone, the people lament his passing and beg his spirit to return.

THEMES, IMAGES, ALLUSIONS, AND METAPHORS

In both *The Woman Warrior* and *China Men* Kingston invents a hybrid form of memoir, one that combines the distinct genres of autobiography, biography, fiction, myths and legends, and historical reconstruction. The narrator of *The Woman Warrior,* in each of the five named chapters, explores a character that is represented as a model of femininity. The figure of Brave Orchid, for example, incorporates the dutiful daughter, the brilliant student, the triumphant warrior, the powerful shaman, and the enthralling storyteller. She is compared with the legendary Fa Mu Lan, whose story precedes that of Brave Orchid, and contrasted with her delicate and fragile sister Moon Orchid, whose story follows. *China Men* similarly contrasts the stories of ancestors with parables and characters from myth. This play with multiple roles is why the form of the narrative is convoluted; Kingston refuses to represent personal and cultural identity in anything less than its true complexity. Not only is her theme the conflicts that have shaped her sense of identity, but the structure of the text itself represents the disjunctions that have formed her sense of self: between China and America, the remembered past and the present, and the mythic and the real.

During much of the narrative in *The Woman Warrior,* the heroine tries to find a voice with which to express herself, especially in relation to her mother. She strives to reach an understanding of how women can relate to each other within the terms of a brutally misogynistic Chinese culture and an American culture characterized by pervasive sexual and racial discrimination. In *China Men* the young female narrator confronts the difficulty of overcoming gender and age barriers in order to tell the stories of her father and grandfathers. Kingston's strategy in both books is to use traditional myths and legends to transcend the historical distance that separates the past from the present. Therefore, she does not simply repeat or record the myths but uses them to tell a new, modern story. Kingston uses the legend of Ch'ü Yüan to represent the complex quality of her father's depression. Ch'ü Yüan, a man defeated by his own integrity through his incorruptible nature, was only appreciated by others after his death. Only after witnessing her father's deep distress is she able to appreciate that her father, like herself, feels pain. In *The Woman Warrior* she uses the legendary character of Fa Mu Lan to represent the heroic quality of her mother who, like the warrior woman, triumphs over all adversaries. Brave Orchid makes a successful life for herself both in China and among foreigners in America. The legendary character of T'sai Yen, who lived among barbarians and wrote poems of her experience, is also used to express the nature of Brave Orchid's achievement.

The feminist theme of the narrative centers upon Kingston's representation of the forms of institutionalized servitude to which women were subject under traditional Chinese patriarchy. *The Woman Warrior* begins with a story in which this theme is prominent. The No Name Woman is persecuted by villagers and implicitly required to kill herself and her illegitimate baby because her act of adultery has violated one of the basic laws of patriarchy: that is, the inheritance of property by the male heir. This law of inheritance makes it essential that a man knows that the child who will inherit his property is in fact his own child. This certainty is possible only through the strict control and regulation of feminine sexuality, and particularly by the rigorous punishment of adultery, which introduces illegitimate children and threatens the proper line of descent and inheritance. The real crime that the No Name Woman commits is not so much the act of adultery but the conception of an illegitimate child; the pregnancy threatens the entire social fabric, which is made up of clearly defined kinship relations. The narrator describes this baby as a "child with no descent line" (15). For this reason, the entire village punishes the No Name Woman. All the villagers join in her punishment by raiding and destroying her family's house and livestock. They do not kill her—at least, not directly—but they focus their outrage upon the property that this illegitimate child may one day claim.

An adulterous woman has no place in a patriarchal society. Her unrestrained expression of her sexuality is a rejection of the patriarchal regulation of women and femininity in general. Under traditional Chinese patriarchy, gender relations are organized according to Confucian principles—women are obedient to the men in their family; their role within the family gives women their identity; marriage is a woman's life and her fate, for no viable alternative lifestyles for women exist outside marriage. Girls are given over to their husband's families, permanently leaving their own parents upon marriage. The exclusion of women from patterns of inheritance, together with the low status of newly married brides within their husband's families, gives rise to the degrading proverbs about women that Kingston finds so offensive. When Brave Orchid first arrives at medical school, she unpacks her belongings and the narrator remarks, "She owned more—furniture, wedding jewelry, cloth, photographs—but she had left such troublesome valuables behind in the family's care. She never did get all of it back" (61). Presumably her husband's family regarded her property as more properly their own, and so they kept it for themselves. Shortly after, as Brave Orchid is savoring the luxury of having, for the first time in her life, a private space of her own, the narrator observes, "Free from families, my mother would live for two years without servitude. She would not have to run errands for my father's tyrant mother with the bound feet or thread needles for old ladies" (62). Brave Orchid's experience encapsulates the low status accorded to young married women within their husbands' families specifically and in patriarchal society in general.

The pervasive nature of antifemale prejudice and male domination within traditional Chinese culture extends even to the language, which the heroine finds embodies the assumption of feminine inferiority. In her early experience, the words 'girl' and 'bad' are assumed to be synonymous: her mother recalls, "When you were little, all you had to say was 'I'm not a bad girl,' and you could make yourself cry" (46). She grows up feeling guilty for having been born a girl, for eating the food, for being "useless, one more girl who couldn't be sold" (52). These feelings of guilt are continually reinforced by the immigrant Chinese of their community who, she recalls, "shook their heads at my sister and me. 'One girl—and another girl,' they said, and made our parents ashamed to take us out together" (46). Much of the narrative is concerned with the narrator's attempt to determine whether her parents express similar misogynistic attitudes because they believe them or because these attitudes are a matter of custom. She admits that while she believes that her parents do love her, the experience of hearing them repeat sayings like, "When fishing for treasures in the flood, be careful not to pull in girls" (52), fills her with hatred. As an adult she seeks to understand the difference between the personal and the cultural by making sense of the old sayings and stories, and how they relate to her.

At the same time, she tries to understand the conflicting demands made upon her by her Chinese ancestry and American childhood. She is critical of China and the culture that belittles her for her gender. The narrator observes that "Crazy Mary" was raised in China until she was almost twenty but by that time, when her parents could afford to send for her to join them in the United States, she was already going mad (187). Her brothers and sisters born in America were perfectly normal and could translate from English to Chinese and from Chinese to English for their parents. This ability to translate between cultures, to operate and to be articulate in the two languages, is the key to survival. Kingston represents herself as caught between the two cultures: the sexism of traditional Chinese culture and the pervasive racism of American culture. She is also caught between two opposed value systems. This conflict is explored extensively in terms of voice—the Chinese expect that she will talk loudly but Americans expect that she will talk softly, in a style that she calls "American-feminine" (47). She is aware of her difficulties in understanding Chinese culture but she is also aware that she does not belong entirely to American culture. The same prejudice she finds ingrained in sexist Chinese sayings, she also finds in such racist American terms as the color "nigger yellow" (48).

In *China Men,* Kingston explores the relationship between gender and racial oppression in terms of the emasculation experienced by Chinese men upon reaching America. There, once their work in the sugar fields and on rail construction gangs was finished, they could find only menial work in laundries, restaurants, and as cleaners. Work such as laundry and cooking was perceived by men like Tom Hong as demeaning "women's" work that men would never be expected to do in China, where domestic work was the responsibility of women and slaves. Her father's gradual decline after the loss of his share of the New York laundry business, she attributes to his loss of status, his becoming a slave (or like a woman) and outstripped by his wife: "Her energy slammed BaBa back into his chair. She took over everything; he did not have a reason to get up" (250). With the return of her father's spirit the narrator perceives a parallel between the legendary figure of Ch'ü Yüan and BaBa: both men live in exile, both have been reduced from a position of high status to no status at all, and both are remembered in stories for their suffering and wisdom. The parallel between these two characters can be contrasted with the comparison between Ch'ü Yüan and the No Name aunt, her father's sister. Both Ch'ü Yüan and the nameless aunt drown themselves in despair at their rejection by society. Whereas the aunt is deliberately forgotten by her family, when Ch'ü Yüan drowns himself, the people regret and do penance for the injustice they have done him.

Silence is both expected of women and is part of their punishment for having been born inferior. The No Name Woman gives "silent birth" (11) just as she refuses to name the father of her illegitimate child. Her family punishes her with silence; they break the silence while the villagers ransack the house only to tell her that henceforth she is disowned. To them it is as though she had never been born. Her mother invites her daughter to join the family's historical punishment of this woman by keeping the family's silence, by denying her existence. The breaking of silence is, however, a necessary part of fighting back against the inferiority that is imposed upon women. So the narrator tells her aunt's story. In the same way, the immigrant Chinese keep silent about their personal histories, their names, and their birthdays in case these details should be used against them by the immigration authorities. Where female silence is a key feature of Chinese sexism, so Chinese silence is an important element of American racism. By denying their historical experiences, Chinese immigrants reduce their own reality. Consequently, she also speaks the truth about her parents and their personal histories. Silence contributes to the effacement of oppressed groups—women and Asians—but the breaking of those silences is a kind of noncooperation with sexism and racism that demands these discriminatory practices be acknowledged and brought to an end.

The power of silence to enforce discrimination compels the heroine to bully one of her classmates who refuses to talk; she feels that ending the silence of this young Chinese girl will end her own oppression by racism and sexism. Later, her aunt Moon Orchid is unable to talk about the difficulty she experiences adapting to a new life in America, and she goes mad. The narrator reflects, "I thought talking and not talking made the difference between sanity and insanity. Insane people were the ones who couldn't explain themselves" (186). Kingston is haunted by a constant anxiety that she will be thought insane. As she thinks about the Chinese families in her community, she observes that each family has its madwoman and she fears that she will be the madwoman of her family. In the final chapter she makes a list of grievances to tell her mother—make her mutilated tongue work in the cause of her own liberation.

The ability of a woman to express herself is related to the motif of mutilation that recurs throughout the narrative. The woman warrior who bears the injustices suffered by her village carved into her back is both a heroine and also an object whose body can be used as a text that accuses her village enemies of their many crimes even after she is dead. Her interpretation of the significance of her mother's act when she cut her daughter's frenum also has two dimensions. Either her mother sought to silence her by repressing her ability to speak—one of the immigrant Chinese sayings about girls is that "a ready tongue is an evil tongue" (164)—or else her mother was speaking truly when she explained that she cut her frenum to prevent her from being tongue-tied, to enable her to pronounce any sound she might wish to say, and to free her to learn many languages.

The theme of resistance and rebellion dominates *The Woman Warrior*. Various rebellions are represented in the narrative. The heroine rebels against the influence of her powerful mother. She rebels against the forces of gender and racial oppression that confront her. Part of that rebellion is her resistance to the inherited gender and racial stereotypes that others seek to impose upon her. Finally, she rebels against the history to which she is subject as her inheritance. Physical violence and resistance, however, are represented as ultimately inadequate weapons with which to engage her ideological enemies. When the warrior woman returns from the scene of battle, she returns to the customary life of a dutiful wife and daughter. She frees the old women whose feet are bound and crippled; she brings to justice the evil baron and even the corrupt emperor; but she does so in the guise of a man, and her efforts do nothing to transform gender relationships or to forge new possibilities for gender identity. A different kind of resistance is needed to battle psychological, ideological, and emotional enemies.

In *China Men* these ideological and psychological enemies are treated largely in historical terms, as the narrator seeks to re-create her father's earlier life. At the beginning of the narrative, she speaks to her absent father and proposes: "I tell you what I suppose from your silences and few words, and you can tell me that I'm mistaken. You'll just have to speak up with the real stories if I've got you wrong"

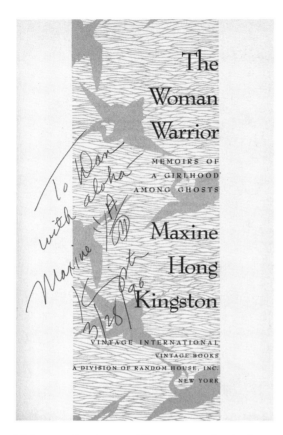

Title page for the 1989 Vintage paperback of Kingston's memoir, inscribed by the author

(15). She attempts to include all the influences that together have created her father's sense of himself and his life. She does not limit herself, therefore, to telling just the story of her father's childhood and early life in China. In addition, she tells the stories of his father, her paternal grandfather, and other older male relatives who immigrated to the United States. Through their shared experiences she gains insight into the forces that shaped her father's life. In this way, *China Men* rewrites the history of Chinese America by claiming an important role for Chinese efforts in the creation of America. In so doing, Kingston reinvents the notion of American national identity to incorporate the Chinese immigrant experience and its cross-cultural legacy. Consequently, Kingston challenges exclusive definitions of American nationality. She exposes the mechanisms of racial discrimination in several ways. In the chapter titled "The Laws," for example, she exposes the legislative means by means of which Chinese immigration to the United States has been restricted. She challenges the influence of racial stereotypes that deny the diversity of Chinese ethic groupings. Kingston describes the historical relationship between Chinese and Westerners that has been shaped by such experiences as the brutal treatment of indentured Chinese laborers on the sugarcane plantations, and the "The Driving Out" (145)—the term for the expulsion of Chinese laborers from California once the building of the railroad was complete.

The most dominant image of *China Men*, framing the narrative at the beginning and end, is that of America as the Gold Mountain—an image which represents America in a mythical perspective. The journey to the Gold Mountain is accepted by the father's family as a part of a man's life. In *The Woman Warrior* Kingston describes the mass village wedding where all the single men about to depart for America were married to women who would provide living links between the sojourners and their home in China. In *China Men* she tells of her father's increasing enthusiasm for travel, as he listens to the stories told by older men about their time spent in America. The first story of *China Men*, however, presents a bleak prospect for any man intending to seek the Gold Mountain. Tang Ao finds not the Gold Mountain but a Land of Women, where he himself is transformed into a woman, violated, and emasculated. Rather than discovering wealth and riches, Tang Ao loses even his own sense of self-worth. This story suggests some of the dangers that confront all the men who travel to the Gold Mountain to seek their fortunes. Not one character depicted in *China Men* finds in America the destiny he has sought. The closing story of the narrative likens the Gold Mountain to the image of a gold needle, lost in the haystack of lived experiences. What the sojourners do not realize, but is seen quite clearly by Kingston, is that they are themselves the treasure that they seek. The labor they expend upon developing the American nation—by clearing wilderness for cultivation and by building railroads—is the source of great wealth. Though these men have no share of the wealth they create, their descendants benefit by living in the nation they helped to build, a legacy bequeathed to the narrator by her forefathers.

The significance of the Gold Mountain is different for the various characters of the narrative. For Ah Goong, the Gold Mountain is synonymous with hardship, discrimination, and isolation. For him, life in America means forgetting his past life in China. He makes a deliberate decision during the time he spends in detention, waiting for his visa application to be processed, that he will make a new start in this new country and no longer be subject to Chinese superstitions or the influences of his Chinese past. To his daughter, he can "only look and talk Chinese. . . . No stories. No past" (14). In contrast, characters such as Bak Goong and Uncle Bun, who fears persecution in America for his communist views, become consumed with the desire to return to China.

Both *China Men* and *The Woman Warrior* are characterized by Kingston's extensive use of the imagery of ghosts and demons. For example, Bak Goong and the other Chinese laborers on the sugar plantation refer to the brutal British overseers as demons, or devils. Also in *China Men*, Sao's mother and Say Goong haunt the relatives who settle permanently in America. For the immigrant Chinese, the white Anglo-American world is the world of ghosts, a world more like that represented in myths and tales than historical reality. Ghosts represent aspects of the loss of identity more than the loss of life. The No Name Woman refers to her newborn child as a ghost because the baby's illegitimacy means that all her family disowns her. The baby has no claim upon a family identity. Consequently, even before her mother kills her, this child is referred to as a ghost. Brave Orchid routinely refers to the white Americans she encounters on a daily basis as ghosts. These people to her are completely foreign and mysterious. Just how foreign white Americans appear to her is emphasized when Moon Orchid, during her first walk around Stockton's Chinatown, remarks that the people passing by her are not so foreign as she had expected. Brave Orchid tells her impatiently that she has not yet seen a Caucasian—they are immigrant Chinese that Moon Orchid has mistaken for Americans.

In *The Woman Warrior* ghosts are of three kinds: in addition to the familiar supernatural figures, Kingston's ghosts may be either figures from the distant past, or figures from a mysterious, foreign Anglo culture. Kingston's ghosts threaten Chinese ethnic identity by drawing people away from the values and customs of traditional Chinese culture. No Name Aunt is called a ghost, a "dead ghost" (14) by her family for having violated the rule of patriarchy, and for this reason Moon Orchid thinks of her sister's children as ghosts; she refers to Brave Orchid's two children who were born in and died in China as the "real Chinese babies" (132). The American children she treats as if they belong in a separate realm. Moon Orchid follows them around the house, speaking aloud a commentary on their every action and repeating their words. Later the narrator reveals that all the immigrant Chinese call their American-born children ghosts, or "Ho Chi Kuei," though she admits that the term may be "Hao Chi Kuei, which could mean they are calling us 'Good Foundation

Ghosts'" (204). When finally she confronts the husband she has not seen for thirty years, Moon Orchid discovers that to him she has become a ghost: "Her husband looked like one of the ghosts passing the car windows, and she must look like a ghost from China. They had indeed entered the land of ghosts, and they had become ghosts" (153). She herself becomes a ghost; when Brave Orchid begins to fear that her sister has already departed her body and is uttering the insane words, she takes the first steps to having Moon Orchid committed to an asylum. Caucasian Americans, who exist outside the confines of the Chinese American community, are referred to as ghosts: Taxi Ghosts, Police Ghosts, Grocery Ghosts—in this way, threats to traditional Chinese culture are rendered void and deprived of reality.

The most-terrifying ghosts that the heroine encounters are the images of the dead and tortured Chinese her mother conjures. Not so much the aunt whose thumbs are screwed off as she is tortured by the Communists, or the uncle whose murdered body the Communists leave in a tree to be a warning to others, but the images of dead and dying babies that her mother delivered, like the child born with no anus, are transformed in her imagination into "nightmare babies" (86). In China, Brave Orchid encounters real ghosts, like her exorcism of the "Sitting Ghost" (74) that haunts the medical college, or the ghosts that try to tip her off a bridge and which she and her great-uncle agree were "Sit Dom Kuei" (88). As if to testify to the truth and reality of these ghosts, the narrator refers to the time when "the Communists issued their papers on techniques for combating ghosts" (88) and to the proof that her mother triumphed over ghosts: "now I see that my mother won in ghost battle because she can eat anything. . . . All heroes are bold toward food" (88). In an important way Brave Orchid, this exorcist of Chinese ghosts, assists her daughter by taking on and dealing with the metaphorical ghosts of her Chinese American world.

The strategy that Brave Orchid uses to deal with the ghosts and devils she encounters is through storytelling, or "talk-story" (19). She tells stories about the things that frighten or worry her and in this way she understands and resolves her anxieties. Brave Orchid also instructs, warns, and entertains her daughter with stories. When she tells the No Name Woman's story, Brave Orchid does all of these. When her daughter repeats her mother's talk-story in *The Woman Warrior,* she displays what she has learned from her mother. This story demonstrates also that words can make possible a form of vengeance, as she avenges the sacrifice of her aunt to the cause of Chinese patriarchy by breaking the family's silence and telling her aunt's story to the world.

The Woman Warrior can be seen as a feminist *kunstlerroman*, a story of the development of the artist from a child to maturity. The culmination of the narrative, the moment when the protagonist accepts her destiny as a writer who will record the experiences that actually comprise the narrative, comes with her warning: "Be careful what you say. It comes true. It comes true. I had to leave home in order to see the world logically, logic the new way of seeing. . . . Shine floodlights into dark corners: no ghosts" (204). At the end of the narrative, she expresses a new view of herself as a translator, a mediator between cultures, which is based on her inheritance from her mother, Brave Orchid, who was able to live among barbarians—a Chinese woman in Anglo-America—and survive to tell the story.

NOTES

1. Maxine Hong Kingston, *The Woman Warrior: Memoirs of a Girlhood Among Ghosts* (New York: Vintage, 1989), p. 3. Subsequent parenthetical references in the text are to this edition.

2. Maxine Hong Kingston, *China Men* (New York: Vintage, 1989), p. 14. Subsequent parenthetical references in the text are to this edition.

3. Paul Skenazy, "Coming Home," in *Conversations with Maxine Hong Kingston,* edited by Skenazy and Tera Martin (Jackson: University Press of Mississippi, 1998), p. 114.

4. Gary Kubota, "Maxine Hong Kingston: Something Comes from Outside Onto the Paper," in *Conversations with Maxine Hong Kingston,* p. 3.

5. Jody Hoy, "To Be Able to See the Tao," in *Conversations with Maxine Hong Kingston,* p. 49.

THE EVOLUTION OF *THE WOMAN WARRIOR* AND *CHINA MEN*

WRITING *THE WOMAN WARRIOR* AND *CHINA MEN*

Kingston took two years to write her first published book, *The Woman Warrior*. She wrote earlier books that have remained unpublished. Kingston originally wrote much of the material that eventually was published as the two books, *The Woman Warrior* and *China Men,* when she first started writing as a child. In a 1980 interview with Arturo Islas and Marilyn Yalom, she admitted that she had been working on the material since then. She explained, "In a sense you could say that I was working on these books for 20 or 30 years, but in another sense I wrote them just a few years ago."[1] While writing *The Woman Warrior,* she worked in relative isolation, refusing to show the work in progress to friends or colleagues. When she decided it was time to reveal the work to external scrutiny, she chose to approach an agent rather than a publisher. She knew that her knowledge of the literary market was limited, and she was not familiar with any of the small presses that might publish her book. Kingston assumed that the larger presses would likely reject her work, so she decided to approach an agent who would know of small presses that might be interested in *The Woman Warrior*. She told Islas and Yalom, "I didn't realize that New York agents don't know the small presses. So when I found an agent, he looked immediately at the large presses and sold it almost right off."[2] Consequently, Kingston found publication easy to achieve. Although her ambitions for the book were modest, she took the success of *The Woman Warrior* in stride. She was surprised when *China Men* joined *The Woman Warrior* on the best-seller list at the same time in 1980. Like every writer, she had dreamed of writing a best-seller but she had never entertained the possibility of having two best-sellers simultaneously.

The publication of *The Woman Warrior* was met with critical success. Among the most enthusiastic reviewers was John Leonard, who wrote in the *The New York Times* (17 September 1976), "Those rumbles you hear on the horizon are the big guns of autumn lining up, the howit-

Kingston

zers of Vonnegut and Updike and Cheever and Mailer, the books that will be making loud noises for the next several months. But listen: this week a remarkable book has been quietly published; it is one of the best I've read for years."[3] In Leonard's estimation, the appearance of *The Woman Warrior* signaled a change in the direction of American literature, away from the dominant position of male novelists. Both academic and popular readers received this first book, like *China Men* after it, with great acclaim, but Kingston's own reaction to this new fame was modest. In a 1979 interview with Karen Horton, Kingston speculated that her age and maturity (she was in her mid-thirties when *The Woman Warrior* was published) may have explained her simple acceptance of the public praise.

Kingston's technique for the writing of both *The Woman Warrior* and *China Men* depended upon her memory of the stories her family told her as a child rather than upon extensive research. In 1977 after the publication of *The Woman Warrior*, Kingston explained her method to Gary Kubota in the *Hawaii Observer*: "I don't do research when I write. I believe there's some creative source in people, and if they can tap it, they don't need to do research. The stories within the book are based mostly on my past experiences as a child living with my parents in Stockton, California. They operated a laundry in the downtown area, and while growing up, I was constantly listening to them and my relatives talk-story. Their recollections of myths, fables and Chinese history turned out to be amazingly accurate."[4]

An additional reason why Kingston has no need of research is that she does not always know what she will write in advance. She told Kubota, "I feel that something comes from outside through me onto the typewriter paper. Often, I sit at the typewriter and compose stuff I didn't even know I knew. It happens all the time. It's not like I've decided what I'm going to write."[5] In her conversation with Horton, Kingston described her approach to her work as profoundly emotional: "There's a feeling I have, or there are feelings, the way people are in certain circumstances. I feel that it comes from the heightened moments in all our lives when we are really aware of what it feels like to be a person or what life is

KINGSTON ON THE ORIGIN OF *CHINA MEN*

"I've always been a writer. There was always the wanting to tell the stories of the people coming. I remember writing *China Men* stories when I was 8, or 9, 10 years old, but I didn't have the vocabulary and the form because I was just a kid. The emotions and the stories I had already, but not the craft."

Maxine Hong Kingston

From Kay Bonetti, "An Interview with Maxine Hong Kingston," in *Conversations with Maxine Hong Kingston,* edited by Paul Skenazy and Tera Martin (Jackson: University Press of Mississippi, 1998), p. 34.

all about. You don't feel it too often, but every once in a while you feel it. I want to put that feeling into writing or I want to write words so that when somebody reads it, they can have that feeling. All the details are only components to get to this feeling. It's sort of a heightened awareness so that you know what it means to be human."[6] The feelings out of which she wrote *The Woman Warrior* changed in the course of the writing. In a 1983 interview with Phyllis Hoge Thompson, Kingston explained that she shifted points of view as she described her narrator: "I feel different when I write her at different ages. I like her viewpoint and her intensity so much."

The Woman Warrior is characterized by its political themes of sexism and racism. Originally, the narrative formed part of a larger work that also incorporated *China Men*. The importance of the theme of gender, however, contributed significantly to Kingston's decision to divide the work. As she explained to Paula Rabinowitz, "The women had their own time and place and their lives were coherent; there was a woman's way of thinking. My men's stories seemed to interfere. They were weakening the feminist point of view. So I took all the men's stories out, and then I had *The Woman Warrior*."[8] Although her writing expresses a strong feminist commitment, Kingston is aware of the potential dangers facing a political writer. She has remarked of *The Woman Warrior*: "I feel I've written a political and artistic work. It's important for me to show that both are possible. I've always felt that it's easy to fall into propagandizing when one does political writing. It can also be very poor writing. It's important for me to show that racial or feminist writing doesn't have to sound like polemics. It can dramatize events and make them brighter."[9] In the interview with Hoge Thompson, Kingston gave an example of how she would take an ordinary story about which she has heard and transform it into a meaningful narrative:

> I was given this little story about getting lost. A lost Chinese sees another Chinese across the street, and calls to him, "Sook Ah." A bystander thinks he said "sugar," and he says, "Oh, you want to find the sugar plantation." Now, I think that's a nothing story. It has no shape, no dramatic suspense, no plot, no chase . . . it's just not very interesting. And yet it was fervidly remembered. So it becomes my task to write about this little nothing story, to try to give it a literary importance. If *they* were so interested, *I* must be interested too.[10]

This little story became a part of Bak Goong's experience of Hawaii in *China Men*. In the chapter, "Great Grandfather of the Sandalwood Mountains," Kingston tells how early one evening, Bak Goong finds himself lost in an unfamiliar part of town and about to be approached by a policeman when he thinks to call "Sook-ah"—meaning "Father's Younger Brother" (111)—to a passing Chinese man. Bak Goong is saved by the policeman's misinterpretation of the sound as the word "sugar" which he assumes is a request for directions to the waiting wagons which will take the laborers back to the sugarcane plantation. The shaping of her materials is a key challenge for Kingston, especially in view of the autobiographical nature of *China Men* and *The Woman Warrior*. In the interview with Hoge Thompson, Kingston explained that events rarely conform to a dramatic structure, though occasionally they do. The example of this dramatic structuring of events that Kingston isolates is the chapter with Moon Orchid's story, "At the Western Palace." Kingston described how this series of events lent themselves to narrative structure: "There's a right number of characters, there's the confrontation towards the end. There's a denouement. But in life that seldom occurs. In fact, in all the stories of those two books, that's the only place where life unfolded like a short story. But that hardly ever happens. So I had to figure out new ways of arranging the material."[11]

KINGSTON ON CREATIVITY

"It's really strange the way creativity sees the world. I think what happens is that you set out to see something, and you've already made up an idea of what it is you want to find. You've already set yourself up to find it because you have the image of it. But then on a larger level, I think that we can actively control this by making up a vision of a better society, by making up a vision of what it is to be a good human being. And when you make that up abstractly, that gets you ready to find it out there, or to build it out there."

Maxine Hong Kingston

From Paul Skenazy, "Kingston at the University," in *Conversations with Maxine Hong Kingston*, edited by Skenazy and Tera Martin (Jackson: University Press of Mississippi, 1998), p. 151.

In writing *China Men* Kingston approached her material somewhat differently than with *The Woman Warrior*. In a 1980 interview with *The New York Times Book Review*, she explained, "The style is much simpler.... I was wrestling with language in the first book, so the sentences are sometimes quite convoluted. After I wrote that book, I had a strong desire to write simple sentences."[12]

The language of *The Woman Warrior*—Kingston's blending of realism, myth, and fantasy—is both distinctive and innovative. An example of the ambiguous nature of Kingston's style in *The Woman Warrior* is found in the "White Tigers" chapter, where the distinction breaks down between reality, dream, and fantasy. When the narrator claims that it was not until she could "point at the sky and make a sword appear" (33) that the old couple who are her teachers and mentors will allow her to leave them, the significance of this claim as real, fantasy, or metaphor is uncertain. The ability to make a sword appear through force of will could signify metaphorically her great power or it could be a real ability within the mythical terms of the woman warrior's story. The convoluted and ambiguous style of *The Woman Warrior* does, however, enable Kingston to forge a compromise between the style of storytelling that inspired her and the written style of her narrative. The talk-story upon which Kingston drew for the substance of *The Woman Warrior* is an oral tradition of storytelling; as a spoken form, talk-story does not exist in a single version. Rather, the same stories exist in many different versions; they differ from one telling to the next according to the storyteller, the occasion, and the effect the teller wants to achieve. In the interview with Islas and Yalom, Kingston described how each story "changes according to the needs of the listener, according to the needs of the day, according to the interest of the time, and the story can be different from day to day. So what happens when you write it down? Writing is so static. The story will remain as printed for the next two hundred years and it's not going to change. That really bothers me, because what would be really neat would be for the words to change on the page every time, but they can't. *So the way I tried to solve this problem was to keep ambiguity in the writing all the time.*"[13] For example, at the beginning of the section titled "A Song for a Barbarian Reed Pipe," the narrator confesses the unreliable source of her information about Moon Orchid's story, which has just been told in the preceding section. In this way she introduces doubt about the accuracy and authenticity of the preceding narrative.

The image of writing that is represented in *The Woman Warrior* is neither positive nor negative. The ability of writers to effect the resolution of conflicts or to transform the world is limited. Kingston said to Hoge Thompson, "the frustration I feel is that writers have the power to change the world only a little bit at a time. We conquer a reader at a time. We change the atmosphere of the world, and we change moods here and there, whereas the people who have the guns and the bombs have so much direct power."[14] As a writer, Kingston creates characters and scenes that are also outside the realm of direct power, big government, and state-waged war. The characters about whom Kingston writes in *The Woman Warrior* are individuals who are insignificant from a broad historical perspective—these are not people who alter the course of history, and Kingston is aware of that. She told Hoge Thompson, "When I write about real people I write to see what they would do with their own small consciousness, their insignificant lives. If I compared them to big public events and personalities, then I would have nothing because they're nobody. I try not to make note of what year a person is born, but instead to see all those flickering lights, and then the lights evolving into some kind of meaning and picture."[15] The characters about whom she writes in *China Men*, however, are characters who have played a significant role in the historical development of America as a nation yet have been removed for the most part from the historical chinamen. The Rock Springs Massacre began in a large coal mine owned by the Union Pacific; the outnumbered chinamen were shot in the back as they ran to Chinatown, which the demons burned. They shot chinamen forced out into the open, demon women and children threw the wounded back in the flames. (There was a rumor of a good white lady in Green Springs who hid China Men in the Pacific Hotel and shamed the demons away.) The hunt went on for a month before federal troops came. The count of the dead was inexact because bodies were mutilated and pieces scattered all over the Wyoming Territory. No white miners were indicted, but the government gave $150,00 in reparations to victims' families. There were many family men, then, were families settlers. Ah Goong was running elsewhere during the Driving Out of Tacoma, Seattle, Oregon City, Albania, and Marysville. The entire chinamen population of Tacoma was packed into boxcars and sent to Portland, where they were run out of town. China Men returned to Seattle, though, and refused to sell their land and stores but fought until the army came; the demon rioters were tried and acquitted. And when the Boston police imprisoned and beat 234 chinamen, it was 1902, and Ah Goong had already reached San Francisco or China, and perhaps San Francisco again.

In Second City (Sacramento), he spent some of his railroad money at the theater. The main actor's face was painted red with thick black eyebrows and long black beard, and when he strode onto the stage, Ah Goong recognized the hero, Guan Goong; his puppet horse had red nostrils and rolling eyes. Ah Goong's heart leapt to recognize hero and horse in the wilds of America. Guan Goong murdered his enemy—crash! bang! of cymbals and drum—and left his home village—sad, sad flute music. But to the glad clamor of cymbals entered the friends—Liu Pei (pronounced the same as Running Nose) and Chang Fei. In a joyful burst of pink flowers, the three men swore the Peach Garden Oath. Each friend friend sang an aria to friendship; together they would fight side by side and live and die one for all and all for one. Ah Goong felt as warm as if he were with friends at a party. Then Guan Goong's archenemy, the sly Ts'ao Ts'ao, captured him and two of Liu Pei's wives, the Lady Kan and the Lady Mi. Though Ah Goong knew they were boy actors, he basked in the presence of Chinese ladies. They traveled to the capital, the soldiers waving horsehair whisks, signifying horses, the ladies walking between horizontal banners, signifying palanquins. All the prisoners were put in one bedroom, but Guan Goong stood all night outside the door with a lighted candle in his hand, singing an aria about faithfulness. When the capital was attacked by a common enemy, Guan Goong fought the biggest man in one-to-one combat, a twirling, jumping sword dance that strengthened the China Men who watched it. Guan Goong's two partners heard about the feats of the man with the red face and intelligent horse. The three friends were reunited and fought until Liu Pei they secured his rightful kingdom.

Ah Goong felt refreshed and inspired. He called out Bravo like the demons in the audience, who had not seen theater before. Guan

Corrected galley proof from *China Men*

KINGSTON ON BIOGRAPHY

"I tell the imaginative lives and the dreams and the fictions of real people. These are the stories of storytellers, and so instead of telling the dates when people are born and where they're born, I tell you what their dreams are and what stories they tell. So what I've written are biographies of imaginative people, and this is culturally correct, because this is the way my people are, my family. People come together and they tell each other their lives, and they make up the stories of their lives."

Maxine Hong Kingston

From Kay Bonetti, "An Interview with Maxine Hong Kingston," in *Conversations with Maxine Hong Kingston*, edited by Paul Skenazy and Tera Martin (Jackson: University Press of Mississippi, 1998), p. 37.

record. They are insignificant only as a consequence of racist historiography, which Kingston aims to correct.

Developing the characters of *China Men* and *The Woman Warrior* presented particular problems for the author, in that many of these people had secret lives: "They didn't want to tell the true story because they were doing something illegal such as gambling. There were lots of illegal immigrants. They made up respectable, legal life stories. They had versions of their lives, and all of them sounded very convincing. Depending on how well you knew them, they would tell you a different version."[16] Kingston felt an obligation to protect these people by maintaining their silence concerning the real events of their lives and by perpetuating the fictions they had invented in order to continue to live their lives in the United States. To do this, Kingston was forced to write in a convoluted, indirect style. To tell the single, "true" story about individuals may be to call down the authorities upon them. As Kingston explained to Hoge Thompson, "this need for secrecy affected my form and my style. I couldn't write things that would hurt these people. There was this ambiguous way I was writing. I would say, this story is what so and so said happened, but it could be it happened this other way. And I'd write two or three versions."[17] She admitted that she does favor particular versions of the stories—though not necessarily the more "true" stories—and these preferences determined how the stories were represented in the narrative: "As I was writing I did try to weight the stories, so that one would appear more true than another one. That's my guess, isn't it? That's why I made myself such a strong character, because knowing this narrator and her biases and her proclivity for colorfulness, you'd say, aha, she *would* think that story's true."[18] By her use of ambiguity and indirection, Kingston seeks to create a realistic representation of the Chinese American community. Of a necessity born of the history of anti-Chinese racism, this community has so much to hide: "They themselves can't afford to tell the truth. So they tell it the way I've told it. When I tell it with all these versions, I'm actually giving the culture of these people in a very accurate way. You can see where the people make up these fictions about themselves, and it's not just for fun. It's a terrible necessity."[19]

REVISING *THE WOMAN WARRIOR* AND *CHINA MEN*

During the writing of *The Woman Warrior* and *China Men* Kingston was neither organized nor disciplined about her working habits. She confessed to Kubota, "Writing is a very painful act. I try to start writing in the mornings, but I fool around and put it off to wash dishes or sharpen my pencils. I'm pretty regular on writing every day, but sometimes I start late and end up finishing in the afternoons."[20] Each text went through an extensive process of revision before Kingston showed her work to anyone. This process of revision continued through each stage of the publication process. For example, *China Men* was subject to at least eight substantial rewritings. She revised the galley proofs so extensively that the book had to be sent back to the typesetters so that all the changes could be accommodated. In the introduction to his 1980 interview with Kingston, Timothy Pfaff described how "snakes of galley proofs line the walls of the living room and small dining room" of her home.[21] At times during the interview he observed Kingston's eyes "wander to the proofs on the nearby table," suggesting that she betrayed some impatience to return to her work of revision.[22]

Kingston preferred to do the writing and the revising of *The Woman Warrior* and *China Men* alone so she could write free from the responses of others. In particular, she could be free to work without the sense that in her writing she was creating a representative picture of Asian American experience. Instead, in these two books she was free to write of her family's history and of her own life. She explained to Pfaff: "The one thing about which I am absolutely sure . . . is that I am a Chinese American woman. That feeling affects my writing in a particular way: I know that what I have to say is what a Chinese American person is thinking. I don't have to go out and make a survey; I don't have to get a committee of peers to correct my work. I see writing as a very solitary thing that I have to do by myself, and polish by myself. It's a very free activity: I can think whatever I want and write in whatever way I want. When I get it into as perfect a state as I can, then I show it to people."[23]

NOTES

1. Arturo Islas and Marilyn Yalom, "Interview with Maxine Hong Kingston," in *Conversations with Maxine Hong Kingston*, edited by Paul Skenazy & Tera Martin (Jackson: University Press of Mississippi, 1998), p. 23.

2. Ibid.

3. John Leonard, "In Defiance of Two Worlds," *New York Times*, 17 September 1976, sec. 3, p. 21.

4. Gary Kubota, "Maxine Hong Kingston: Something Comes From Outside Onto the Paper," in *Conversations with Maxine Hong Kingston*, p. 2.

5. Ibid.

6. Karen Horton, "*Honolulu* Interview: Maxine Hong Kingston," in *Conversations with Maxine Hong Kingston,* pp. 11–12.

7. Phyllis Hoge Thompson, "This is the Story I Heard: A Conversation with Maxine Hong Kingston and Earll Kingston," in *Conversations with Maxine Hong Kingston*, p. 7.

8. Paula Rabinowitz, "Eccentric Memories: A Conversation with Maxine Hong Kingston," in *Conversations with Maxine Hong Kingston*, p. 69.

9. Ibid., p. 3.

10. Hoge Thompson, pp. 3–4.

11. Ibid., p. 8.

12. Timothy Pfaff, "Talk with Mrs. Kingston," in *Conversations with Maxine Hong Kingston*, p. 16.

13. Islas and Yalom, p. 31.

14. Kay Bonetti, "An Interview with Maxine Hong Kingston," in *Conversations with Maxine Hong Kingston,* p. 37.

15. Hoge Thompson, p. 2.

16. Ibid., p. 10.

17. Ibid.

18. Ibid., p. 12.

19. Ibid.

20. Kubota, p. 3.

21. Pfaff, p. 14.

22. Ibid.

23. Ibid., p. 19.

THEMES IN *THE WOMAN WARRIOR* AND *CHINA MEN*

SUMMARY OF THEMES

The themes of *The Woman Warrior* and *China Men* are inseparable from Maxine Hong Kingston's characters and the history through which they lived. Kingston explores the impact of twentieth-century historical changes upon her immigrant parents; however, she does not represent these events directly. Instead, she introduces events as they influenced and shaped her parents' lives. For example, her mother's education is made possible by the reforms of traditional Chinese culture introduced by Sun Yat-sen and the Republican forces. Likewise, the multiple life stories told by members of the Chinese American community who do not dare expose the real circumstances of their lives to immigration authorities are the consequence of a long history of anti-Chinese prejudice that has been expressed in discriminatory immigration laws. Kingston also treats more-contemporary trends and events in American history, such as the Civil Rights movement, the women's liberation movement, and the Vietnam War. While she does not portray these events in a direct fashion, she writes how these movements and the war affected the characters in the books.

Through both *The Woman Warrior and China Men* the effects of sexism, patriarchy, and feminism, in both China and America, form the context within which Kingston's young narrator seeks to determine her mature identity. She experiences the influence of feminist ideas in part through her teachers who encourage her to think about college and a professional career. She determines that she will be more than a wife, a mother, a slave to men. The protagonist searches for a sense of personal worth in a world that devalues her because she is female. She finds this antifemale prejudice most clearly expressed in the practices of traditional Chinese culture about which her parents tell stories. They recall, in passing, the practices of arranged marriage, polygamy, and concubinage. She also hears the stories of female relatives whose lives were blighted by hatred of women: the grandmother who could not walk on her bound

A slave girl in Chinatown in San Francisco, circa 1895–1906, photographed by Arnold Genthe. In *The Woman Warrior* Kingston writes, "There is a Chinese word for the female I - which is slave."

feet, the No Name Woman who loses her life, and Moon Orchid who is treated like a widow by the husband who has abandoned her.

Like the Chinese women whose lives are constrained by the misogyny of their culture, the young heroine discovers that the Chinese in America are constrained by the racism of American culture. Her mother was a doctor in China, but she is forced into manual labor in the United States—Brave Orchid works in the laundry, in the canneries, and in the fields picking fruit. She tells her daughter, "I didn't need muscles in China. I was small in China" (104); and her daughter reflects, "She was. The silk dresses she gave me are tiny. You would not think the same person wore them. This mother can carry a hundred pounds of Texas rice up- and downstairs" (104). Brave Orchid expresses grudging admiration for her sister Moon Orchid's estranged husband because, although he is Chinese, he runs a successful practice as a neurosurgeon. However, his success is achieved at the expense of his Chinese ethnicity. He abandons his Chinese past along with his Chinese wife, Moon Orchid, and his assimilation into American life is represented by his marriage to an American-born Chinese woman from whom he keeps secret such details of his past life in China as his first wife and their daughter. Brave Orchid's own husband is remembered by her sister as a young scholar, but in America he works first in a gambling house and later runs a laundry. Not only restricted employment opportunities limit the lives of the immigrant Chinese. Anti-Chinese immigration legislation, dating from the nineteenth century, restricted the freedom of Chinese people to settle in the United States; consequently, both legal and illegal immigrants developed a widespread suspicion and mistrust of the immigration authorities. Kingston represents individuals who have constructed for themselves complex alternative life stories with which to protect themselves and their families from the threat of deportation. Racism determines the possibilities of life for Chinese immigrants in the United States, as sexism does the lives of women in the China these immigrants left behind.

AUTOBIOGRAPHICAL THEMES

The autobiographical character of *The Woman Warrior* and *China Men* arises from Kingston's use of events and experiences in her own life as the occasion for exploring the major themes of the narratives. For example, in *The Woman Warrior*, the related themes of misogyny, silence, and revenge are explored through Kingston's discovery of her father's sister, the No Name Woman, who was in reality an aunt of Kingston's.

THE NO NAME WOMAN

"In the twenty years since I heard this story I have not asked for details nor said my aunt's name; I do not know it. People who can comfort the dead can also chase after them to hurt them further—a reverse ancestor worship. The real punishment was not the raid swiftly inflicted by the villagers, but the family's deliberately forgetting her. Her betrayal so maddened them, they saw to it that she would suffer forever, even after death."

Maxine Hong Kingston

From *The Woman Warrior* (New York: Vintage, 1989), p. 16.

In this story many characters are motivated by the desire for revenge. The villagers believe that the aunt's illegitimate child threatens the ability of the village to provide sufficient food for all its members in a time of food shortage and hunger. The villagers also perceive that the aunt's adultery threatened the basis of patriarchal culture, in which women are subject to the will of their fathers and husbands. In this culture, feminine sexuality is closely controlled by men through the institution of marriage. Women may be sexually active only within the confines of the marriage relation, and in this way the legitimacy of all children is assured. Their legitimacy is essential for the perpetuation of clear lines of descent and inheritance. In a patriarchal society such as the Chinese society of Kingston's parents, inheritance passes through the male line, from father to son, and the values of society work to ensure that every father knows that his property is inherited by his own son. Thus, adultery and illegitimacy cannot be tolerated, and a harsh penalty is exacted for those found guilty of these crimes. The villagers take revenge upon her family for this crime against the patriarchal values of the community by ransacking and destroying the family's property.

The family then takes revenge upon their daughter for bringing shame and infamy upon the household. They dispossess and disown her, turning her out of the house and treating her as if she were already dead by calling her "Ghost" and "Dead ghost" (14). Kingston has described in an interview the circumstances in which she and her sister confronted their parents with direct questions about the historical existence of this aunt. Her parents were reluctant to break their long silence but finally their mother relented: "'Oh, go ahead and tell her.' And then he said, yes, he had a sister. So that makes me feel that the whole story is true. But that's as much as I know. He did not say what became of her. And just by his silence, I assume that what I surmised is so."[1]

Kingston goes on to explain that by telling the story in all its complexity, including all the possible motivations and circumstances, she finally ends that process of vengeance and restores her aunt's identity and gives her a place in history. Kingston reflected, "I now realize that what I did by writing down her story and giving it my concern and care and finding the words for it, I have saved her. I realize now that this is the power of art. I gave her a life, I gave her a history, I gave her immortality, I gave her meaning. . . . And by finding her meaning and giving that meaning to all of us, I retrieved her from the no-nameness, the nothing, and created her again. And I do feel that your reading it finishes this act of creativity. She lives because of your having read that story and having questions about it."[2] The reader then becomes involved in the act of vengeance as Kingston simultaneously ends her family's historical punishment of the daughter they have cast out of their history and places the blame where it belongs—with the patriarchal value system that requires women be controlled by men or else die. Kingston exacts revenge upon a system of sexual oppression and intolerance that has brought about the injustice that was her aunt's death. She also gives the reader a part to play in this act of vengeance by exposing the circumstances of her aunt's death to the reader as a witness. She is invited by her mother to join in the family's ostracism of her aunt; instead, the reader joins with the author in the breaking of the silence that has surrounded the No Name Woman.

In a 1986 interview Kingston explained the difference between Chinese and American attitudes toward revenge, and the importance of the theme in *The Woman Warrior*: "I come from a culture where revenge is important. So many of the stories and operas I grew up on have that theme of revenge. I think revenge has something to do with justice in our lifetime rather than justice in another reincarnation. But in American culture revenge is really questioned. Christianity says no revenge. The vengeance I will permit myself has to come in a new form. I wrote in *The Woman Warrior* that the Chinese idiom for 'revenge' can also mean 'reporting to five families.' If you can find the words for an injustice and put it in some artistic shape, and let everyone know, then revenge has taken place. It has something to do with broadcasting the reputation of one that you want revenge against. Revenge cannot take the form of an eye for an eye, not like that."[3]

At the end of the chapter "No Name Woman," Kingston introduces one final act of vengeance that completes this drama. The narrator remarks that in drowning herself and her baby in the family well, in the drinking water, the No Name Woman is acting from spite. Kingston calls this a "spite suicide" (16), and she describes the fear with which Chinese superstition receives the figure of the drowned corpse, "whose weeping ghost, wet hair hanging and skin bloated, waits silently by the water to pull down a substitute" (16). In choosing the manner of her death in this way, the No Name Woman exacts a measure of revenge for

KINGSTON ON GHOSTS

"There are people who are people, and there are people that are ghosts doing real things, like selling newspapers and bringing milk and driving taxicabs. So I am describing an actual cultural phenomenon. These books have the artistic problem of how to write the true biographies of real people who have very imaginative minds."

Maxine Hong Kingston

From Jody Hoy, "To Be Able to See the Tao," in *Conversations with Maxine Hong Kingston,* edited by Paul Skenazy and Tera Martin (Jackson: University Press of Mississippi, 1998), p. 61.

---

herself and her child. The narrator also suggests that her aunt killed herself before her family or neighbors could kill her, thus taking something away from the complete fulfillment of their vengeance. After the villagers ransacked their house, her family curses her by ranting, "Death is coming. Death is coming" (13). Perhaps by this they mean to kill her themselves but will wait until her baby is born to ascertain its gender; as the narrator comments, "There is some hope of forgiveness for boys" (15). While the family still sleeps, before they can see her living child, she drowns herself and the baby. In this chapter then, the patterns of revenge are complex and multiple.

The breaking of silence is, for Kingston as a writer, an important aspect of avenging wrongs. Sexism and racism both work to encourage women and members of racial minorities to keep silent. The inability to assert oneself orally, to tell one's story, is to adopt a position of weakness and passivity. As Kingston has remarked: "Language is important to our sanity. *You have to be able to tell your story, you have to be able to make up stories or you go mad.*"[4] The importance of gaining a voice, both as a woman and as a Chinese American woman, has been dramatically demonstrated to Kingston, who, like the narrator of *The Woman Warrior,* suffered a prolonged period of muteness. She admitted in a 1980 interview, "Yes, I went through a time when I did not talk to people. . . you know, it comes and goes. It's still happening to me but not so severely. And also, I'm all right now but I do know people who never came out of it."[5] The Chinese girl who refuses to speak, despite the violent bullying of her, is based partly upon Kingston herself but also someone Kingston knew: "she is a recluse today in that Victorian-woman sense. Even today she is closed off."[6]

The difficulty Kingston experienced as a child with oral expression was at its most intense in her first years at school when shyness, fear, and her inability to speak English caused her not to speak at all. Instead, she painted pictures and then, to express her own inability to communicate, she would paint over the figures and scenes with black paint. The blackness was not intended to obliterate the scenes but to represent the curtain that Kingston felt separated her from the rest of the world. She describes this in *The Woman Warrior:* "I painted layers of black over houses and flowers and suns, and when I drew on the blackboard, I put a layer of chalk on top. I was making a stage curtain, and it was the moment before the curtain parted or rose" (165). The curtain had to be raised to reveal the drama concealed beneath—Kingston refers to the scenes hidden by the black curtain as "operas" (165); just as the curtain of silence that was her parents' silence concerning China and Kingston's Chinese cultural inheritance had to be removed so that she could know and claim her heritage. Though she had difficulty with oral expression, Kingston always wrote and recorded her experiences: as she has said, "While I've had problems speaking, I've always been a writer."[7]

Kingston's inability to speak English resulted in a series of early humiliations described by the narrator of *The Woman Warrior:* "During the first silent year I spoke to no one at school, did not ask before going to the lavatory, and flunked kindergarten" (165). She was not entirely silent, however, and recalls, "I talked at home and to one or two of the Chinese kids in class. I made motions and even made some jokes" (166). The shame of her early failures, however, remains with the narrator, who, at the end of the narrative, accuses her mother, "It's your fault I talk weird. The only reason I flunked kindergarten was because you couldn't teach me English, and you gave me a zero IQ" (201). These same humiliations Kingston, in a 1989 interview, blames upon her mother who did not prepare her adequately for school. "I was just put into school where I flunked kindergarten, where I was given a zero IQ, and where I had to sit in a corner."[8]

Betty Friedan in 1993, whose 1963 book *The Feminine Mystique* galvanized the woman's movement by challenging prevailing gender stereotypes, influencing young women such as Kingston

The narrator's younger sister and other Chinese children also did not speak at the American school. She explains the reason for this as the ignorance of the Chinese children about what they were expected to do and how they were expected to behave at school. In *The Woman Warrior* she writes of her own lack of understanding: "At first it did not occur to

KINGSTON ON MEMORY

"The artist's memory winnows out; it edits for what is important and significant. Memory, my own memory, shows me what is unforgettable, and helps me get to an essence that will not die and that haunts me until I can put it into a new form, which is the writing."

Maxine Hong Kingston

From Paula Rabinowitz, "Eccentric Memories: A Conversation with Maxine Hong Kingston," in *Conversations with Maxine Hong Kingston*, edited by Paul Skenazy and Tera Martin (Jackson: University Press of Mississippi, 1998), p. 67.

me I was supposed to talk or to pass kindergarten" (166). The Chinese children, however, did not have the same difficulties at Chinese school. In a 1989 interview with faculty and students at the University of California at Santa Cruz, Kingston explained the different approach to teaching and learning: "I went to Chinese language school for seven years. The education is very archaic in that the method is the same as in classical times, which is to memorize. They didn't explain anything. It's just rote memory and learning many words that you don't hear used. At about the sixth or seventh year they began giving you literature, but in the beginning, almost everything is taught in forms, so everything was a kind of poetic language."[9] Knowing what was expected made the demands of Chinese school much easier for the Chinese girls, and the protagonist is quite clear that the difficulties she and the other girls encounter with oral expression is a consequence of their femininity: she says, "I knew the silence has to do with being a Chinese girl" (166). In American school, only the exercises that are similar to the teaching methods of Chinese school are manageable. The narrator recalls, "Reading aloud was easier than speaking because we did not have to make up what to say, but I stopped often, and the teacher would think I'd gone quiet again" (166). In the same way, the Chinese girls would excel at spelling but could not participate in the class play; they could memorize spellings but did not have the voice: "Our voices were too soft or nonexistent" (167) to perform in public.

THE AUTHOR'S ERA

The era in which *The Woman Warrior* and *China Men* were composed and published was a time during which the status of women in American society was undergoing rapid change. The feminist movement that gained momentum in the early 1960s and was galvanized by the publication of Betty Friedan's *The Feminine Mystique* in 1963 was forcing real legislative and social changes in the lives of American women. In this book, Friedan identified the economic, political, cultural, and personal pressures that kept women—especially educated middle-class women—out of the public world for which they had been educated and in the home as wives and mothers. Though these women enjoyed all the material comforts they could want, many experienced a sense of frustration and disappointment that they could not describe. Friedan called this "the problem that has no name" and used the phrase as the title of her opening chapter. The reason for this mysterious problem Friedan described as "the feminine mystique," a concept of femininity that finds fulfillment in material wealth but denies women the opportunity for self-fulfillment in the public world of work. In this book and in her political activism, Friedan called for equality of opportunity for all women. This meant, of course, that women were subjected to new pressures and to new expectations. This pressure to succeed in feminist terms complicates the adolescent life of Kingston's protagonist in *The Woman Warrior* and her representation of the experiences of her male relatives in *China Men*. Friedan was writing about the decade of the 1950s, the decade of Kingston's teenage years. The representation of her adolescence in the narrative, however, is complicated by the voice of the mature author who was thirty-seven at the time of the publication of *The Woman Warrior* in 1977. For example, the narrator indicates that twenty years have elapsed between the time her mother told the story of the No Name Woman to her pubescent daughter and Kingston's retelling of it in *The Woman Warrior*.

Kingston's adolescent narrator must be feminine in both Chinese and American terms. She is caught between the two cultures and between changing conceptions of what an American woman should be. The stereotype of the woman who is entirely satisfied to pursue only domestic activities, described by Friedan, still exerted a strong influence over the girls of Kingston's generation. Traditional gender roles were not so much abolished by the women's movement as they were questioned and criticized, and alternative images of femininity were promoted. The heroine feels the burden of these choices. Early in the narrative she describes herself: "Walking erect (knees straight, toes pointed forward, not pigeon-toed, which is Chinese-feminine) and speaking in an inaudible voice, I have tried to turn myself American-feminine. Chinese communication was loud, public. Only sick people had to whisper" (11). The attempt to conform to American expectations of how girls should sound results in the muteness of many of the Chinese girls she meets at school. They must be attractive and feminine in ways that Friedan documents but, at the same time, as a consequence of the advances made by the women's liberation movement, these girls must also live successful lives as more than wives and mothers.

The narrator recalls how her mother taught her the chant that tells the life of Fa Mu Lan: "She said I would grow up a wife and a slave, but she taught me the song of the warrior woman" (20). This double injunction, to be successful in a male-dominated world and on masculine terms but at the same time to be feminine and accomplished as a woman, is the demand that the protagonist struggles to fulfill throughout the narrative. Fa Mu Lan is a brave and successful warrior who leads her army in triumph but she is also a caring and nurturing mother, and upon her return to her parents and her village, she is a dutiful and obedient daughter. The challenge to herself that she reads in this story is the challenge to identify the equivalent in her world to the village that Fa Mu Lan protects and defends. She tries to reassure herself: "I mustn't feel bad that I haven't done as well as the swordswoman did; after all, no bird called me, no wise old people tutored me. I have no magic beads, no water gourd in sight, no rabbit will jump in the fire when I'm hungry. I dislike armies" (49). She has to identify and struggle with different kinds of injustice.

The traditional Chinese prejudice against women is the first injustice against which she rebels. She takes strength from the powerful examples of her grandmother Ah Po, who is introduced in *China Men* as her paternal grandmother and who dominates her husband and her family. She humiliates him in public when she chases him through the village, cursing him as she goes, to the house of the villagers who have swapped their baby girl for Ah Po's baby son. She takes strength from her mother and from the shifting attitudes in America toward the possibilities that are open to women, especially in terms of education and entry into public life through the professions. Like her mother-in-law, Ah Po, Brave Orchid is a contradictory character. She tells her daughters that they are expected to grow up to be wives and mothers, yet she teaches them the example of the woman warrior. She herself represents much more than just a wife and mother. She trains as a doctor and has a successful practice in China before she travels to America. Brave Orchid complains, "I shouldn't have left, but your father couldn't have supported you without me. I'm the one with the big muscles" (104). She ignores the fact that if she had stayed in China, there would have been no American-born children for her to support. She makes the point that she is the central pillar of the household, who by sheer willpower controls and directs all that goes on in the house. She, rather than her husband, is dominant in the house and in the laundry as well. She describes moving her babies around to keep them as far as possible from the dirt that comes from the soiled clothes, working long hours in the terrible heat, and carrying heavy bundles. Like Fa Mu Lan, Brave Orchid combines elements of masculinity and femininity; she has the strength of a man and the nurturing capacity of a woman.

The narrator is influenced by the example of her mother, who is such a powerful and effective person, but her life is also shaped by the political currents of her time, particularly the women's liberation movement. When she imagines a life that is substantially different from the model of a woman's life that is set out in traditional Chinese terms by her mother, she turns to education and imagines for herself a professional career. Toward the end of the narrative finally is able to give expression to all the resentments she has held against her mother. She resents being unable to tell her mother things like how she was involved in fights at Chinese school, how she envied the Catholic girls the ritual of confession, and how she prayed to the Christian God for a white horse that would make all her imaginings come true. Her inability to tell these things and her mother's refusal to listen fuel her resentment. Everything she has suppressed comes out in a torrent of words, sparked off by the fear that her mother is preparing to marry her to the retarded man who haunts the laundry. This fear gives her the strength to voice her objections to the life she assumes her parents have planned for her. To this fear is added outrage when her parents discover that this man carries pornography in the boxes that travel with him everywhere. She finds these magazines and pictures offensive. The image of "the hunching sitter . . . hunching on his pile of dirt" (200) finally causes her throat to "burst open" (201), as she describes it. Pornography was one of the expressions of sexual discrimination against which the women's movement strenuously campaigned. Feminists argued against the representation of women in pornography as objects of exchange, who could be bought and sold, and for sexual purposes that identified women solely with their sexuality, thus depriving women of their full humanity. Her disgust at the sight of the pornography possessed by the man she fears her parents will force her to marry emphasizes to her the way in which the devaluation of women in traditional Chinese culture operates—by identifying women with their sexuality and seeking to control that sexuality, and by using women as objects of exchange (for example, through female slavery).

The women's liberation movement thus shapes the narrator's views of women, in opposition to the views expressed by her parents and the other immigrant Chinese, as well as shaping her ambitions for her own future. Before the reforms of discriminatory economic and social practices promoted by groups such as the National Organization for Women, established by Friedan in 1966, young women could not imagine escape from their parents' control because they did not have access to the resources necessary to live independently. Kingston's protagonist can assume that she will have a college education and that this will give her access to employment in a professional field. The refusal to accept a destiny that involves becoming a slave or a wife and the desire to be independent and self-sufficient are options available to her because of the reform by American feminists of sexist practices that would have denied young women the opportunity to become autonomous individuals.

Kingston's heroine's ambitions contrast with those of her three girl cousins, who are subject to daily verbal abuse from their great-grandfather who holds girls in low esteem. Her grandfather and their great-grandfather, who lived with them, were brothers. She describes how "When my sisters and I ate at their house, there we would be—six girls eating. The old man opened his eyes wide at us and turned in a circle, surrounded. His neck tendons stretched out. 'Maggots!' he shouted, 'Maggots! Where are my grandsons? I want grandsons! Give me grandsons! Maggots!'" (191). The parents of her cousins expect no more for them than that they will grow up to be clerk-typists, yet they will not invest in their daughters' futures even the little it would take to buy them a typewriter. For these parents, such investment in their daughters' futures would be lost, as the daughters would be lost to the family, when they marry and become part of their husbands' families. Her mother, Brave Orchid, buys them the typewriter. Brave Orchid introduces into the narrative stories about the misogyny that characterizes traditional Chinese attitudes toward women. However, in her own life and in her actions, she emphasizes the feminist values that she adopts from the contemporary American women's movement.

EVENTS OF THE DAY

The major historical event in which the United States was involved at the time Kingston was writing *The Woman Warrior* and *China Men* was the conflict in Vietnam. The war in Southeast Asia was, and continues to be, of particular interest to Kingston as a member of the Asian American community. Members of the U.S. armed forces who were of Asian descent found themselves in a difficult position because they were fighting an Asian enemy. To Anglo-Americans, the Chinese Americans and the Vietnamese perhaps did not look different. Kingston explores this issue at length in *China Men*, where she devotes a chapter to "The Brother in Vietnam," but the conflict itself and the peace movement it spawned in the United States provide significant contexts for both *The Woman Warrior* and *China Men*. At the beginning of the chapter "At the Western Palace" in *The Woman Warrior,* Brave Orchid sits in the

This early-twentieth-century advertisement for a washing machine reveals prevailing racist stereotypes by boasting that the new invention would drive Chinese laundry workers out of the country.

San Francisco airport awaiting her sister's arrival from Hong Kong. As she waits, Brave Orchid uses the power of her will to protect her sister and the aircraft in which she is traveling: "Her head hurt with the concentration. The plane had to be light, so no matter how tired she felt, she dared not rest her spirit on a wing but continuously and gently pushed up on the plane's belly" (113). When Brave Orchid catches sight of young men in military uniform, also waiting, she realizes, guiltily, that she has allowed her concern for her sister to distract her from the effort she has been expending on behalf of her son: "She sat up suddenly; she had forgotten about her own son, who was even now in Vietnam. Carefully, she split her attention, beaming half of it to the ocean, into the water to keep him afloat. He was on a ship. He was in Vietnamese waters. She was sure of it" (114).

Brave Orchid's need to assure herself that her son is on a ship and in Vietnam arises from her children's desire to protect her from worrying about her absent son. She tells the niece who waits with her in the airport that she had told her son to flee to Canada. There, he would have been safe from conscription into the U.S. armed forces. Conscription is one of the ways in which Fa Mu Lan's family and villagers are oppressed by the corrupt warlord who rules over them. Her husband and her brother both put themselves forward to take the place of her elderly father when he is called, against his will, to do military service. Eventually, when no one else can take his place, the warrior woman puts herself forward; she says, "I saw the baron's messenger leave our house, and my father was saying, 'This time I must go and fight.' I would hurry down the mountain and take his place" (33). Later, conscription is one of the many wrongs committed against her family of which she accuses the captured baron.

The narrator's brother refuses to take his mother's advice to escape conscription by fleeing to Canada, and so he joins the military. To save their mother from constant worry about her son's whereabouts and his safety, her other children attempt to hide from her the fact that her son is fighting in Vietnam. Brave Orchid is able to see through their attempts: "They had said he was in Japan, and then they said he was in the Philippines. But when she sent him her help, she could feel that he was on a ship in Da Nang. Also she had seen the children hide the envelopes that his letters came in" (114). The brothers and sisters are concerned about their mother rather than their brother, but the fact that they feel the need to protect her from news about her son indicates that they are aware of the danger in which he finds himself in Vietnam.

When the narrator writes that she "went away to college—Berkeley in the sixties—and I studied, and I marched to change the world" (47) she is referring to the marches that protested America's involvement in the Vietnam conflict. She sets this in the context of her desire to transcend the discrimination she experiences within her family; she wishes that she would be welcomed by the family with a celebration of "chickens and pigs. That was for my brother, who returned alive from Vietnam" (47). She is not a boy and the assumption she learns from her family is that as a girl she is inadequate. She observes wryly, "If I went to Vietnam, I would not come back; females desert families" (47). Here, Kingston conflates or combines the psychological violence done to girls in a misogynistic culture, such as that of her parents, and the military violence of the conflict in Southeast Asia. She refers to the Chinese attitude that upon marriage a woman is lost to her family; she belongs entirely to her husband and his family. Kingston means that metaphorically if she left home to fight, her parents would not wait vigilantly for her return because she is not so valuable to them as her brother.

Kingston also juxtaposes misogyny with militarism because the causes for which she marched in Berkeley in the 1960s were against war and sexual discrimination. The campaign against the Vietnam War, or the Peace Movement as it was sometimes called, was part of a program of social reform that embraced opposition to the injustices done to women by the forces of sexism and gender prejudice as well as protest against the impact of racial prejudice in the form of segregation and widespread racial discrimination. The historical background of *The Woman Warrior* and *China Men* is broadly composed of these protest movements. The anti-authoritarian motivation of these protest movements of the 1960s also informs Kingston's narratives.

REPRESENTATIONS IN OTHER LITERATURE

The themes of sexism, racism, and the difficulty of living in two cultures—an immigrant culture and an American culture—are explored by several contemporary Chinese American women writers, such as Amy Tan and Fae Myenne Ng. Ng's novel *Bone* (1993) is a first-person narrative that tells how a Chinese American family copes with the trauma of a daughter's suicide. Each member of the family—mother, father, elder half sister, who is the narrator, and younger sister—reacts differently, and in this way Ng represents a wide range of contemporary Chinese American experience.

Much of the narrative in *Bone* that is concerned with the parents explores the disappointment experienced by Chinese immigrants whose dreams of a good life in America have been unfulfilled. As he searches for someone or something to blame for his daughter's death, the narrator's stepfather, Leon, complains that the good life promised him when he immigrated to America has never materialized: "he blamed all of America for making big promises and breaking every one. Where was the good job he'd heard about as a young man? Where was the successful business? He'd kept his side of the bargain: he'd worked hard. Two jobs, three. Day and night. Overtime. Assistant laundry presser. Prep cook. Busboy. Waiter. Porter. But where was his happiness? 'America,' he ranted, 'this lie of a country!'"[10] Her mother, Mah, shares this disappointment, though on her own terms as a wife and mother. The narrator explains why her mother feels ashamed when she travels with her youngest daughter to visit her family in Hong Kong: "I felt for Mah; I felt her shame and regret, to go back for solace and comfort, instead of offering banquets and stories of the good life. Twenty-five years in the land of gold and good fortune, and then she returned to tell her story: the years spent in sweatshops, the prince of the Golden Mountain turned into a toad, and three daughters: one unmarried, another who-cares-where, one dead. I could hear the hushed tones of their questions: 'Why? What happened? Too sad!'" (24).

America fails to fulfill the expectations of life on the Gold Mountain attributed to it in Chinese culture. Consequently, Chinese immigrants find themselves caught between the two cultures: living in an American social system but equipped culturally with Chinese expectations and values. Leila, the narrator, experiences this disjunction acutely. She works as a community liaison officer with a school in San Francisco's Chinatown. Just as the narrator, in *The Woman Warrior,* does not understand at first what is expected of her at American school—that she should talk and pass her assessments—so Leila encounters Chinese children and parents who do not know how American education works. The parents bring Chinese assumptions to their dealings with teachers and the school, and Leila finds herself explaining that different assumptions apply in America: "I invite them to the parent-teacher meetings, the annual potluck. At the evaluation conferences, I tell them that their participation is important. They tell me, 'That's your job. In China, the teacher bears all responsibility.' I use my 'This isn't China' defense. I remind them 'We're in America.' But some parents take this to heart and raise their voices. 'We're Chinese first, always.'. . . I try to tell them I can't take the full responsibility for the education of their children. But they keep on with their beliefs. 'You're the teacher. Hit them if they don't obey. Scold them until they learn.'" (16–17). Leila also finds it depressing that this new generation of Chinese immigrants struggles with the same difficulties that faced her parents.

Leila recalls that as a child she resented having to translate for her parents; now, she translates for these immigrant families with their weak English and inability to understand American bureaucracy—"A call to the tax man, a quick letter to the unemployment agency" (17). When Leila convinces her stepfather, Leon, to apply for social security, however, she encounters a whole new set of problems. Like the immigrant Chinese of Kingston's neighborhood in Stockton, Leon has told multiple versions of his life story in order to escape notice by immigration authorities. He is then unable, and unwilling, to prove his identity as an American citizen when, with Leila along as his translator, he is interviewed at the social security office. The narrator describes the interviewer: "He was polite, and patient. He asked Leon why he had so many aliases? So many different dates of birth? Did he have a passport? A birth certificate? A driver's license? Leon had nothing but his anger" (56). Leila observes wryly, "the laws that excluded him now held him captive" (57). Leon went to great lengths first to enter the United States and then to remain in the United States by defying discriminatory immigration laws that sought to keep him out. The story of how he outwitted the immigration authorities is well known by Leon's family. Leila recalls, "One hundred and nine times I've heard Leon tell it. How buying the name Leong was like buying a black-market passport. How he memorized another man's history to pass the interrogation on Angel Island" (57). Brave Orchid, in *The Woman Warrior,* and her husband, in *China Men,* also remember the interrogation they underwent upon their arrival in the United States. For example, Brave Orchid recalls that she was asked in what year her husband cut off his pigtail, "and it terrified her when she could not remember. But later she told us perhaps this lapse was for the best: what if they were trying to trap him politically? The men had cut their pigtails to defy the Manchus and to help Sun Yat-sen, fellow Cantonese" (96).

The anti-Chinese racism that is represented by these legal constraints upon Chinese immigration is represented throughout *Bone.* For example, the story rarely moves outside San Francisco's Chinatown; the characters live, work, and socialize within a geographical space that is racially defined. At one point, Leila resists the suggestion that she and her boyfriend, Mason, should go out for dinner with his best friend, Zeke. She argues, "Going outside of Chinatown with Zeke was never a good idea" (45), and to illustrate her point she recalls an occasion when they all went to a comedy club in San Francisco. Zeke objected loudly to the racist jokes told by one of the comics; "Later, walking to the car, I'd whispered to Mason, 'Can't he even take a joke?' But Mason'd answered, 'How many chink jokes do you have to take?'" (46). Within the confines of Chinatown Leila is able to feel protected against this kind of racial confrontation.

Also indicative of the segregation of Chinese Americans from the American mainstream is the representation of the Chinese cemetery in *Bone.* Leon believes that the bad luck that has culminated in his daughter's suicide originates with his failure to keep his promise to his "father"—the man who sold him an American birth certificate and claimed him as his son—to return his bones to China for a traditional burial. Leon has great difficulty locating Grandpa Leong's bones in the Chinese cemetery. The cemetery itself is chaotic: "They could see the grass and stones and long shadows of the cemetery through a locked chain-link gate. Leon led Mason along the fence until he found a torn section large enough to crawl through. It was a messy-looking place, with overflowing garbage cans and half-singed funeral papers from Chinese burning rituals stuck in the bushes" (72). Leila discovers that the reason Leon cannot find the correct grave is that the Chinese cemetery has run out of space for the dead, and so Grandpa Leong, along with many others, has been disinterred and his bones reburied in a communal grave with all the others who bear the family name "Leong." Even in death, the Chinese are confined to a small and overcrowded space of American soil.

As in *The Woman Warrior* and *China Men,* in *Bone* the theme of racism is interwoven with the theme of sexism. The novel begins, "We were a family of three girls. By Chinese standards, that wasn't lucky. In Chinatown, everyone knew our story. Outsiders jerked their chins, looked at us, shook their heads. We heard things" (3). Ng explores the antifemale attitudes of the Chinese in America just as she explores the anti-Chinese attitudes of Anglo-Americans. These attitudes are placed in context by her passing reference to the stories she and her sisters heard about the fate of girls in China. The narrator remarks, "We're lucky, not like the bondmaids growing up in service, or the newborn daughters whose mouths were stuffed with ashes. The beardless, soft-shouldered eunuchs, the courtesans with the three-inch feet and the frightened child brides—they're all stories to us" (35).

The women of China that Mah and Leon left behind do not all represent a negative image. The group of women with whom Mah worked in the sweatshop are referred to collectively by Leila as the "sewing ladies" and they are able to bring reassurance and comfort, especially to Mah, during times of crisis. When Mah finds Grandpa Leong dead and must organize his funeral alone because Leon is working on a cruise liner, the sewing ladies give advice and support. When news of Ona's suicide reaches them, these women bring food and consoling words to calm Mah's inconsolable grief. Leila reflects, "how often the sewing ladies were a gossiping pain and equally how often they were a comfort. Bringing the right foods was as delicate as saying the right words. The sewing ladies knew, in ways I was still watching and learning from, how to draw out Mah's sadness and then take it away" (105).

The sewing ladies are also the accidental witnesses to Leila's confession of her secret marriage to Mason. Leila resists a traditional Chinese wedding, yet she feels obliged to get married in the style her mother wishes. As a consequence, she is unable to agree to Mason's repeated requests that they marry rather than continue to cohabit. She confesses her dilemma to her youngest sister, Nina, who responds: "I know about *should*. I know about *have to*. We should. We want to do more, we want to do everything. But I've learned this: I *can't*" (33). Leila summons the courage to defy her mother and marry in her own way, without the grand Chinese banquet, quietly and anonymously in city hall. What Leila does not tell her sister is that Mah blames Leila's sexuality for her disappointment in her other daughters: "Mah said something about how everything started with me, since I was the first one, the eldest, the one with the daring to live with Mason when I wasn't married. She said it in that irrational way she has, 'That's why Ona went bad. That's why Nina left'" (41).

Sexuality, especially feminine sexuality uncontrolled by the constraints of marriage, is the danger against which patriarchy guards itself. In *The Woman Warrior*, traditional Chinese attitudes toward marriage are represented in precisely these terms; marriage is a mechanism for controlling feminine sexuality. Unrestrained feminine sexuality, such as expressed by the No Name Woman, is severely punished.

The relationship between Chinese mothers and their Chinese American daughters is a major theme of Amy Tan's novels *The Joy Luck Club* (1989) and *The Kitchen God's Wife* (1991). In *The Joy Luck Club*, as in *The Woman Warrior* and *Bone*, first-person narrators tell their own stories. Cross-cultural relationships are therefore represented impressionistically as personal experience rather than objectively as sociological fact, as would be the effect produced by a third-person, omniscient narrator. The limitations and partialities of the narrators become apparent when those characters are reported as actors in the narrative told by another. For example, the character Jing-mei in Tan's novel *The Joy Luck Club* reports her mother's theory of five personal elements and uses her aunt An-mei as an example:

Passengers arriving in 1924 at Angel Island, the major port of disembarkation for Chinese immigrants. Passengers were subject to a quarantine inspection and a lengthy interrogation process. (California Department of Parks and Recreation)

"Too much fire and you had a bad temper. That was like my father, whom my mother always criticized for his cigarette habit and who always shouted back that she should keep her thoughts to herself. . . . Too little wood and you bent too quickly to listen to other people's ideas, unable to stand on your own. This was like my Auntie An-mei."[11] Jing-mei describes An-mei as having no spine but in fact it is An-mei who later tells her own daughter, Rose, that she has no spine and that she lacks wood. In this way Rose is able to explain to herself the passivity and lack of self-assertion that plague her life: "My mother once told me why I was so confused all the time. She said I was without wood. Born without wood so that I listened to too many people. She knew this, because once she had almost become this way" (191). Tan's characters also learn about themselves from the stories told by others.

Each chapter of *The Joy Luck Club* concerns a crucial incident in the life of the character who tells her story. Consequently, the novel does not present a comprehensive historical account of Chinese American experience in the twentieth century; rather, it is focused thematically upon the issue of generational change and the possibility of communication between mothers and daughters across the generation gap. This gap between the generations is exaggerated by the cultural distance separating Chinese-born mothers from their American-born children. The lesson for each individual is that self-identity is inseparable from family identity and that the maternal bond is the single most formative influence upon a daughter's sense of self.

Similarly, this recognition of the importance of the narrator's relationship with her mother emerges at the end of *The Woman Warrior* as she retells the story of Ts'ai Yen. The tale of the poetess abducted by barbarians and held captive by them for twelve years, during which time she has two barbarian children, is powerfully reminiscent of Brave Orchid's story. Her children are to her like barbarians. She can scarcely communicate with them, and they live in a different world than hers; the United States is a barbarian land in Brave Orchid's experience and as she grows older she laments having left China. Brave Orchid, however, like the captive Ts'ai Yen, acts as a mediator between the culture of her birth and the barbarian culture in which she is forced to live. Brave Orchid makes a life in the United States but brings to it the richness of her Chinese culture. Not only Brave Orchid but her daughter also resembles Ts'ai Yen. She learns her artistry and poetry from her mother's powerful talk-story. Her artistic ambition, to unite East and West, Asia and America, through her writing, is possible because of the example set by her mother. The formative influence of Brave Orchid upon her daughter's developing sense of self emerges from the implicit comparison between them that is made through the figure of Ts'ai Yen.

In a 1990 interview with Katherine Henderson, Tan explained the importance of mothers and daughters in her writing: "the [metaphorical] umbilical cord . . . gets stretched over time; whether it's the mother or daughter who severs it or tries to pull it tighter, part of that is individual and part is cultural. In a Chinese family the mother pulls very tightly on the bond to a point where [the daughter] asks, 'Why can't I know about such and such?' and the [mother answers], 'Because I haven't put it in your mind yet.' The notion that your mother puts every thing in your mind—the blank slate theory—is part of Chinese culture."[12] This kind of thinking informs the relationship between Waverly Jong and her mother, Lindo, and the power struggle between them. Waverly believes that her mother pushes her to succeed as a national chess champion so that through her daughter she can achieve the triumphs that eluded her younger self. Finally, Waverly accuses her mother of using her in vicarious ways, of living through her daughter: in the crowded street Waverly shouts at her mother, "Why do you use me to show off? If you want to show off, then why don't you learn to play chess?" (99). Waverly is punished with a protracted silence. She also loses her talent for playing chess. Her mother's advice before each match had seemed trivial and insignificant to her. Only after her mother has withdrawn her support does she begin to realize what she has lost. She describes this realization: "I could no longer see the secret weapon of each piece, the magic within the intersection of each square. I could see only my mistakes, my weaknesses. It was as though I had lost my magic armor" (172). The empowering influence of her mother is her secret weapon and her magic armor. To challenge maternal authority as Waverly does is to transgress an invisible boundary; this challenge is met with silence in both *The Joy Luck Club* and *The Kitchen God's Wife*. In the latter novel, for example, the narrator, Pearl, suggests to her mother that she stop complaining about her close friend Helen and just tell Helen what is bothering her. The consequence of this advice, this challenge to her mother's habitual way of conducting her relations with other people, is dramatic: "when I said that, my mother looked at me with a blank face and absolute silence. And after that, she did stop complaining to me. In fact, she stopped talking to me for about two months."[13] This silence, like the silence with which Waverly Jong's mother punishes her, is a punishment for failing to see what is the case, a failure to understand a method of communication that works effectively, even if it cannot be appreciated by American-born daughters.

The theme of silence in Tan's writing is related to the theme of communication across the generational and cultural gaps that separate Chinese-born mothers from their American-born daughters. Kingston uses the theme of silence to explore the experience of living between cultures when, in *The Woman Warrior,* she represents the narrator bullying the silent schoolgirl who she fears is just like her and her subsequent period of hysterical muteness; or in *China Men* when she describes the prohibition against speaking among the Chinese laborers that is enforced by the white overseers both on the sugarcane plantation and on the railroad construction gangs. In *The Woman Warrior,* however, the theme of silence relates also to the manner in which the narrative is structured. Silence is a way of keeping secrets, and the breaking of silence is a necessary act of narrative violence against those whose secrets are preserved by silence. In this respect, Kingston has compared her narrative with Alice Walker's novel *The Color Purple* (1980) and Toni Morrison's *The Bluest Eye* (1971). In a 1996 interview with Eric J. Schroeder, Kingston described the opening injunction from her mother to keep the following story secret, to join in a conspiracy of silence: "There has to be a way into the story. And there are obstacles in the way, including orders from one's own mother not to tell. So I thought if I began the book stating what that order was, I could confront it directly and disobey the order. And in that way I could free myself and my voice to be able to tell the story. Since writing that I've seen that there are other people who use the same technique. Alice Walker begins *The Color Purple*: 'You better not never tell nobody but God.' Toni Morrison begins *The Bluest Eye*: 'Quiet as it's kept'—then proceeds to tell the community's secrets."[14] In each of these narratives, by Walker, Morrison, and Kingston, silence serves the interests of those who are motivated by violent racist and sexist prejudice. In each case the writer who breaks this silence acts in the interests of justice and freedom.

NOTES

1. Paul Skenazy, "Kingston at the University," in *Conversations with Maxine Hong Kingston,* edited by Paul Skenazy and Tera Martin (Jackson: University Press of Mississippi, 1999), p. 119.
2. Ibid.
3. Arturo Islas and Marilyn Yalom, "Interview with Maxine Hong Kingston" (1980), in *Conversations with Maxine Hong Kingston,* p. 30.
4. Ibid.
5. Ibid.
6. Ibid.
7. Kay Bonetti, "An Interview with Maxine Hong Kingston" (1986), in *Conversations with Maxine Hong Kingston,* p. 35.
8. Skenazy, p. 128.
9. Ibid.
10. Fae Myenne Ng, *Bone* (New York: HarperCollins, 1994), p. 103. Subsequent parenthetical references in the text are to this edition.
11. Amy Tan, *The Joy Luck Club* (London: Heinemann, 1989), p. 31. Subsequent parenthetical references in the text are to this edition.
12. Katherine Henderson, "Amy Tan," in Mickey Pearlman and Katherine Usher Henderson, *Inter/View: Talks with America's Writing Women* (Lexington: University Press of Kentucky, 1990), p. 16.
13. Amy Tan, *The Kitchen God's Wife* (London: HarperCollins, 1991), p. 13.
14. Eric J. Schroeder, "As Truthful as Possible: An Interview with Maxine Hong Kingston," in *Conversations with Maxine Hong Kingston,* p. 215.

CRITICAL RESPONSE TO *THE WOMAN WARRIOR* AND *CHINA MEN*

CRITICAL SUMMARY

The innovative style of Maxine Hong Kingston's work has drawn critical attention, especially her use of the two dimensions of autobiographical form and traditional Chinese myths in the subject matter. Since its publication in 1976, *The Woman Warrior* has embroiled its author in debates over the nature of autobiography. Conventionally, the autobiography involves a realistic portrayal of the events of the subject's life; however, Kingston adds to this factual information the stories she has heard, the heroic feats she has imagined, and the lives she has created for various members of her family. Kingston then adds conjecture, myth, and fantasy to the realistic narrative and produces a work that is different from conventional autobiographies.

The idea that women's autobiography may constitute a distinct style of writing, a subgenre of autobiography, is relatively recent. One of the most cogent and persuasive analyses of the tradition of women's autobiography is offered by the critic Sidonie Smith in her 1987 study *A Poetics of Women's Autobiography: Marginality and the Fictions of Self-Representation*. Smith identifies a tradition of feminine autobiography that originates with the fifteenth-century mystical writings of Margery Kempe, develops through the seventeenth-century writing of Margaret Cavendish, Duchess of Newcastle, and continues through the eighteenth century with the work of Charlotte Charke and through the nineteenth century with philosopher Harriet Martineau. Smith locates Kingston's innovative work within this tradition. Smith points out that all autobiographical writing depends upon two assumptions: that it is possible to tell the truth in language and that there exists a single, authoritative sense of self to be communicated in language. These assumptions have been questioned by critics who use structuralist and poststructuralist theories to question the referential power of language and the singular sense of personal identity that language can represent. Smith explains, "The autobiographical text becomes a narrative arti-

Chinese men in a laundry in the United States. Though her parents operated a laundry business, the adolescent Kingston questioned whether or not her experience was representative of the Chinese American immigrant experience.

fice, privileging a presence, or identity, that does not exist outside language. Given the very nature of language, embedded in the text lie alternative or deferred identities that constantly subvert any pretentions of truthfulness."[1] This notion of an autobiographical text that resists the assertion of a single, true life told unproblematically by the writer describes the ambiguous and playful quality of *The Woman Warrior*. This tension is especially so in those passages such as the beginning of the chapter "A Song for a Barbarian Reed Pipe," where Kingston's protagonist deliberately undermines the reality and reliability of the preceding narration. Kingston's representation of multiple characters who have influenced her or who offer instructive comparisons with her life—Fa Mu Lan, T'sai Yen, Brave Orchid, Moon Orchid, the No Name Woman—also undermines the idea of a single and authoritative autobiographical voice.

Smith argues that the women who write in the autobiographical tradition all represent a feminine challenge to the patriarchal construction of women's literary voices, lives, and identities. Indeed, she argues that the existence of women's autobiography constitutes a feminine assertion of self-worth by claiming that women's lives are sufficiently important to record and to read as literary works. She argues that the female autobiographer's "very assumption of the power of public self-promotion challenges the ideals and norms of the phallic order and represents a form of disorder, a kind of heresy exposing a transgressive female desire. Stealing words from the language, she would know and name herself, appropriating the self-creative power patriarchal culture has historically situated in the pens of man."[2] In other words, by writing about their own lives women act outside the restrictions placed upon them by a male-dominated culture and reveal the suppressed desire of women to go beyond or transgress the limits placed on them as women.

The Woman Warrior is located in this transgressive autobiographical tradition because, in Smith's view, it "exemplifies the potential for works from the marginalized to challenge the ideology of individualism and with it the ideology of gender."[3] Smith goes on to argue: "Recognizing the inextricable relationship between an individual's sense of 'self' and the community's stories of selfhood, Kingston self-consciously reads herself into existence through the stories her culture tells about women. Using autobiography to create identity, she breaks down the hegemony of formal 'autobiography' and breaks out of the silence that has bound her culturally to discover a resonant voice of her own."[4] Smith suggests that in this way Kingston challenges the stereotypical construction of women's identities in the traditional Chinese culture of her parents, as well as the prescriptions for feminine behavior to which she is subject in modern America.

The challenge to feminine stereotypes is, in Smith's view, the primary motivation of Kingston's autobiographical style of writing. In her work Kingston seeks a way to speak authentically as herself, rather than as a representative woman or Chinese American individual. Ironically,

NARRATIVE STYLE

"I try to be convoluted. Life is convoluted. I know there are some people who have a certain expectation of a linear kind of story where everything is explained to them and it goes at a slower pace and it's more of an accessible, popular kind of writing style. If they expect that, then they can't get into a more complicated book. I think that people like that miss out on something because they are not willing to work harder."

Maxine Hong Kingston

From Karen Horton, "Honolulu Interview: Maxine Hong Kingston," in *Conversations with Maxine Hong Kingston,* edited by Paul Skenazy and Tera Martin (Jackson: University Press of Mississippi, 1998), p. 11.

therefore, the style of writing characterized by Smith in terms of its ability to create fictions of identity should be used by Kingston to seek a sense of her own authentic individuality, in isolation from stereotypes of her race and gender. This refusal to claim the public status of a representative Chinese American woman, however, has created problems for Kingston. Some Asian American critics have accused her of dishonesty, precisely because they do interpret her representing herself and her family as indicative of the Chinese American experience. This accusation is fueled by Kingston's assertion that she invented none of the material used in the writing of *The Woman Warrior* and *China Men*. All the characters, settings, and events represented in the narratives she recalled either from her own memories or the stories her family told her. Thus, the materials she used were at the same time real but not objectively true. The myths, legends, and stories that were transformed in Kingston's imagination possessed the reality of memories and "talk-story" but were not true in any sociological sense.

The first essay to explain the controversy over Kingston's representations was Sau-ling Cynthia Wong's 1992 essay "Autobiography as Guided Chinatown Tour? Maxine Hong Kingston's *The Woman Warrior* and the Chinese American Autobiographical Controversy." Wong explains that the reason for the controversy about Kingston's book is located in the distinction between fiction and reality that is blurred in autobiographical writing. Asian American critics feared that while Asian readers possessed the cultural understanding required to identify the points in the narrative where history gives way to fiction, Caucasian readers would lack this contextual knowledge and so would read the entire narrative as being factually true. In this view, Kingston risks creating a situation where Western readers of her work would believe that they had an authoritative access to Asian American culture simply by reading her books. For this reason Frank Chin accused Kingston of being an assimilationist writer. This accusation assumed that Kingston was trying to make the Asian American experience comprehensible to Western readers by simplifying and translating features of Asian American experience into Western terms.

Kingston herself objected strenuously to the suggestion that she had set out to represent her family as typical of Chinese Americans. In *The Woman Warrior*, for example, the narrator describes her own concern about her experiences: "I asked my sister, just checking to see if hearing voices in motors and seeing cowboy movies on blank walls was normal" (190). Of course, she finds that this is not "normal." Kingston never set out to write an account of typical Chinese American life. In a 1980 interview she conceded that there were such writers: "writers who set out to represent the rest of us; they end up with tourist manuals—chamber-of-commerce relations whitewash."[5] In *The Woman Warrior* Kingston writes about one village in the south of China, which is hardly representative of China as a whole. Of her experience as a Chinese American, Kingston recalled, "I have asked my sisters, 'On a range of 1 to 10, how odd do you think we were? How odd was our upbringing?' My sister said it was 8. That means pretty odd, which is saying that we are not very representative."[6]

Kingston's use of traditional Chinese myth has also proved controversial. She has been accused by Chin, Jeffery Paul Chan, and Benjamin Tong of simplifying and misrepresenting the traditional stories in order to make them appeal to an Anglo-American audience. In a 1992 interview Kingston answered Chin and other critics with several questions:

KINGSTON ON HER CRITICS

"We have to do more than record myth.... That's just more ancestor worship. The way I keep the old Chinese myths alive is by telling them in a new American way. I can't help feeling that people who accuse me of misrepresenting the myths are looking at the past in a sentimental kind of way. It's so easy to look into the past.... It's harder to look into the present and come to terms with what it means to be alive today."

Maxine Hong Kingston

From Timothy Pfaff, "Talk with Mrs. Kingston," in *Conversations with Maxine Hong Kingston*, edited by Paul Skenazy and Tera Martin (Jackson: University Press of Mississippi, 1998), p. 18.

> "What are the important issues at stake? I have identified two. One of them is the racial and cultural myths. Whom do they belong to? Frank would say they belong to real Chinese such as himself. And they do not belong to, for example, the Caucasians. My feeling is, if somebody goes to a bookstore and buys my book, then they have bought the myths, and they can have the great myths of China by reading them. The only way that myths stay alive is if we pass them on. He has also been saying that there is a true text, including the chant of the Woman Warrior. Now I know that myth is not passed on by text; it's mostly passed on by word of mouth, and every time you tell a story and every time you hear it, it's different. So there isn't one frozen authentic version; there are many, many authentic versions different from person to person."[7]

Kingston also identified the gender issue as separating her from Chin: "That explains, why, as a woman, it's absolutely clear to me that we have the freedom of creating alternate myths, and for Frank Chin, as a male, there is a monolith, one monument of a myth."[8]

In Chin's view even the form of Kingston's writing is suspect. In the essay "This is Not an Autobiography," Chin argues that the genre of autobiographical writing is essentially a Western, Christian, literary genre and as such has no place in the canon of Chinese American literature.[9] Wong summarizes the assumptions underlying the accusations made against Kingston: "the autobiographer's work should be innocent of material that might be seized upon by unsympathetic outsiders to illustrate prevalent stereotypes of the ethnic group; the author should stress the diversity of experience within the group and the uniqueness and self-definition of the individual. Ideally, an ethnic autobiography should also be a history in microcosm of the community, especially of its sufferings, struggles, and triumphs over racism."[10] Critics attacked Kingston for writing about subjects other than the shared racial experience of Chinese Americans. Kingston's choice of her own experience and that of her immediate family as her subject in *The Woman Warrior* and *China Men* has been judged by critics as a betrayal of her community and her race. Ironically, then, Kingston is attacked by these critics not because her work is "insufficiently factual but it is insufficiently fictional."[11] Wong goes on to explain, "an ethnic autobiographer should be an exemplar and spokesperson whose life will inspire the writer's own people as well as enlighten the ignorant about social truths."[12] This attempt to dignify the group does mean, however, that the writer's desire to explore modes of self-representation or self-definition must be sacrificed to the requirements of representing the community.

The representation of the self in relation to others within the generic context of autobiography has concerned critics of both *The Woman Warrior* and *China Men*. For instance, in her 1991 essay "Autobiography in a Different Voice: *The Woman Warrior* and the Question of Genre," Joan Lidoff claims that contemporary "women's autobiographies are often written as biography."[13] In other words, many women write about their lives rather than about their selves, narrowly defined. The stories of their lives involve family, friends, colleagues, indeed the entire society in which they live rather than focusing introspectively upon their own inner emotional and intellectual experiences. Hence, in Lidoff's view the term "biography"—the story of a character's life—is more appropriate to describe women's autobiography than the term "autobiography." She locates Kingston's style of autobiography within a tradition of autobiographical writing that represents the self in relation to significant others, especially the family. As she explains, this "form of female autobiography validates a speaking voice by placing it in the service of another; it does not place itself center stage but understands itself in context by trying to recreate the parent as other—to see the mother in her own terms and not just as mother."[14] Lidoff argues that in *The Woman Warrior* Kingston tells the life story of her mother, just as she tells her father's life story in *China Men*, in order that she might come to understand herself. This attempt to know the self by placing the emphasis of the autobiographical narrative upon understanding the individuals who have exerted influence over the shaping of that self, Lidoff argues, is exemplified in Kingston's work but is characteristic of women's autobiography in general.

Kingston's exploration of her identity as a Chinese American woman has, of course, two dimensions: gender and race. Where critics such as Smith and Lidoff focus on the gender implications of Kingston's autobiographical style, Shirley K. Rose address the racial dimensions of Kingston's work. In her essay "Metaphors and Myths of Cross-Cultural Literacy: Autobiographical Narratives by Maxine Hong Kingston, Richard Rodriguez and Malcolm X," Rose compares Kingston's work with that of the Chicano writer Richard Rodriguez and the African American writer Malcolm X. According to Rose, these three writers "create cultural roles for themselves. They read and write their own lives."[15] Through the conventions of literacy, the myths, metaphors, and plot structures arising out of a cultural consensus, the writer is able to share the cultural meanings that give meaning to the lives of individuals in society. Literacy, therefore, becomes a mechanism by which the member of an ethnic minority is able to participate in the mainstream culture. As Rose explains, "The writer who claims autonomy reinforces his participation in a culture when he exploits its conventions for literate discourse. The writer who describes her participation in literate culture constructs an autonomous self in the act of writing."[16] Kingston's achievement in writing the lives of herself and her family in *The Woman Warrior* and *China Men* is seen by Rose as having two dimensions: the achievement of personal autonomy and also the achievement of social integration. The process of creating a life story therefore gives voice to racial and gender conflicts that otherwise cannot be expressed in literate form. The conventions of literacy itself lend Kingston this power, in Rose's interpretation.

CRITICAL SURVEY

Kingston presented her own account of the initial critical reception of *The Woman Warrior* in the 1982 essay "Cultural Mis-readings by American Reviewers."[17] Kingston objected to the emphasis placed by reviewers upon the idea of Chinese people as exotic and inscrutable. Some critics, Kingston observed, emphasized the mythic elements of the narrative at the expense of the historical and autobiographical dimensions, and some used the word "inscrutable" to describe the tone of her work. Kingston suggested that "inscrutable" would be a more appropriate characterization of the ignorance of the reviewers. She was not unaware of the dangers of being considered a representative Asian American writer, someone who produced stereo-

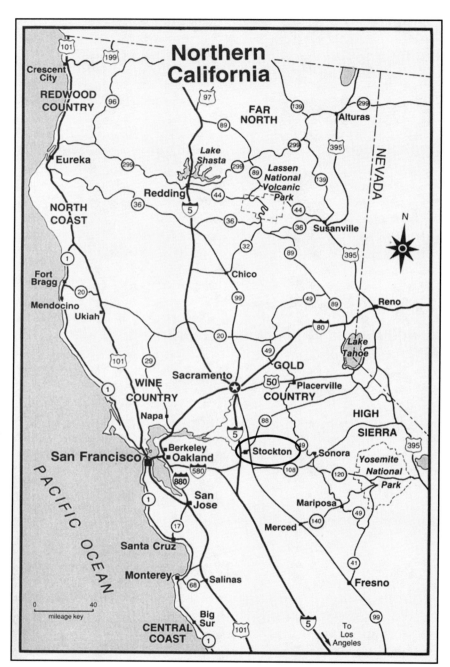

Map of Northern California showing the location of Stockton, Kingston's hometown in the San Joaquin Valley. Kingston has noted that early reviewers of *The Woman Warrior* confused Stockton with the better-known Chinese community in San Francisco.

types. She knew that if she failed to create the kind of stereotypes expected of her, then her work would be doubly condemned. Kingston remarked, "The most upsetting example of this school of reviewing is Michael T. Malloy's unfavorable review in *The National Observer:* 'The background is exotic, but the book is in the mainstream of American feminist literature.' He disliked the book *because* it is part of the mainstream. He is saying, then, that I am not to step out of the exotic role, not to enter the mainstream. One of the most deadly weapons of stereotyping is the double bind, damned-if-you-do-and-damned-if-you-don't."[18]

What Kingston objected to most strongly was the implication that somehow she was not American and that her work was Chinese. Her exclusion from the ranks of American writers and placement in a class of "oriental" writers angered Kingston because this literary exclusion repeated the various forms of racial exclusion about which she wrote. In response to a remark by the reviewer Alan McMahon, who referred to "the rank and file of Chinese living in their native land," Kingston exclaimed, "I do not understand. Does he mean Chinese Americans? What native land? Does he mean America? My native land is America."[19] Kingston explained that her objections were based upon the biased reading of *The Woman Warrior* that was expressed in these reviews. Reviewers regarded her as Chinese and failed to see that she was also American. The fundamental problems of identity and cultural assimilation that she explored in the narrative arose precisely because Kingston operated within two cultures—Chinese and American. She complained, "Another bothersome characteristic of these reviews is the ignorance of the fact that I am an American. I am an American writer, who, like other American writers, wants to write the great American novel. *The Woman Warrior* is an American book. Yet many reviewers do not see the American-ness of it, nor the fact of my own American-ness."[20] As a consequence of this inability to understand Kingston's work as that of a Chinese American writer, some critics failed to perceive the American quality of her language, settings, and stories. These critics only noted the non-Western elements and failed to see that being represented within an American context changed those elements.

Not only did these early reviewers ignore Kingston's dual cultural heritage, but they also confused the Chinese community in Stockton with the more famous one in San Francisco. In her essay Kingston explained the shortsightedness of the reviewers:

> New Yorkers seem to think that all Chinese Americans in California live in San Francisco. Even my publisher did not manage to correct the dust-jacket copy completely, and part of it says I am writing about Stockton, and part says San

Francisco. The book itself says that the Chinese Americans in the San Joaquin Valley town, which is its setting, are probably very different from the city slickers in San Francisco. I describe a long drive *away from* San Francisco to the smaller valley town, which I do not name; I describe Steinbeck country. Yet, *New West,* which published an excerpt, prefaced it by twice calling it a San Francisco story—ironically, it was the very chapter about the San Joaquin valley. How geographically confused their readers must have been. *New West* is a California magazine; so the theory about New York provincialism applies to more places than New York."[21]

The confusion of Stockton, a town largely unknown to Kingston's reviewers, with the stereotypical Chinatown of San Francisco may be interpreted as a consequence of the debate over Kingston's authenticity as a Chinese American writer. These issues of authenticity, her identity as an American, and the quality of Kingston's work as representative of the Chinese American experience all have been developed in the critical literature that has appeared since these early reviews.

CRITICAL SELECTIONS

Suzanne Juhasz, "Maxine Hong Kingston: Narrative Technique and Female Identity," in *Contemporary American Women Writers,* edited by Catherine Rainwater and William J. Scheick (Lexington: University Press of Kentucky, 1985), pp. 177–178.

The Woman Warrior is "messy" insofar as its narrative patterns are several and intertwined. *Complex* is really a better word for the dynamics of the mother-daughter relationship. The move to individuate and the move to connect both arise from the essential attachment between daughter and mother, the need for separation thus exists in the context of connection. In consequence, the identity that the text establishes for its narrator is achieved through a process involving both individuation and attachment.

The largest narrative pattern has a linear direction. The first three stories move toward defining the mother, thereby distinguishing her from the daughter; the two final stories go on to define the daughter, distinguishing her from the mother. But within each of the stories other movements occur in alternating patterns, maintaining the necessary tension between separation and connection. The text as a whole, for example, can be seen as an alternation between the stories the mother tells and the stories the daughter tells. Each teller's stories, in turn, alternate between true stories and stories that are not true.

The mother creates her relationship with her daughter through the kinds of story she tells her, stories whose purpose is sometimes to keep the two women alike and sometimes to make them different, as when, for example, the mother tries to offer her daughter a life other than her own. Seeking to know her mother, the daughter begins by thinking that what she has to understand is the difference between her mother's "truths" and "lies." Ultimately, however, she comes to discover not so much which ones are lies but why they are lies, and it is this kind of awareness that helps her to see her mother as another person.

At the same time, the daughter's own narrative style also alternates between "truths" and "lies." Her truths are her actual memories of her own past; but to write her history beyond herself, she invents or imagines stories—of her dead aunt in China, of her mother's young womanhood, of the woman warrior. This process of imaginative empathy should be understood not as prevarication but as fiction. It is, however, not the literal truth, and it establishes both connection with her subject, by means of empathy, and separation as well—the story is, after all, her own creation.

In each of the stories, these alternating rhythms create the double movement of individuation in the context of connection that enables the narrator to establish identity. In the first story, "No Name Woman," for example, the mother's telling of the aunt's story gives rise to her daughter's version of it, yet the daughter's version is revisionary. The daughter's story, in turn, both deepens her connection to her female heritage and creates some separation from it and thereby control over it.

Veronica Wang, "Reality and Fantasy: The Chinese-American Woman's Quest for Identity," *MELUS*, 12 (1985), p. 23.

Maxine Hong Kingston explores with uncanny frankness and sensitivity in her first autobiographical novel, *The Woman Warrior: Memoirs of a Girlhood Among Ghosts*, the dilemma of the Chinese-American woman as she struggles for selfhood in a chaotic and hostile environment. Straddling two cultures, Maxine, the author/heroine, has to confront the reality or fiction of her Chinese heritage that reaches her mainly through her mother's mythical yet authoritative "talk-stories," and the equally puzzling realities of her American birth, education, and experience. Both heritages impose external limitations and demand prescribed behaviors even though she is constantly aware of the remoteness of ancestral China and her essential separation from it, as well as her marginal status of exclusion and alienation in American society. As a Chinese-American woman, Maxine must come to terms with her past and present, with China and America, with woman-as-slave and woman-as-warrior, and thus find her own identity and voice, one that is not externally imposed but self-expressive, born painfully out of the experience of alienation and suffering. This journey necessarily involves a rejection of all superficial authorities and restrictions, either Chinese or American, in order for her to open the way toward individual growth and self-expression that fuse the past with the present, the Chinese simultaneously with the American. This quest for selfhood must involve a deliberate act of self-assertion. She must deal with her Chinese-American-ness in the depth of her own being in order to know who she is and where she belongs. Values and behaviors deemed meaningful and valid to other women may turn out to be myths and falsehoods to her. She must examine established values and behaviors and then evaluate them in terms of her own perception and experience.

Sidonie Smith, "Filiality and Woman's Autobiographical Storytelling," *A Poetics of Women's Autobiography* (Bloomington & Indianapolis: Indiana University Press, 1987), pp. 151–152.

The Woman Warrior: Memoirs of a Girlhood Among Ghosts . . . an autobiography about women's autobiographical storytelling. A postmodern work, it exemplifies the potential for works from the marginalized to challenge the ideology of individualism and with it the ideology of gender. Recognizing the inextricable relationship between an individual's sense of "self" and the community's

KINGSTON'S FA MU LAN

"The heroic figure of Fa Mu Lan thus represents a certain kind of woman warrior, a culturally privileged 'female avenger.' Embedded in Kingston's fantasy autobiography, however, lies a truly 'subversive' story of female empowerment. Imaged as tiny, foot-bound, squeaky-voiced women dependent on male authority for their continued existence, the wives of warriors, barons, and emperors who haunt the interstices of the textual landscape are, in one sense, conventional ghosts."

Sidonie Smith

From Sidonie Smith, "Filiality and Women's Autobiographical Storytelling," in *A Poetics of Women's Autobiography* (Bloomington & Indianapolis: Indiana University Press, 1987); reprinted in *Maxine Hong Kingston's* The Woman Warrior: *A Casebook,* edited by Sau-ling Cynthia Wong (New York & Oxford: Oxford University Press, 1999), p. 66.

---

stories of selfhood, Kingston self-consciously reads herself into existence through the stories her culture tells about women. Using autobiography to create identity, she breaks down the hegemony of formal "autobiography" and breaks out of the silence that has bound her culturally to discover a resonant voice of her own. Furthermore, as a work coming from an ethnic subculture, *The Woman Warrior* offers the occasion to consider the complex imbroglios of cultural fictions that surround the autobiographer who is engaging two sets of stories: those of the dominant culture and those of an ethnic subculture with its own traditions, its own unique stories. As a Chinese American from the working class, Kingston brings to her autobiographical project complicating perspectives on the relationship of women to language and to narrative.

Considered by some a "novel" and by others an "autobiography," the five narratives conjoined under the title *The Woman Warrior* are decidedly five confrontations with the fictions of self-representation and with the autobiographical possibilities embedded in cultural fictions, specifically as they interpenetrate one another in the autobiography a woman would write. For Kingston, then, as for the woman autobiographer generally, the hermeneutics of self-representation can never be divorced from cultural representations of woman that delimit the nature of her access to the word and the articulation of her own desire. Nor can interpretation be divorced from her orientation toward the mother, who, as her point of origin, commands the tenuous negotiation of identity and difference in a drama of filiality that reaches through the daughter's subjectivity to her textual self-authoring.

Preserving the traditions that authorize the old way of life and enable her to reconstitute the circle of the immigrant community amidst an alien environment, Kingston's mother dominates the life, the landscape, and the language of the text as she dominates the subjectivity of the daughter who writes that text. It is Brave Orchid's voice, commanding, as Kingston notes, "great power" that continually reiterates the discourses of the community in maxims, talk-story, legends, family histories. As the instrument naming filial identities and commanding filial obligations, that voice enforces the authority and legitimacy of the old culture to name and thus control the place of woman within the patrilineage and thereby to establish the erasure of female desire and the denial of female self-representation as the basis on which the perpetuation of patrilineal descent rests. Yet that same voice gives shape to other possibilities, tales of female power and authority that seem to create a space of cultural significance for the daughter; and the very strength and authority of the maternal voice fascinates the daughter because it "speaks" of the power of woman to enunciate her own representations. Hence storytelling becomes the means through which Brave Orchid passes on to her daughter all the complexities of and the ambivalences about both mother's and daughter's identity as woman in patriarchal culture.

Storytelling also becomes the means through which Kingston confronts those complexities and ambivalences. In dialogic engagement with her mother's word, she struggles to constitute the voice of her own subjectivity, to emerge from a past dominated by stories told to her, ones that inscribe the fictional possibilities of female selfhood, into a present articulated by the fictional possibilities of female selfhood, into a present articulated by her own storytelling. Her text reveals the intensity of that struggle throughout childhood and adolescence and the persistence of those conflicts inherent in self-authoring well into adulthood; for, not only is that effort the subject in the text; it is also dramatized by the text. In the first two narratives she re-creates the stories about women and their autobiographical possibilities passed on to her by her mother: first the biographical story of no-name aunt, an apparent victim and this a negative model of female life scripts, and then the legendary chant of the woman warrior Fa Mu Lan, an apparent heroine and positive model. But as she explores their fates, Kingston questions the very basis on which such distinctions are predicated. Uncovering layer by layer the dynamics of and the consequences of her mother's interpretations as they resonate with the memories of her past, the daughter, as she too passes them on to posterity, circles around them, critiquing them, making them her own. Next she reconstructs out of the autobiographical fragments of Brave Orchid's own Chinese experience a biography of her mother, discovering by the way the efficacies of powerful storytelling for the woman who has fallen in status with her translation to another culture. In the fourth piece, an elaborate fabrication played on actual events, she becomes even more keenly attentive to all autobiographical and biographical representations, including her own. Looking back to the beginnings of her own struggle to take a voice, she traces in the final narrative the origins of her own hermeneutics. The apparent line of progress, which as it ends returns us to the beginning, becomes effectively a circle of sorts, a textual alternative to the constricting patriarchal circle Kingston has had to transgress.

Frank Chin's parody of *The Woman Warrior,* "The Unmanly Warrior," was written in 1988, the year that David Henry Hwang's play *M. Butterfly* premiered on Broadway. Hwang based his play upon a real incident which involved the revelation that a French diplomat engaged in a twenty-year love affair with a Chinese spy who was actually a man. Hwang explains how the Chinese agent is able to pass as a woman by using the image of Asian femininity as mysterious, exotic, and above all modest, an image famously represented in Giancomo Puccini's opera *Madame Butterfly.* Chin objects to the feminization of Asian manhood in Hwang's play, just as he objects that Kingston represents Chinese men as powerless and emasculated. In "The Unmanly Warrior" Chin parodies Kingston's narrative by retelling the Fa Mu Lan myth as a version of the story of Joan of Arc. In Chin's narrative, Joan of Arc becomes a man forced to dress and act as a girl; in the preface to the story Chin explains that Joan of Arc is in fact a complex autobiographical metaphor for the experiences of a young French girl living in China. The liberties Chin takes with the story of Joan of Arc are intended to upset a Western reader in the same way that Chin is upset by the liberties he feels Kingston has taken with the story of Fa Mu Lan. Chang Apana, mentioned in Chin's final paragraph, was a Chinese detective with the Honolulu Police Department whose exploits in 1919 came to the attention of the writer Earl Derr Biggers, who then used Officer Apana as the model for the character "Charlie Chan".

Frank Chin, "The Most Popular Book in China," *The Chinaman Pacific and Frisco R. R. Co.: Eight Stories* (Minneapolis: Coffee House Press, 1988), reprinted in *Maxine Hong Kingston's* The Woman Warrior: A Casebook, edited by Sau-Ling Cynthia Wong (New York & Oxford: Oxford University Press, 1999), pp. 27–28.

> None of the historical facts and legendary heroes and touchstones violated beyond recognition by Maxine Hong Kingston and David Henry Hwang for white approval and entertainment are anywhere near as obscure and esoteric to the Chinese as Joan of Arc is to the French.
>
> The violation of history and of fact and of Joan of Arc makes no difference to the pleasure and stimulation the Chinese get from *Unmanly Warrior* [Chin's parody of *The Woman Warrior*], so why should the falsification of history, the white racist stereotypes and slurs in Kingston's prose and Hwang's theater mean anything to the pleasure whites derive from reading and seeing their work? They don't, of course. People who know nothing about China, about Chinese-Americans, the railroad, the opera and who don't want to know more than they know—know Kingston and Hwang, and that's all they care to know. How Kingston and Hwang make them feel about Chinese and Chinese-Americans.
>
> Well, folks, it's that same old feeling. Fu Manchu, Charlie Chan, Pearl Buck, Shangri-la of the Thirties has become Maxine Hong Kingston and David Henry Hwang in the Eighties, providing whites with an escape from the immediate and pressing terror of hard times, of empty gas tanks and payments to make. Whites have been using the Chinese as the metaphorical out for all their perversions and debilitating insecurities since the thirteenth century. The popular stereotype of the Chinese in white publishing, white religion, Hollywood and TV is a sickening pastiche of white perversions and socially unacceptable fantasies made speakable by calling them Chinese. Kingston and Hwang confirm the white fantasy that everything sick and sickening about the white self-image is really Chinese. That is their service to white ego. Reviewers and critics ripe for the cycle of Christian Chinese-American autobiography and Charlie Chan become accomplices to making the fake China and Chinese America of Kingston and Hwang real with the force of history. The source of their vision of Chinese-American art and history is white fantasy, not Chinese-American history. They're more Charlie Chan than Chang Apana.
>
> Charlie Chan was short and fat and walked with the light, dainty steps of a woman, in white fantasy. Chang Apana was tall and wiry, and he walked through sun and shadow with a bullwhip over his shoulder, in Chinese-American myth and history.

Leslie Rabine discusses the gender dimension of Kingston's work initially in terms of a comparison with two other American ethnic women writers: the Jewish-American writer Anzia Yezierska and the Mexican-American writer Sandra Cisneros. Yezierska came to prominence in the 1920s for her autobiographical stories of feminine immigrant experience. Cisneros, writing in the 1980s and 1990s, also explores themes of cultural conflict and alienation from an often autobiographical feminine perspective.

Leslie W. Rabine, "No Lost Paradise: Social Gender and Symbolic Gender in the Writings of Maxine Hong Kingston," *Signs,* 12 (Spring 1987), pp. 477–479.

The Woman Warrior is structured in a double and simultaneous movement that traces the girl's anguished but never totally completed struggle to break away from her girlhood world and the incomplete return after the incomplete break. The narrator, in telling her story, simultaneously relives the young girl's negative feelings for her mother, her family, the community, and its myths and also measures the distance that bestows on them their positive and irreplaceable value: "I looked at their ink drawings of poor people snagging their neighbor's flotage with long flood hooks and pushing the girl babies on down the river. And I had to get out of hating range.... I refuse to shy my way anymore through our Chinatown, which tasks me with the old sayings and the stories. The swordswoman and I are not so dissimilar. May my people understand the resemblance soon so that I can return to them." A double voice writes these words, a voice that is at the same time both in and out of hating range, the voice of a writer who in a certain sense has already returned to write about her people, to claim and transform their stories, but who writes as the girl who cannot return. Throughout *The Woman Warrior,* these two voices, while remaining two, never really separate from each other any more than Kingston can really separate from her mother and her people. Her story, like those of Cisneros and Yezierska, is about separation and the impossibility of separation.

In the works of all three writers, women's contradictory attitude toward their culture has both social and psychological reasons. The culture of each—Chinese-American, Jewish-American, Chicano—in addition to providing their personal identity, also provides an area of resistance against the dominant culture that dehumanizes people not only through racism but also through a homogenizing and sterile rationalism. Yet the childhood culture, infused in the works of all three writers with what Kingston calls "woman hatred," provides small haven. [Kingston, "Reservations About China," *Ms. Magazine* (October 1978), pp. 67-70] The myths that nourish the imagination and the spirit also relegate women to an inferior position; and the community, instead of suffusing them with warmth, suffocates them, limits them to a role serving men, and hinders their growth. "Living among one's own emigrant villagers can give a good Chinese far from China glory and a place.... But I am useless, one more girl who can't be sold." A woman from an immigrant group in the United States can find that between the two cultures she has no place.

This insoluble ambivalence can be explored through psychoanalytical theories about mother-daughter relationships, theories that analyze the way that male and female infant relationships to the mother affect the development and structure of the masculine and feminine psyche. Boys separate completely from the mother, developing a subjective structure based on lack (or as Freudians have

ETHNIC IDENTITY

"It is, in fact, essential to recognize that the entire *Woman Warrior* is a sort of meditation on what it means to be a Chinese American. To this end, the protagonist appropriates whatever is at hand, testing one generalization after another until a satisfactory degree of applicability to her own life is found."

Sau-ling Cynthia Wong

From Sau-ling Cynthia Wong, "Autobiography as Guided Chinatown Tour? Maxine Hong Kingston's *The Woman Warrior* and the Chinese American Autobiography Controversy," in *Multicultural Autobiography: American Lives,* edited by James Robert Payne (Knoxville: University of Tennessee Press, 1992); reprinted in *Maxine Hong Kingston's* The Woman Warrior: *A Casebook,* edited by Wong (New York & Oxford: Oxford University Press, 1999), p. 45.

---

said, on castration) and, therefore, on the desire to fill it. Fulfillment is fantasized as a return to the lost unity with the mother and the state of nature she represents or, in other words, to a lost paradise. But girls do not go through this complete separation, so that their subjectivity is shaped not by a linear desire for something imagined as lost, but by a conflict between two needs: they desire both to remain close to the lost mother and to break into autonomy.

Luce Irigaray, in her poetic work *Et l'une ne bouge pas sans l'autre* (1979), expresses the violence and insolubility of this conflict. For the narrator, the acultural, asymbolic unity with the mother suffocates and paralyzes her: "And I can no longer run toward what I love. And the more I love, the more I become captive, held in sluggish fixity." (Irigaray, 7) With great effort, she gains autonomy from the mother, but her only alternative is to turn to the father. She becomes a "mechanical scholar," (Irigaray, 12) learning the sterile power-hungry culture of the father, which for Kingston, Cisneros, and Yezierska would also be the racist or anti-Semitic dominant culture. Irigaray explores constructing a new cultural relationship with the mother, but only as an impossible fantasy, or at least for now.

The narrator of *The Woman Warrior* weaves her ambivalence to her community and culture into her ambivalence toward her mother, who communicates to her the culture and its myths and who interprets the community for her. In a scene relating an interchange between the adult Maxine and her mother, the narrator says, "How can I bear to leave her again?" And in the same scene she also expresses the contrary desire to get away: "'When I'm away from here,' I had to tell her, 'I don't get sick. . . . I can breathe. . . . I've found some places in this country that are ghost free. And I think I belong there.'" Yet it is the mother's ghosts who breathe life into the daughter's writing.

Sau-ling Cynthia Wong, "Necessity and Extravagance in Maxine Hong Kingston's *The Woman Warrior:* Art and the Ethnic Experience," *MELUS,* 15 (Spring 1988), pp. 3–5, 7, 23.

Maxine Hong Kingston's *The Woman Warrior,* by its very commercial success and its popularity with the literary establishment and the mainstream audience, seems to have become ideologically suspect to some Asian-American critics. Jeffery Paul Chan faults Kingston for mistranslating the Cantonese term "ghost" and giving a distorted picture of Chinese-American culture based on her "unique" experiences. He also expresses distress at the fact that the publisher passed *The Woman Warrior* off as nonfiction when it is obviously fiction, a practice he attacks as belittling of Chinese-American experiences and creative efforts. Chan sees Kingston's sensibility as having been "shaped by a white culture predisposed to fanciful caricature of a Shangri-la four thousand years wise, but feudally binding." Benjamin R. Tong goes even further than Chan and accuses Kingston of being "purposeful" in mistranslating Chinese terms to suit white tastes so that her book would sell better. "She has the sensibility but no conscious, organic connection with [Cantonese] history and psychology," Tong concludes. "[I]f she and I were ever to meet, she would know that I know she knows she's been catching pigs [tricking whites out of their money by giving them what they think is Chinese] at too high a price"—"the selling out of her own people."

These are grave charges. They are worth examining in some detail since the unspoken assumptions on which they rest pertain to the important issue of how one conceives of Chinese-American literature, and, by extension, ethnic literature in America. First, the depiction of "unique" experience in literature is deemed reprehensible because it threatens to "distort" Chinese-American reality. Secondly, fantasy drawing on traditional Chinese culture (in which *The Woman Warrior* abounds) is considered exotic "fanciful caricature," presumably because social reality is given short shrift. As for the translation of Chinese terms, while most translators would agree that a word may be variously rendered depending on context, the Chinese-American writer is proscribed from exercising such discretion. A weightier task awaits her, namely, educating the reader about the reality of Chinese-American life. To this end, only one translation, with all the "right" connotations, is acceptable.

A Chinese American boy in 1952 practices writing Chinese characters. Chinese schools, such as the one Kingston attended, helped perpetuate Chinese traditions for immigrant families in the United States.

Implied in all such accusations of "selling out" is the premise that a definitive version of the life of an ethnic group exists, one which it is the ethnic writer's moral responsibility to present. To do anything else is unconscionable, and crass ulterior motives are the only explanation. Presumably, this definitive version would represent the given ethnic group in a favorable light, purged of annoyingly "unique" features, and free useless fantasy which diverts attention from the sordid facts of oppression in American society.

In what does the "standard" version of Chinese-American reality—which Kingston is supposedly guilty of distorting—consist? Who, in Chan and Tong's view, is to legislate for the writer in choice of subject matter, adoption of tone, sifting of cultural traditions, portrayal of sex roles, degree of explicitness in expressing opposition to racism, and a myriad other issues likely to surface in ethnic literature? When one scrutinizes the concept of typicality—which, for racial minorities, is notoriously vulnerable to the vagaries of the dominant ideology, as Chan and Tong are no doubt aware—one realizes a simple truth. While one can speak of *the* Chinese-American experience, *the* Asian-American experience, or *the* minority experience for convenience, in contexts where generalization is needed and not detrimental to the nature of the discipline, no such thing exists in literature, where (to borrow from William Blake), "to particularize is alone distinction of merit." Without the particular—the author's multifarious experiences, some frequently encountered in her ethnic group, some not, filtered through the idiosyncrasies of her sensibility and style, and above all, competently evoked—our apprehension of the general is merely cerebral, our claim of empathy a sham.

That said, however, it should be acknowledged, in equally certain terms, that given the realities of current American society, no ethnic writer, however privileged individually, can totally escape the collective historical experience of oppression, and that the very act of writing and getting published is itself a political statement. We have, then, two apparently contradictory claims on the ethnic writer: one, a fundamental human need to affirm the specificities of one's personal experience, however "atypical," especially when the redemption of a painful past is at stake; and the other, a no less compelling imperative to express solidarity with those whose sufferings take similar forms from similar causes, such that one's gift of writing becomes more than a tool for individual therapy or gratification.

Interestingly enough—perhaps surprisingly to those critics for whom *The Woman Warrior* is merely a capricious if highly readable personal chronicle—Kingston is by no means silent on how these competing claims on the ethnic writer might be resolved. The major terms of the protagonist's struggle toward a balance between self-actualization and social responsibility are here identified as "Necessity" and "Extravagance," after two key passages in the opening sections of the book.

It is only by meditating on what the aunt went through . . . that the young Maxine is able to determine what degree of concession to Necessity and what degree of commitment to Extravagance would *feel* right. She cannot arrive at an answer intellectually, nor can any ready-made answer handed over to her serve in her complicated navigations through the perilous landscape of her Chinese-American girlhood. Everybody knows that a certain amount of concession to Necessity is inevitable, but at what point does the "work of preservation," which "demands that the feelings playing about in one's guts not be turned into action" (9), become tyrannical? . . . Extravagance will have its say somehow—if not accompanied by creative joy, then by a tragic sense of dedication to a cause which, in the last analysis, may be the only worthwhile one: doing something not because one has to but because one wants to. Easily mistaken for hedonism, Extravagance in this sense is actually the essence of being human; without this kind of Extravagance, life is bondage, drudgery, mere animal existence.

When Kingston expressed, through the protagonist, a desire to be accepted by her people—"The swordswoman and I are not so dissimilar. May my people understand the resemblance soon so that I can return to them" (62)—was she anticipating the kind of charges about "selling out" that the book drew from hostile Chinese American critics? A work that begins "You must not tell anyone . . . what I am about to tell you" (3) is perhaps bound to be fraught with misgivings. If the ethnic writer, by virtue of belonging to a misunderstood group, is saddled with the duty of disseminating a kind of average version of the group's image, then Kingston has obviously avoided this Necessity. Her imaginative penetrations of particular experiences relevant to her unique struggles can be viewed as a kind of Extravagance, easily interpreted as frivolous, self-alienating, self-serving or worse. However . . . the ethnic writer has no other choice but to honestly seek the balance between Necessity and Extravagance which feels right to a person of her particular temperament, background and capabilities. The Higher Necessity for the sake of which she withholds cruder if more immediately tangible judgments on the sources of injustice concerns, ultimately, all humanity. Without a profound faith in the ability of human beings to understand each other despite their differences, the act of writing and getting published would not make much sense for the ethnic writer or, for that matter, for any other writer, since even within a socially recognized category such as an "ethnic group," diversity is necessarily great. The story of T'sai Yen, the Chinese woman poet who spent twelve years in exile among barbarians and brought back a song which "translated well" (243), concludes *The Woman Warrior,* hinting that effective art should be able to reduce the effects of cultural differences and touch upon common human feelings. Both the "barbarian" flute-players and the "civilized" singers were, after all, engaged in the same search for that clear, high note—"an icicle in the desert" reconciling paradoxes—which would have the power to disturb and communicate.

Elise Miller, "Kingston's *The Woman Warrior:* The Object of Autobiographical Relations," in *Compromise Formations: Current Directions in Psychoanalytic Criticism,* edited by Vera J. Camden (Kent, Ohio & London: Kent State University Press, 1989), pp. 138–141.

Autobiographies—narratives defined by the need to assert, "I am"—can tell us a great deal about the aggression required to claim our existence and the dangers of defining our identity and of celebrating our separateness from others. Maxine Hong Kingston's *The Woman Warrior* (1977) is no exception. Indeed, her unconventional text, structured largely around the third-person point of view, reveals something most autobiographies obfuscate: that the process of composing an autobiography inevitably entails a regression to one's earliest stages of development. The autobiography is thus a reenactment of infantile modes of being and relating to the world. The unusual structure of *The Woman Warrior* reflects Kingston's interest in fantasy, dreams, and unconscious memories, and more importantly, reveals, as Margaret Mahler states, that an "old, partially unresolved sense of self-identity and of body boundaries, or old conflicts over separation and separateness, can be reactivated (or can remain peripherally or even centrally active) at any or all stages of life." [Margaret Mahler, *The Psychological Birth of the Human Infant,* New York: Basic Books, 1975.]

The Woman Warrior has been seen as a feminist exploration of a woman's efforts to discover her identity and especially to disentangle her sense of self from the significant women around her. Kingston's text has also been read as a commentary on the cultural dislocations experienced by Asian-Americans. What I hope to show is that alongside Kingston's conscious political intentions is a more powerful struggle, a struggle every person—and every author of an autobiography—experiences. Our infantile battles for power and boundaries, our primitive grief over separations and abandonments, our earliest efforts to tolerate fragmentation and dislocation must, I believe, predate and predetermine any later alienation Kingston felt as a woman or as an Asian-American. Instead of challenging feminist or cross-cultural readings, I will thus complement them with a psychological approach that underlines how the pieces of Kingston's story evoke different aspects of infantile development and experience. . . . These primitive experiences of ego—rendered accessible via the writer's fantasies—are as intimately connected to an adult's discovery and enjoyment of a self in the act of writing as they are in life and in therapy.

The Woman Warrior, subtitled "Memoirs of a Girlhood Among Ghosts," is a working through of many ghosts: the ghosts of her parents, the ghosts from

China, and, even more profoundly, the ghost of her earliest self—the traces of her most primitive experience of boundaries, mergings, separations. *The Woman Warrior* is a palimpsest: every conscious and adult search for definition and identity resonates with a prior yearning for differentiation, a past hunger for a sense of self, bounded by a stable, real world. Kingston's conscious and current explorations of the boundaries between America and China and between her self and her mother are repetitions of these primitive conflicts and fantasies.

The Woman Warrior begins with Kingston's mother's statement: "'You must not tell anyone . . . what I am about to tell you'" (4). By beginning with Brave Orchid's admonition, Kingston reveals that her text is the stuff of stolen secrets, betrayed confidences, and surreptitious intentions, and she also prepares us for the ubiquitous presence of Brave Orchid, who will be the source and nemesis of her daughter's identity. From the very beginning, we see that Kingston's search for self takes place in the context of the mother (or of other women who take the place of the mother). In remembering these m/others, Kingston can uncover forgotten or never known aspects of Brave Orchid and of her self.

Like No Name Woman and her child, Kingston's self at this point in the text has no name, no place, no definition. Like the newborn's, Kingston's new identity is hypothetical, symbolic, projected. And it will remain so throughout the autobiography, because for Kingston the very quest for identity throws every aspect of the self into question. The quest erases boundaries, challenges definitions, and leaves Kingston, as writer, in an undifferentiated state, structured only by the boundaries of the autobiographical text and task. Thus, the image of the baby conveys the tentativeness, the creativeness, the malleability of identity, and is typical of the ways characters throughout the text are described, transformed, renamed, reborn, replaced, recreated. Not only does Kingston infuse her narrative with the fragile quality of the infantile self, but she also suggests that identity is always ephemeral, illusory, fictional.

Though No Name Woman nurtures Kingston's identity, she also threatens it, and in doing so, she epitomizes the paradox of identification—the dangers, especially for women, inherent in mirrored and reflected selves. Identity is explored as a form of mirroring throughout *The Woman Warrior*. Identity, for Kingston, is always being speculated about and is always specular. Indeed, for most of the text, Kingston is present only as a projection or reflection. In a sense, she is in pieces. Eschewing the conventional autobiographical first-person report, Kingston informs her text not as actor, but as witness and as third-person narrator of the stories of women who function as fragments of Kingston's self, as displaced versions of Kingston's "I," as alienated pieces of Kingston's potential identity. In the same way that a mother functions simultaneously as the other and as part of an infant's ego, so these female figures are both merged with and alienated from Kingston's autobiographical self. They exist as transitional objects, neither subjects nor objects.

Kingston thus creates and sustains a self through these specular relationships, but she also exemplifies the radical decentering and otherness of the human subject. Conscious of her self only in these alienated fragments, Kingston recalls what Lacan describes as the "first months of life" when the infant recognizes itself in the mother and thus "*out there* as a unified whole in contrast to" its own "fragmented and chaotic jumble of impulses and sensations." These simultaneous recognitions of self and object "*split* the subject in the moment of his own specular capture" and thus establish what Lacan sees and Kingston vividly dramatizes as the essential dual nature of identity (in Evans [Martha Noel Evans, "Introduction to Jacques Lacan's Lecture: The Neurotic's Individual

Myth," *The Psychoanalytic Quarterly,* 48 (1979)] 394–395). Kingston's identifications with figures like No Name Woman are thus simultaneously comforting and fragmenting. These symbiotic bonds are remnants of the "complete" self experienced during infancy, a self that seemed more true, perfect, or whole because not yet distinguished from m/other. By inhabiting these symbiotic states, by remaining in her hall of mirrors, Kingston can forestall, as the infant does, the tragedy of differentiation.

David Leiwei Li, "*China Men:* Maxine Hong Kingston and the American Canon," *American Literary History,* 2 (Fall 1990), pp. 482–483.

Maxine Hong Kingston's 1980 book *China Men* is a work that unequivocally engages the major canonical issues—the notion of America/Americanness, for one, either in its ideological or aesthetic sense, particularly captures her imagination. She is "claiming America" in her Chinese American way and retelling "the American myth" as "poetically" and "truly" as William Carlos Williams's *In the American Grain* (Pfaff 1, 25). Picking up where Williams's precursor text left off in about 1850, Kingston has unfolded in *China Men* more than a century of Chinese American experience and constituted an oppositional voice to official American history. Kingston deliberately blurs the boundaries of history as the master record of events and the canon as the container of privileged literary texts, for she sees an analogy in the law of inclusion and exclusion operating in the structuring of both history and canon that needs to be dealt with simultaneously: the historical presence of a people is always intricately woven with its literary presence. *China Men* challenges the problematic democratic nationalism of the canonical paradigm and endeavors to write into the existing canon the possibilities of change within the canon itself.

Since America/Americanness is a geopolitical concept motivated by interests and materialized in canonical texts, historical as well as literary, Kingston has devised an agenda of what I call "the discovery of origins"—first establishing the root and the precedence of the concept for a later redesignation, then tracing the formative hegemonic processes for adaptation and appropriation, and finally positing a set of advantageous relationships with the available canon that will valorize her own text's position—only to anchor the origin of America in her original formulation. This discovery procedure is a formal strategy hinged upon linguistic and textual mediation, subversion, and transformation. It is a discovery of given meanings and combinations of new meanings; it works out problems of culture in words and signs; and it emerges with new perspectives on the American Literary canon and American historical identity.

Shirley Geok-lin Lim, "Twelve Asian American Writers: In Search of Self-Definition," in *Redefining American Literary History,* edited by A. LaVonne Brown Ruoff and Jerry W. Ward (New York: Modern Language Association of America, 1990), pp. 245–246.

Open representations of Chinese American identity unfold with the openness of form in *The Woman Warrior* and *China Men*. In these works Kingston eschews conventional narrative structure; instead she brings together collective tales (for example, the stories of fantastic eaters, Kao Chung, Chau Yi-han, Chen Luan-feng, and Wei Pang, in *The Woman Warrior* 88–90); racial myths (the feminist tale of Fa

Mulan, in the same work, 20–53; or the legend of Ch'u Yuan in *China Men* 256–260); and autobiographical (her childhood is described in *The Woman Warrior* 164–206), biographical (her parents' life stories appear in that work, 57–87, and in *China Men* 15–73), and historical materials (for example, the chapter on anti-Asian legislation in the United States, in *China Men* 152–159). These diverse subjects form a pastiche made coherent and persuasive through a narrative voice that is at turns puzzled, enraged, fearful, reportorial; it is consistently honest. In what is only the appearance of memoir, the images move from legendary past to childhood past to narrative present to family past, and so on, creating a surreal sense of identity in which myths, history, and invented and biographical narratives exist on the same plane of truth or imagination. The commingling of reality and unreality is organized by a self-conscious narrator who sometimes uses a personal, subjective voice and at other times assumes the impersonal viewpoint of the mythopoeic historian.

Kingston's books are marked by intertextuality—that is, by layers of reinterpretations of earlier literatures and, consequently, by a stylistic inventiveness. The various stories on which the books are built are written in a variety of modes: realistic, satirical, allegorical, heroic, comic, tragic, tragicomic, journalistic, and fabled. Fluidity replaces conventional form, and juxtaposition remains the only consistent narrative device. The range of materials and styles, quirky unpredictability of narrative movement, and disturbing juxtapositions imply an authorial mind at work, arranging, organizing, and arriving at a form that reflects an indeterminate cultural content. Paradoxically, Kingston's works are largely self-referential, appealing not only to external historical and sociological validations but to insights that come from the confrontation of invented, historical, and biographical selves.

The stories in *The Woman Warrior,* many of them based in a mythic or historic China, are strained through the sensibility of an Asian American narrator who is fascinated and repelled by aspects of the culture that she explores. The idiosyncratic author reads her Chinese mother's tales for significance and operates in the dual role of narrator and interpreter, with herself as audience, agent, and participant. The legend of Fa Mulan, the woman warrior, for example, is retold in a feminist light, as an expression of and a means to the author's understanding of her female position in a male chauvinist society.

Kingston is also out to discover the meaning of her ethnicity; the tone is intelligent, ironic, and angry. Ethnicity is a puzzle: "Mother would pour Seagram's 7 into the cups and, after a while, pour it back into the bottle. Never explaining. How can Chinese keep any tradition at all? They don't even make you pay any attention . . ." (185). And it can be barbarously oppressive. "I looked at their ink drawings of poor people snagging their neighbor's flotage with long flood hooks and pushing the girl babies on down the river. And I had to get out of hating range" (52). Beginning with the familiar position of authorial alienation, Kingston assumes the role of storyteller, which, shamanlike, is also the role of meaning maker. Re-creating and responding to family and racial stories, Kingston does not so much reflect ethnicity as make her own realities. After all, the narrator tells us, "maybe everyone makes [meaning] up as they go along" (185).

Betty Ann Bergland, "Representing Ethnicity in Autobiography," *Yearbook of English Studies,* 24 (1994), pp. 83–84.

Among Asian-American autobiographies, *The Woman Warrior* may be the most well known; indeed, one scholar argues that "many readers who otherwise do not concern themselves with Asian-American literature have read Kingston's book." Max-

A Chinese railroad worker in the Sierra Nevada Mountains, 1867. In *China Men*, Kingston tells the story of her grandfather, Ah Goong, who came to the United States to work on the transcontinental railroad.

ine Hong Kingston's *Woman Warrior* has generated intense debate about ethnic identity, complicated by gender politics. Sau-ling Cynthia Wong discusses the battle she describes as the "pen wars," noting that Chinese-American critics have charged the work with misrepresenting the Chinese language, folklore, and culture. For example, critics argued, the translation "ghosts," for the Chinese word *kuei* neutralized the hostile attitude toward whites suggested in other meanings, such as "spirit of death," "demon," or "asshole" (Wong, p. 252). Furthermore, critics charge, Hong Kingston's Fa Mu Lan story (parodied in Frank Chin's "The Unmanly Warrior") is a greatly distorted version of Chinese folklore. In addition, Hong Kingston is attacked for stereotyping Chinese, emasculating Chinese men, being too personal, and being "fashionably feminist" (Wong, pp. 255–256). Wong writes: "In the final analysis, the main reason critics attack *The Woman Warrior* is not that it is insufficiently factual but that it is insufficiently fictional: that the author did not tamper more freely with her own life story" (p. 260). Wong suggests what the critics really wanted was the "Chinatown tour," a Chinese-American autobiographical form white Americans demanded since the nineteenth century, which offered, presumably, a microcosm of the Chinese-American community.

Ethnic subjects living in multiple worlds receive cultural signs quite unlike any of the worlds imagined separately. Complex and contradictory, the cultural signs for male and female also remain significantly different, evident in the first

ON MYTH

"I was sort of disturbed when I read the review [of *China Men*] in *The New York Review of Books* where the critic said that I was trying to connect my family and Chinese Americans to the great high tradition of China by writing its myths; these people tell the peasant myths to each other, they pass them on and derive their strength from them. They also derive their doubts by comparing themselves to heroes of the past. I know all of these great heroes and they're not helping me in my American life. These myths are integrated into the peasant's life and into Chinese American life. And also, myths change from one telling to another. It really bothered me that that wasn't getting through."

Maxine Hong Kingston

From Arturo Islas with Marilyn Yalom, "Interview with Maxine Hong Kingston," in *Conversations with Maxine Hong Kingston*, edited by Paul Skenazy and Tera Martin (Jackson: University Press of Mississippi, 1998), p. 29.

---

words of the autobiography, "You must not tell anyone"—her mother's instructions to the narrator about the silenced Chinese aunt who threw herself into the family well in China. The aunt and all the memories signified in her silencing haunt the story. Thus, silence and talk become prevailing metaphors throughout the autobiography, associated with the struggle simply to live. In the final chapter, the narrator asks, "What do our villagers do? They would not tell us" (p. 213). How does one represent past traditions in the absence of talk, literal or figurative, or with language that is inadequate to explain the chaos of signs? Talk-story comes to represent efforts to explain the world, yet mingles memory with imagination. The narrator writes: "I continue to sort out what's just my childhood, just my imagination, just my family, just the village, just movies, just lies" (p. 239). Maxine Hong Kingston attempts to explore those marginal locations bell hooks [sic] refers to, those spaces where ethnic women can become human, yet remain committed to liberatory struggle. The stakes remain high, however, since for her critics, she lies.

LeiLani Nishime, "Engendering Genre: Gender and Nationalism in *China Men* and *The Woman Warrior*," MELUS, 20 (1995), pp. 67–69.

China Men, Maxine Hong Kingston's book on the history of Chinese-Americans, followed closely on the heels of the publication of her much-acclaimed autobiography, *The Woman Warrior*. Kingston has said that she first envisioned the two volumes as one book; yet if we view these books as companion works, then it is curious how differently they represent what might be called the Chinese-American experience (Talbot, 12). While the first, most obvious divide may be at the level of gender, as evidenced by the two books' titles, another equally important division takes place at the level of genre. When Kingston allies generic distinctions, i.e. history and autobiography, with particular genders she both explores and exposes that underlying alliance, raising questions about the role genre plays in defining both gender roles and Chinese-American identity. At the same time, she raises questions about the meaning of the public and private in relationship to history and autobiography and how notions of public and private give those genres a gendered status. By locating gender in Kingston's manipulations of genre and mythology and looking at the gendered categorization of generic forms, we can also locate the place of Chinese-American identity in her conception of gender and genre.

Much of the power of these two works lies in Kingston's attempt to intervene in and undermine a "master narrative" of history and identity in America. Although Kingston does skillfully parody and disrupt accepted notions of history and autobiography and destabilize those categories with her introductions of gender and race, her ability to escape the boundaries of genre remains in question.

Perhaps the question that must be asked is: How complete is the connection between genre and the ideology that gave rise to it? Does Kingston's repetition of these genres, albeit in altered forms, merely contribute to reinforcing those forms or, as Judith Butler claims, can there be "repetition with a difference?" In other words, as Gayatri Spivak might ask, "Can the subaltern speak?" Kingston never fully escapes genre because she must write within and against the constraints of generic forms in order to comment upon them and manipulate them. If she abandons the forms completely, the cultural resonances so crucial to her disruption of hegemonic conceptions of Chinese-American identity, gender and history, would be lost, but her adherence to those forms raises questions about her ability to fully subvert or escape the ideologies that inform those genres.

Whether Kingston speaks without being consumed by the "epistemic violence" of her writing tools, namely language and genre, is my central question. My search is not for Kingston's "authentic" voice hidden within these forms, but an examination of how she engages with and uses these forms to her own ends. By examining Kingston's deconstruction of the opposition between fictional and non-fictional forms, such as autobiography and history, her use of mythology to explore issues of national identity, and her manipulation of genre and mythology through the introduction of race and gender, I hope to delineate constraints of genre and the meaning of the subversion of these forms at the intersection of gender and Chinese-American identity.

Looking at the opposition between these two books' genres proves to be no easy matter, as Kingston rarely lets any clear opposition stand. Instead, what was a matter of black and white, autobiography and historiography, slips away into a hazy area where both generic boundaries are difficult to define. Although both books blur the boundaries between the two genres, they do not find a common third term, and instead they present examples of two very different approaches to both history and autobiography.

These unstable oppositions are apparent even before one cracks the binding of either book. Although both books now can be found in the fiction or Asian American literature section, the generic distinctions given to them by their publisher betray their earlier distinctions. *The Woman Warrior* falls under the rubric of autobiography while *China Men*, a work of history, is categorized as non-fiction/literature. But the books do not remain within the two distinct genres of autobiography and history, much less maintain their mutual exclusivity. Perhaps some of the loudest uproar over *The Woman Warrior* centered upon Kingston's blurring of the boundary between non-fictional autobiography and a fictional retelling of her life story. She insists on an eccentric voice, telling her memoirs from a highly personal point of view and making no attempt to "objectively" review her subjective, skewed vision of her world. *China Men* also participates in this transgression of generic boundaries, for this history makes room for fables, myths, family lore and personal accounts as well as official laws and documents. In both cases, Kingston questions and undermines the status of "truth" and "facts" by questioning the concepts of universality and objectivity.

Shirley Geok-lin Lim, "Immigration and Diaspora," in *An Interethnic Companion to Asian American Literature,* edited by King-Kok Cheung (New York & Cambridge: Cambridge University Press, 1997), p. 302.

> Kingston repeatedly asserts that in her books she is claiming America for Chinese Americans, a proposition that can be restated to mean claiming Chinese Americans for America. The double movement of appropriation is marked in the critical reception of her work, chiefly praised for making accessible to American readers the strange world of Chinese living in the United States. The accessibility works more in one direction than the other. Americans of Chinese ancestry, or even Chinese living in the United States, do not find that *The Woman Warrior* has made the United States more accessible to them, or that the book helps them to negotiate the dominant culture and to appropriate it for their needs. The book's popular reception in the universities suggests that it is the dominant culture which is incorporating Kingston's version of the Chinese into its transcultural psyche.
>
> Rather than breaking, interrupting, or challenging the hegemony of U.S. mainstream culture, the popular adoption of selected Asian American texts—illustrating, for example, Western feminist notions of Asian patriarchal modes, or Western literary ideas of the postmodernism [sic]—points to the dispersal of their strangeness, and finally to the Americanization of Asia (Lim 1993). The transformation of the natal country, China, in the reception of *The Woman Warrior,* through the interpretative affiliations that make it the national text it is today (read under the grids of U.S. feminism, U.S. immigrant history, U.S. ethnographic community, U.S. literary experimentation, and so forth), underlines its power as a text of assimilation.

Teresa C. Zackodnik, "Photography and the Status of Truth in Maxine Hong Kingston's *China Men,*" *MELUS,* 22 (1997), p. 55.

> In her (auto)biographical narrative *China Men,* Maxine Hong Kingston searches for and reconstructs the history of her (fore)fathers through a complex narrative that accesses memory, "talk-story," imagination, historical "facts" and documents, photographs, Chinese legends and folklore, and newspaper articles. Hong Kingston's narrative arrives at a knowledge of her (fore)fathers' identities and histories, as well as her own, via these sources, and in so doing equalizes the truth value of memory, "factual" accounts, imagination, and documented "proof." Her treatment of photographs in *China Men* is not confined to a reconstruction of her male ancestors' past and history, but also plays a prominent role in the narrative of her immediate family's more recent past. Moreover, Hong Kingston's own apparent view of the photographs is a diverse and often seemingly contradictory one: as a child she tells of innocently believing that a photograph may lie; yet, as an adult she seems to hold the equally naive belief that the photograph is capable of telling the truth. Hong Kingston also interrogates the multiple functions of the photograph in both American culture, and within her own family. In her narrative, photographs are documents of self-evident proof and silent communications from the past which speak only when she names them. In addition, Hong Kingston examines the status of the photograph as document, a document that can attest to a personal and communal history of Chinese American presence, as well as contribute to an erasure of that presence in America. Finally, photographs in *China Men* are both failed attempts to capture an event or person(s) as unchanged and present ("as they are"), and tools for fabricat-

ing a successful "American" to send home to loved ones in China. Far from undermining the history she discovers and creates, Hong Kingston's plural and contradictory treatment of the photograph parallels the multiple and self-contradicting versions of the histories she presents, exposing and challenging dominant American history as a monologue that has silenced and erased the histories of Chinese Americans.

Yuan Yuan, "The Semiotics of China Narratives in the Con/texts of Kingston and Tan," *Critique: Studies in Contemporary Fiction*, 40 (Spring 1999), p. 292.

How "'Chinese' is *The Woman Warrior*?" Sau-ling Cynthia Wong asks in her essay "Kingston's Handling of Traditional Chinese Sources" (27). The nativeness of ethnic American literature is a complex issue that deserves serious consideration and intelligent discussion. I have noticed that to date it is not the nativeness of our ethnic narratives that has escaped critical attention but the narrative reconfiguration of nativeness in literary representation. That is to say, the whole issue of nativeness in literary texts requires careful examination in the context of cultural differences and in relation to subject positions. In this essay, I explore the theoretical implications of that "native" issue by inquiring into the semiotics of "China experiences" in terms of "China narratives" within the contexts of Maxine Hong Kingston's *The Woman Warrior* and *China Men* and Amy Tan's *The Joy Luck Club* and *The Kitchen God's Wife*.

The "China experiences" presented by Kingston and Tan emerge as narratives of recollection—which means that in their novels they have reconstructed various narratives of experiences in China against the background of American society and within the context of American culture. Their China narratives emerge in the "other" cultural context informed by a complex process of translation, translocation, and transfiguration of the original experiences in China. In fact, China experiences are generally transfigured into "China narratives" only after they have lost their reference to China; thus they are related more to the present American situation than to their original context in Chinese society. The present American context provides meaning and determines the content of the China narrative. Only under such circumstances as loss of origin can China experiences emerge as a China narrative—a text reconfigured within other contexts. "China narrative," therefore, differs from China experiences and signifies a specific kind of self-reflexive discourse that is reinscribed within another cultural context to serve specific purposes: self-affirmation or self-negation, remembrance or repression. Eventually, in the novels of both Kingston and Tan, China as a geographical location is transliterated into a semiotic space of recollection; China as personal experiences is translated into a cultural repository for reproduction; and, as a text, China is reconfigured into a variety of discourses: myth, legend, history, fantasy, films, and talk-stories.

The China narrative in both Kingston and Tan serves as an undercurrent but central text that structures the present relationship between mothers and daughters because of the specific position it occupies in their lives. Therefore, the cross-cultural hermeneutics of China is conducted within that domestic space, between two generations in general and between the Chinese mothers and their American-born daughters in specific. As products of different cultures and histories, mothers and daughters abide by different cultural values and possess different modes of interpretation. In fact, they speak entirely different languages whenever they talk about China. "My mother and I spoke two different languages, which we did," Jing-Mei Woo says in *The Joy Luck Club,* "I talked to her in English, she answered back in Chinese"(23). The bilingual conversation turns into a game of translation; and in that translation, meaning is transfigured, displaced, and occasionally, lost. As Jing-Mei Woo says: "We translated each other's meanings and I seemed to hear less than what was said, while my mother heard more" (27).

Both mothers and daughters constantly have to re-evaluate their respective China narratives that are grounded in entirely different cultural contexts, with different historical references and subject positions. For the mothers, China narratives inform a process of recollection (history or loss of it) whereas for the daughters, who have never been there, China narratives become a text of culture. In other words, China experiences as semiotic texts are reconstituted through a choice of two modes of discourse: history or culture. Eventually, China becomes a semiotic site where culture and identity are fought over, negotiated, displaced, and transformed. Instead of being a static ontological presence of a unitary category, China becomes a hermeneutic space for articulating identity and difference, a process that governs the cultural and historical reconstitution of the subjects.

APPROACHES OF THE CRITICS

Early interpretations of *The Woman Warrior* focused upon two main issues: Kingston's innovative narrative technique and her feminism. Critic Suzanne Juhasz points to the necessary connection between the two issues, arguing that in order to represent the condition of women in a patriarchal society—China or the United States—Kingston could not use inherited literary forms which carry a masculine bias but had to create for herself a new feminist literary voice. The structure of *The Woman Warrior,* in Juhasz's view, is based upon the relationship between mother and daughter, and the daughter's attempts to distance herself from her mother's influence while at the same time preserving a connection with her mother. The opposing forces of separation and connection, then, generate the narrative structure that alternates between mother and daughter as the narrator tries to reach an understanding of her mother as an individual, and of her own mature individuality. Within the daughter's storytelling, the narrative shifts between autobiography and fantasy as the young narrator seeks to understand the broader context of her feminine heritage, within which her individual identity is located.

The powerful autobiographical element of *The Woman Warrior* has interested critic Sidonie Smith, who sees Kingston's narrative as exemplifying a postmodernist form of the autobiographical genre. This postmodern quality is identified with the indeterminacy of the narrative, as when the narrator confesses that the story of Moon Orchid's confrontation with her estranged husband is based on her imaginative reconstruction of the situation rather than objective fact or direct witness, and also the self-reflective nature of the narrative which reflects upon the influence of storytelling or talk-story in people's lives. The ways in which the individual's sense of self are embedded in cultural and community values are revealed as Kingston's young protagonist measures herself against the stories told about women in her family and community. As a Chinese American, she does more than this because she invokes the values and attitudes of both the Chinese and the mainstream American cultures toward women.

Feminist approaches to *The Woman Warrior* and *China Men* highlight Kingston's representation of antifeminine, misogynistic attitudes. Leslie Rabine, for example, directs attention to the two narrative voices that echo throughout the text—the voice of separation and the voice of belonging. In her account, *The Woman Warrior* represents the young Kingston's desire to escape from the influences of her family and the immigrant Chinese community, but even as she grows up and leaves she finds that she can never be completely apart from this world that formed her. This world, the ethnic subculture of her parents, not only has had an inescapable influence upon her developing sense of self, it has also provided a refuge, Rabine argues, from the racism of Anglo-American society. This refuge is, however, limited. The ethnic woman can find herself trapped between the misogyny and woman-hating of her ethnic culture and the racism of mainstream culture. Between these two cultures she has no place.

Rabine uses the work of the French feminist Luce Irigaray to conceptualize the process of separation that always remains incomplete. Irigaray invokes the legacy of Sigmund Freud's psychoanalytic theories, particularly the theory of the Oedipal complex. Freud theorized that as boys mature they recognize their common masculinity, which they share with their fathers. Their early attachment to their mothers is therefore surrendered for a new identification with the father, which provides the basis for the mature masculine gender identity. Women, however, cannot identify with their fathers because they do not share a common gender identity with them. Consequently, when women surrender their infant identification with the mother, this surrender can never be completed. Women, in this view, remain always tied to their infant selves through their identification with the mother. Women may desire independence and autonomy but they are unable to achieve this autonomy because of the bond they retain with their mothers. Rabine interprets the ambivalence expressed by the narrator of *The Woman Warrior* toward her mother in these terms. The mother transmits to her daughter the stories, myths, and values of the Chinese community; the daughter's attempts to distance herself from the community are also her way to gain a mature distance from her mother. She discovers that she cannot escape completely from either her mother or the Chinese community. Both have shaped her in important ways and to both she must keep returning.

Psychoanalysis is used in readings of *The Woman Warrior* in order to highlight Kingston's complex representation of the formation of gender identity. Elise Miller uses the insights of psychoanalysis to describe the process of individuation that lies at the heart of the narrative. She argues that the autobiographical style of *The Woman Warrior* represents a regression to early infantile modes of relating to the world. The elements of fantasy, dreams, and unconscious imagery reveal the ambivalence of Kingston's narrator—and of Kingston herself—toward gender identity and the boundaries that separate the individual from family and the community. According to Miller, Kingston's narrative is also concerned with representing the early processes of ego formation (the formation of self-identity or a sense of "I") that underlie the more mature development of gender and racial identity.

THE WOMAN WARRIOR AND CHINA MEN CRITICALLY ANALYZED

The determination of gender identity is the theme most often highlighted by feminist approaches to *The Woman Warrior* and *China Men*. Kingston's narrator seeks to define herself as a woman in relation to the powerful figure of her mother and also in relation to the antifemale and woman-hating attitudes expressed by both men and women within her ethnic community. What makes this quest for self-definition so difficult are the stories of feminine worthlessness that the narrator must contest. These misogynistic narratives would have her believe that she too is worthless, destined to be a wife and a slave; she must challenge and triumph over these narratives and the cultural values they encode if she is to succeed in her quest for self-possession. As a warrior woman, she must battle against the forces of misogyny that would control her mind by controlling her body and her sense of herself as a woman.

A radical feminist analysis of *The Woman Warrior* highlights the nature of the narrator's battle for the right to define herself as a woman through control of her feminine sexuality. Radical feminism is a form of feminist analysis that focuses upon the oppression of women through their sexuality. Radical feminism analyzes the relationship between the social inequality of men and women and sexual difference. The domination of women by men provides the foundation of social inequality, and the sexual oppression of women underlies the economic, cultural, and social subordination of women.

Radical feminism views women as the most fundamentally oppressed class within misogynistic patriarchal cultures. Gender is viewed as a system that operates to ensure continued male domination. Domination is achieved and maintained through the control of feminine sexuality by males and the diversity of forms of male sexual violence against women. What radical feminists term "compulsory heterosexuality," or the refusal of lesbian sexuality, and masculine sexual violence are then prime strategies of control within the power structure of patriarchy. Forms of patriarchal violence include sexual mutilation and the imprisonment of women in their bodies (so women are unable to walk or run and are constantly in pain). Kingston's description of Chinese foot-binding in *China Men* is particularly vivid. The threat posed by rape and violent assault keeps women confined in terms of where they can go and when. Pornographic images of sexual torture and violence represent the values of gender violence. Intimidation, terrorism, fear—these strategies, and not the innate inferiority or passivity of women, keep women in a subordinate position where they are dominated by men.

By viewing gender in this way, radical feminists are able to treat gender as a system. The systemic nature of gender ensures continued male domination through the masculine control of feminine sexuality. The control of feminine sexuality is also achieved through restrictions upon the right to contraception and abortion and the control of reproductive technologies, including sterilization, and male sexual violence. Other strategies include the objectification of women—the creation of cultural artifacts from women's bodies. As Leslie W. Rabine comments in her essay "No Lost Paradise: Social Gender and Symbolic Gender in the Writings of Maxine Hong Kingston": "Sexed bodies become the visible signs through which a system of hierarchical social roles is enforced by economics, politics, the family, religion, and other institutional constructs so that individuals whose bodies are visibly marked 'female' find themselves forced into oppressive positions."[22]

Coming to terms with the abuse of oppressed feminine bodies is an important aspect of Kingston's fiction. Even more central is the exploration of the ways in which women are led to identify with the interests of the ruling patriarchy and to express this allegiance by mutilating their own bodies. In both *The Woman Warrior* and *China Men*, Kingston represents women engaged in the activity of mutilating other women. Women perform the foot-binding, women wield the depilatory string, the mother cuts her daughter's frenum to free her tongue and

Members of the National Organization for Women (NOW) protesting at the White House. Published in 1977 at a time of renewed political activity by women, *The Woman Warrior* was celebrated by feminists for its challenge to prevailing gender stereotypes.

forces her hands through tight jade bangles, no matter how she weeps with pain. Self-oppression is perceived by Kingston as operating between or among women as much as it operates through cultural discourses, including language itself. The narrator notes with outrage, "There is a Chinese word for the female I—which is 'slave.' Break the women with their own tongues!" (47). This denial of the self is the complete victory of patriarchy, to have women embrace the inferiority of their position to the extent that they will impose upon other women the strategies of patriarchal control.

In her account of her father's upbringing in *China Men*, Kingston dramatizes the nature of feminine self-oppression. Her father's mother, Ah Po, possesses attitudes toward other women that are violently misogynistic in comparison to her husband's views. This woman, who is outraged that her husband would exchange his youngest son for the baby girl he has always wanted, has fully assimilated the antifeminine assumptions of her society. She is distressed not so much by the loss of her son as by the intrusion of a worthless girl into her otherwise perfect family, which is comprised of three sons.

The difference between Brave Orchid, the dutiful daughter, and her sister-in-law, the No Name Woman, in terms of their attitudes to beauty and disposition of their bodies, reveals the extent to which they have internalized the patriarchal control of their sexuality. The free exercise of feminine sexuality, the sensual life, and sensual enjoyment are condemned by the patriarchal village society. In one of the versions of her story, No Name Woman rejects the strictures placed upon her sexuality; she adorns her body, she liberates her sexuality from the confines of patriarchal marriage, and ultimately she uses her body to exact revenge upon the people, and the system, that oppress her. Her aunt's story is told to the narrator only in order to make her mistrust her new mature femininity, and particularly her feminine sexuality; to make her view negatively menstruation as a curse and sexuality as a threat.

In her essay, "Necessity and Extravagance in Maxine Hong Kingston's *The Woman Warrior:* Art and the Ethnic Experience," Sau-ling Cynthia Wong shows how the conflicting impulses toward self-expression and social responsibility are explored in the thematic substance of *The Woman Warrior*, but these twin themes also appear in the rhetoric of this text and *China Men*, particularly in the symbolism associated with the body.[23] The willing submission to bodily mutilation, such as Ah Po and Brave Orchid demonstrate, signifies the acceptance of a conventional lifestyle, with personal identity largely inscribed by conservative cultural forces. On the other hand, the impulse toward self expression and the bodily representation of a distinct and private personal identity, such as Moon Orchid's and the No Name Woman's, is differently and often violently treated. In Kingston's work, tradition is frequently represented by bodily symbolism; departures from it are also represented physically. The adolescent protagonist tries out for herself various incarnations of femininity—the No Name Woman, Moon Orchid, Ts'ai Yen—trying to find a way to negotiate the patriarchal demands placed upon her.

Sau-ling Cynthia Wong discusses at length the contrast between Moon Orchid, with her passion for feminine ornamentation of the body, and Brave Orchid, whose utilitarian values will not permit her to decorate her body. Moon Orchid is the "lovely useless type" according to her sister, who, upon seeing her for the first time in thirty years, immediately thinks, disapprovingly, "she wore pearls around her neck and in her earlobes. Moon Orchid *would* travel with her jewels showing" (117). Moon Orchid, as her sister clearly understands, is rendered powerless by the passion for fine dainty things, dresses, and jewelry that consumes all her energy. The narrator offers a contrast between the sisters by comparing Moon Orchid's hands to Brave Orchid's: "The kitchen light shined warmly on the gold and jade rings that gave her hands a completeness. One of the rings was a wedding ring.

Brave Orchid, who had been married for almost fifty years, did not wear any rings. They got in the way of all the work. She did not want the gold to wash away in the dishwater and the laundry water and the field water" (127). Moon Orchid's jewelry, the narrator suggests, is a sign that she has never needed to work in her life; more than this, it is a symbol of the forces that prevent her from working. Moon Orchid has been kept by her husband, protected from the need to make her own way in the world, so that now she is unable to look after herself. She is comfortable with her place within the patriarchy, though she needs someone to take care of her.

Like the women of the previous generation, such as Brave Orchid's mother-in-law, who were reduced to inactivity by the crippling of their bound feet, Moon Orchid is also incapable of action because she is unable to act as the agent of her own destiny. She needs a man—father, brother, or husband—to tell her what to do. She can decide what to wear, but she cannot decide what to do. Moon Orchid is a product of patriarchy, a woman who exists to serve men. This attitude explains why she is so terrified at the prospect of confronting her estranged husband. She knows that by coming to America without his explicit instructions she is somehow betraying him. When her sister suggests they must tell him that Moon Orchid has arrived in America, she shrinks into a childlike passivity: "Moon Orchid's eyes got big like a child's. 'I shouldn't be here,' she said" (124). This knowledge, combined with the feminine passivity that is one of her strong character traits, reduces Moon Orchid to a kind of moral paralysis. Her sister is constantly advising her to go to her husband and demand her rights—but Moon Orchid has never thought of her life or herself in terms of her "rights." Her inability to think in terms of sexual politics (her rights in relation to her husband) is a consequence of her inability to think in any terms beyond the physical. Moon Orchid is effectively trapped in her own femininity—the passivity and the physical frailty that is expected of women and the overriding concern with physical appearance.

These characteristics of Moon Orchid's oppression become apparent through the contrast she presents with her sister, Brave Orchid. Brave Orchid is physically strong, she is the active agent and shaper of her own destiny, and she is unconcerned about her physical appearance. Brave Orchid represents a strange kind of androgyny, a mix of masculine and feminine characteristics that becomes a contradictory blend of feminism and misogyny. In China, Brave Orchid participates in the harassment of her sister-in-law, the No Name Woman; she shapes her body to conform to social expectations of how a married woman's body should appear; she takes a girl slave and, in her role of midwife, possibly commits female infanticide. In these ways, she is agent of but also subject to the misogyny of her patriarchal culture. In the

United States, however, Brave Orchid works like a man—the narrator recalls how her mother works from 6:30 A.M. until midnight—possessing the strength of body and mind that is expected of a man. Brave Orchid is also relentless in the pursuit of what she perceives to be her rights. So when the delivery boy mistakenly brings a consignment of medicine to the laundry, bringing a curse of sickness and death upon them, in Brave Orchid's terms, she will not rest until her daughter brings her candy from the druggist as reparation, or compensation for the harm he has done. Likewise, when thinking about how her sister has been treated by the husband who has neglected her for thirty years, Brave Orchid is outraged and, on her sister's behalf, grows in her determination to ensure that Moon Orchid's rights are respected. As Linda Morante asserts, "Brave Orchid embodies the selfhood that she insists women can never possess."[24]

Brave Orchid demonstrates that it is possible for women to resist the debilitating impact of patriarchy, though they cannot escape altogether. Even Brave Orchid is subject to the power of the ideology of male domination. So, when Moon Orchid's husband tells the sisters to their faces that he will not take his Chinese wife into his American household, Moon Orchid is reduced to a stuttering silence and even Brave Orchid can only respond with the muted demand that he buy them lunch, after their long journey from San Francisco to Los Angeles. In the face of direct male authority, even Brave Orchid gives way.

To the forms of intimidation that keep women afraid and willingly confined to the protective confines of the house—the threat of violence and sexual violence especially—Brave Orchid expresses no fear. The narrative is framed by instances of sexual violence: the first story concerns the rape of the No Name Woman; the final story concerns the abduction of Ts'ai Yen by a barbarian warlord, who then keeps her as his "wife" and mother of his children until she is ransomed. The narrator refers to Ts'ai Yen as a wife but since she is a hostage, used for sexual purposes by her captor, the term "wife" seems to be a euphemism for Ts'ai Yen's true status of sexual slave. This kind of violence does not touch Brave Orchid. In China she travels freely as a doctor to visit her patients; in the United States she shields her children from the sight of dead bodies in the street and advises her sister how to avoid the tramps. Even supernatural threats hold no terror for Brave Orchid. She is able to dispel malignant spirits and even to exorcise the ghost that haunts the medical college, a ghost who has claimed many victims in the past.

All the female characters of *The Woman Warrior* experience to some extent a dislocation between mind and body. A humorous instance is the meeting of Brave Orchid and Moon Orchid after a period of many years. At the airport, Brave Orchid is looking for a woman who resembles her sister as she knew her, as a young woman. Both women are shocked that the image each held of the other in her mind is so different from the reality before her. They argue,

> "You're an old woman," said Brave Orchid.
>
> "Aiaa. *You're* an old woman."
>
> "But you are really old. Surely you can't say that about me. I'm not old the way you're old."
>
> "But *you* really are old." (118)

Finally Moon Orchid jokes, to her sister's annoyance, "You're wearing an old mask to tease me" (119). The distinction between how these women think of themselves, the private image they carry in their minds, and the public image they display in the physical appearance they show the world is, in Moon Orchid's case, a consequence of patriarchy. In a patriarchal culture, women live with the requirement that they sacrifice self-image for society's conventional image of femininity. Brave Orchid resists this imperative. Looking at her reflection in a shop-front window, she thinks, "She used to be young and fast; she was still fast and felt young. It was mirrors, not aches and pains, that turned a person old, everywhere white hair and wrinkles" (147). Brave Orchid does not look into mirrors, but her sister does. When her husband exclaims, "Look at her" (153), Moon Orchid sees herself through his contemptuous eyes, as an old woman who has stepped outside the role assigned to her by this male-dominated culture. "Moon Orchid was so ashamed, she held her hands over her face. She wished she could also hide her dappled hands" (153). Her impulse is self-effacement, to render herself invisible, nonexistent, in the face of her husband's dominating stare.

The No Name woman discovers that as a consequence of her betrayal of patriarchal law she no longer has a place in the world; Moon Orchid betrays the unwritten law that she should always be obedient to her husband's will and similarly finds that she has lost her place in the world. Both women are betrayed by their femininity: No Name Woman by her feminine sexuality and Moon Orchid by her feminine passivity. The figure of Fa Mu Lan, the Woman Warrior, however, symbolizes the psychological needs of narrator. She represents the power of androgyny, of masculine strength combined with feminine delicacy, and a willing submission to discipline that is feminine together with the masculine freedom of selfhood. This discipline practiced within the context of freedom constitutes what Sau-ling Cynthia Wong calls a "Higher Necessity" and importantly Fa Mu Lan's disciplined freedom represents a positive interpretation of bodily mutilation with which to cancel the stories of bound feet and other abuses.[25] She freely chooses her mutilation and disciplines her body both to withstand the pain and to remain active despite it. Fa Mu Lan trains her body so that it coincides perfectly with her mind; there is no disjunction between her self-image and her public image. Rather, her body represents the fulfillment and completion of her humanity. Her gender "difference," her femininity in a masculine-dominated society, is represented as an essential and creative cosmic principle. As Rabine argues, in the representation of the woman warrior, "The 'difference between,' the logic of opposition, the law of gender that protects patriarchal genealogy, gives way to the difference within."[26] So the difference between men and women that is the foundation of patriarchal society in the figure of the woman warrior becomes a reconciliation of her male and female powers.

Patriarchal violence then gives way to righteous vengeance, and also the revelation, or exposure, of injustice: Fa Mu Lan's parents carve their grievances into her body, and in this way she uses her body to complete her life story. The invisibility that women such as Moon Orchid seek is akin to the silence that hides and perpetuates injustice, the inscription of those injustices is a breaking of silence. So the narrator finds that she must tell her mother all the injustices to which she has been witness if she is to end the pain in her throat and overcome her sense of alienation. She needs the unifying power of art, the voice of her genuine self, rather than list to achieve this completion. Words are powerful, as she discovers; "Be careful what you say. It comes true," she advises (204). Words endow their possessor with the power to speak truthfully and to see accurately the shape or meaning of their own lives. Words are able to shape and communicate reality—words, more than anything else, are able to embody realities. The maturing protagonist discovers that as an artist she is compelled to represent her people and the injustices they suffer, just as Fa Mu Lan represents her people as a warrior. Her people, however, are the community of women. The example of the female poet, Ts'ai Yen, who was able to communicate across the lines of difference with the barbarians, provides a fitting role model. In Ts'ai Yen, she finds an example of female power that is wielded through language and narrative. Stories of sexual violence, exclusion, invisibility, powerlessness—the strategies by which patriarchal culture oppress women by transforming feminine sexuality into a weapon against women—become themselves weapons with which to attack patriarchal injustices when these linguistic weapons are in the hands of a woman warrior.

NOTES

1. Sidonie Smith, *A Poetics of Women's Autobiography: Marginality and the Fictions of Self-Representation* (Bloomington & Indianapolis: Indiana University Press, 1987), p. 5.

2. Ibid., p. 42–43.

3. Ibid., p. 150.

4. Ibid., pp. 150–151.

5. Kay Bonetti, "An Interview with Maxine Hong Kingston," in *Conversations with Maxine Hong Kingston,* edited by Paul Skenazy and Yera Martin (Jackson: University Press of Mississippi, 1998), p. 41.

6. Arturo Islas and Marilyn Yaom, "Interview with Maxine Hong Kingston," in *Conversations with Maxine Hong Kingston,* p. 21.

7. Neila Seshachari, "Reinventing Peace: Conversations with Tripmaster Maxine Hong Kingston," in *Conversations with Maxine Hong Kingston,* p. 202.

8. Ibid., p. 203.

9. Frank Chin, "This is Not an Autobiography," *Genre* 18, 2 (1985), p. 112.

10. Sau-ling Cynthia Wong, "Autobiography as Guided Chinatown Tour? Maxine Hong Kingston's The Woman Warrior and the Chinese American Autobiographical Controversy," in *Maxine Hong Kingston's* The Woman Warrior: *A Casebook,* edited by Sau-ling Cynthia Wong (New York & Oxford: Oxford University Press), p. 37.

11. Ibid., p. 38.

12. Ibid., p. 37.

13. Joan Lidoff, "Autobiography in a Different Voice: *The Woman Warrior* and the Question of Genre," in *Approaches to Teaching Kingston's* The Woman Warrior, edited by Shirley Geok-lin Lim (New York: Modern Language Association of America), p. 117.

14. Ibid.

15. Shirley K. Rose, "Metaphors and Myths of Cross-Cultural Literacy: Autobiographical Narratives by Maxine Hong Kingston, Richard Rodriguez and Malcolm X," *MELUS,* 14 (1987), p. 4.

16. Ibid., p. 14.

17. Maxine Hong Kingston, "Cultural Mis-readings by American Reviewers," in *Asian and Western Writers in Dialogue,* edited by Guy Amirthanayagam (London: Macmillan, 1982), pp. 55–65.

18. Ibid., p. 56.

19. Ibid.

20. Ibid., pp. 57–58.

21. Ibid., pp. 60–61.

22. Leslie W. Rabine, "No Lost Paradise: Social Gender and Symbolic Gender in the Writing of Maxine Hong Kingston," in *Signs: Journal of Women in Culture and Society* 12, 3 (1987), p. 473.

23. Sau-ling Cynthia Wong, "Necessity and Extravagance in Maxine Hong Kingston's *The Woman Warrior*: Art and the Ethnic Experience," *MELUS,* 15 (1988), pp. 3–26.

24. Linda Morante, "From Silence to Song: The Triumph of Maxine Hong Kingston," *Frontiers,* 9, no. 2 (1987), p. 80.

25. Wong, p. 19.

26. Rabine, p. 475.

THE WOMAN WARRIOR AND CHINA MEN IN HISTORY

PUBLIC RESPONSE

From its initial publication in 1977, *The Woman Warrior* has been hailed as a masterpiece. In 1979 *The Woman Warrior* was named by *Time* magazine as one of the top ten nonfiction works of the decade, and ten years later, in 1989, the book was still listed as a best-seller on the trade paperback lists.[1] Commenting on Kingston's significance as a contemporary author, Sau-ling Cynthia Wong described *The Woman Warrior* as "one of the most widely circulated and frequently taught literary texts by a living American author."[2] Kingston was also aware of just how popular her work had become; in her "Personal Statement," included in Shirley Geok-lin Lim's collection of essays on *The Woman Warrior*, Kingston observed that on college campuses young women were referring to *The Woman Warrior* simply as "the book" that they carried with them like a badge or talisman.[3] *The Woman Warrior* has been honored with prestigious literary prizes, such as the 1976 National Book Critics Circle Award, and *China Men* won the 1981 National Book Award for nonfiction. Kingston's work is also popular with nonacademic readers in both English and Chinese.

Kingston has a large readership in China; both *The Woman Warrior* and *China Men* have been published in China, Hong Kong, and Taiwan in legal editions and also in pirated editions that feature what the author described as some bad translations. In the People's Republic of China, the Language Institute translated *The Woman Warrior* into the national standard language and also into Cantonese. According to Kingston's own estimates, some twenty translations have been made of *The Woman Warrior*.[4] In China her work is so important that Kingston is perceived to be part of the Chinese literary tradition. In an interview with Marilyn Chin, Kingston explained how her work was received by contemporary Chinese writers. She recalled that during her 1988 trip to China she was impressed with the response of one poet in particular:

> He said that I was writing in the tradition of the past. And, . . . they were telling us that there was a "roots literature" movement in China—because in the Cul-

Chinese men working for the Southern Pacific Railroad Company near Sacramento, California, in 1877. With the completion of the railroad, Chinese laborers were expelled from the area.

---

tural Revolution they cut off the roots. . . . So they had cut off their ties to the West, and cut off the bindings of feudalism, the imperial arts and all that. But then they weren't left with anything. So, as I came to the end of the trip, when we got to Shanghai, they were crying and talking about all this Cultural Revolution stuff. Then I thought, I know why they invited us American writers there, especially me, because they felt I was working in free conditions. Here I was in America, where I had free speech and free press. And I spent this lifetime working on roots. So what they were saying was that I was their continuity. And they wanted help in figuring out where to go.[5]

Despite her awareness of the importance of her work in contemporary China, Kingston described her approach to her Chinese roots as "tentative."[6] Her primary contribution is to the traditions of American literature, as an American writer of Chinese ancestry. In these terms, her achievement is to have created a space for Chinese American writers within the American literary canon and, at the same time, to have stimulated a readership for Chinese American literature.

HISTORICAL REFLECTIONS

The Woman Warrior and *China Men* reflect disparate aspects of Kingston's dual Chinese and American cultural heritage. The major historical events of twentieth-century China—the history of Chinese immigration to the United States, the changing history of race relations in the United States in the mid twentieth century, particularly the Civil Rights movement, and the changing status of women through the efforts of the Women's Liberation movement—all are reflected in these narratives.

The lives of the narrator's parents are shaped by the events of Chinese history and by the history of legislative constraints to which Chinese immigrants to the United States have been subject since the nineteenth century. Brave Orchid was born in 1898 and her husband was born in 1903; they both lived to witness and to be shaped by the tumultuous historical changes that took place in China in the twentieth century.

Early in the twentieth century the Chinese imperial system of government, which had lasted for centuries, finally was brought to an end. Despite attempts to reform the imperial government, the republican movement, led by Sun Yat-sen, gained force. In 1912 the Republic of China was created under the new president, Yuan Shih-k'ai. His government was soon exposed as corrupt, and the former revolutionaries reorganized as the Kuomintang (Nationalist Party) to oppose the new republican government. Yuan Shih-k'ai's corrupt attempts to reestablish the empire and to style himself as emperor failed and, with the Nationalists in exile in Japan, the real power in China fell to the provincial warlords. These warlords were not unlike the evil baron who is destroyed by Fa Mu Lan in *The Woman Warrior*. During this time, in 1924, Kingston's father, Tom Hong, left China to work in the United States.

In 1928 the Nationalists, led by Chiang Kai-shek, defeated the warlords and the Chinese Communists, and united China under a single government. In 1931 the Japanese occupied Manchuria and extended their military influence in northern China; the war against Japan weakened the Nationalist government and allowed the Communists to gain in strength and influence. In 1934 and 1935 Mao Zedong led the Chinese Commu-

EXCLUSION

"Exclusion plays right into the hands of the American writer. There have been amazing coincidences of exclusion, so that I become a person who is able to look at everything from an interesting perspective. The alienated, individualistic writer or hero or heroine is a tradition in American literature. I take that stance very easily: I don't worry whether my voice is "our" voice. Even though I have a peculiar voice I'm able to speak to everyone from my stance of exile, as outsider, and then I can make my way in."

Maxine Hong Kingston

From Jody Hoy, "To Be Able to See the Tao," in *Conversations with Maxine Hong Kingston,* edited by Paul Skenazy and Tera Martin (Jackson: University Press of Mississippi, 1998), p. 50.

FROM "WHITE TIGERS" IN THE WOMAN WARRIOR

"To avenge my family, I'd have to storm across China to take back our farm from the Communists; I'd have to rage across the United States to take back the laundry in New York and the one in California. Nobody in history has conquered and united both North America and Asia."

Maxine Hong Kingston

From Maxine Hong Kingston, *The Woman Warrior* (New York: Vintage, 1989), p. 49.

nists on their long northern march to Shensi, and by the end of World War II the Communists controlled a large area of northern China. In 1939, before the outbreak of widespread conflict, Kingston's mother, Brave Orchid, left China to join her husband in the United States. Full-scale civil war broke out in 1946, and in 1949 the Chinese Communists established the People's Republic of China. *The Woman Warrior* and *China Men* describe the suffering of the family members who remained in China during this time and the deaths of two paternal uncles, Dai Bak and Ngee Bak, who were both killed by Communists in 1949. In 1953 China began its first Five Year Plan for economic growth, and in 1958 the Communists launched the Great Leap Forward, the second Five Year Plan, to accelerate economic development by reforming the peasant agricultural communes. In fact, the Great Leap Forward retarded China's development by bringing economic depression and food shortages that lasted until 1962. In *The Woman Warrior* and *China Men*, the narrator describes the letters sent to her parents by their Chinese relatives begging for money for food and other necessities. In *The Woman Warrior* she recalls that "the adults wept over the letters about the neighbors gone berserk turning Communist. . . . the aunts kept disappearing and the uncles dying after unspeakable tortures" (190). At this time, Chinese people living in the United States were prevented by law from sending financial aid to relatives in Communist China.

The Cultural Revolution of 1966 to 1969 was Mao Zedong's attempt to ensure that China remained a radical Communist state based upon the principle of a classless society. During the Cultural Revolution universities were closed; many provincial governments were seized by radicals; and all aspects of life in China were disrupted. Finally, in 1967 Mao called out the army to restore order. In 1971 U.S. Secretary of State Henry Kissinger traveled secretly to Peking to explore the possibility of establishing diplomatic relations between the United States and China. In that year, China was admitted to the United Nations when the United States dropped its opposition to Chinese membership, and in 1972 President Richard Nixon made an official visit to China. There, the United States and China signed the Shanghai Communiqué that anticipated the establishment of normal diplomatic relations.

During the 1960s the United States did not repeal punitive legislation that prevented most Chinese from immigrating. The historical experience of the Chinese in the United States is largely a history of prejudice and discrimination, but also an invisible history of which most Americans are unaware. Kingston seeks to expose the true history of the Chinese in the United States. In *The Woman Warrior* Kingston describes some of the measures taken by the Chinese community to avoid notice by immigration authorities that the people cannot trust: "Lie to Americans. Tell them you were born during the San Francisco earthquake. Tell them your birth certificate and your parents were burned up in the fire. Don't report crimes; tell them we have no crimes and no poverty. Give a new name every time you get arrested; the ghosts won't recognize you. Pay the new immigrants twenty-five cents an hour and say we have no unemployment. And, of course, tell them we're against Communism" (184). In *China Men,* exploitation and brutal discrimination characterize the experience of Ah Goong, described in the chapter "The Grandfather of the Sierra Nevada Mountains." Once the building of the railroad is complete and the labor of Chinese workmen like Ah Goong is no longer needed, these Chinese laborers are driven out of California upon pain of lynching. The narrator tells how Ah Goong, aware of the murderous racial hostility that surrounded him, drifted from place to place until he finally returned to China, having discovered that there was no place for him in America.

This sense of not belonging, as an Asian man in the United States, was codified historically in a series of acts of legislation that minimized the migration of Chinese people to America and restricted the permanent settlement of Chinese communities in America and in California in particular. These laws are listed chronologically in *China Men* in the chapter that follows Ah Goong's story, titled "The Laws." In this chapter Kingston tells the story of racial prejudice that characterized relations between the U.S. government and Chinese individuals. This drama was largely played out through the medium of immigration laws and procedures. The Burlingame Treaty of 1868 is Kingston's starting point. This treaty was an agreement between the U.S. government and the emperor of China to allow free movement between the two countries "for the purposes of curiosity, of trade, or as permanent residents" (152). The Burlingame Treaty was modified in 1880 and suspended in 1881. Only two years after the first signing of the treaty, the 1870 Nationality Act excluded Chinese and other Asians from migrating to America by specifying that only "free whites" and "African aliens" could apply for U.S. naturalization. Chinese were prohibited from entering California by a law passed in 1878 by the California Constitutional Convention. At the same time, Chinese already residing in California were excluded from state schools; they could no longer own land; and they became subject to special taxes applicable only to Chinese. The first of many Chinese Exclusion Acts was passed by Congress in 1882. The 1882 Exclusion Act was extended in 1892 and again in 1904; in 1943 the Chinese Exclusion Act of 1882 was finally repealed. The effect of this law was so great that, as Kingston remarks, in 1943 "Japanese invaders were killing Chinese civilians in vast numbers; it is estimated that 10 million died. Chinese immigration to the United States did not rise" (157). The quota system for immigration applications was abandoned in 1978 in favor of a worldwide limitation on immigration to the United States. There remained, however, special quotas for Southeast Asian refugees.

Kingston continues, in "The Laws," to document other immigration restrictions, such as the law passed in 1924, the year that her father came to the United States, which prohibited Chinese women from immigrating. This attempt to curtail the establishment of Chinese families in America was complemented by the prohibition against marrying a Chinese person. Any man or woman who married a Chinese person did so at the risk of losing his or her own citizenship. After the passage of the War Bride Act of 1946, even the Japanese wives of returning servicemen were given priority over the wives of Chinese Americans. During this period the narrator of *The Woman Warrior* describes her mother, Brave Orchid, as working extra jobs in order to send money to relatives who were suffering in China but were unable to flee to the United States.

In *China Men* Kingston gives an account of the legislative response by the United States to the Chinese Communist Revolution of 1949. In 1949 Congress passed a series of Refugee Relief Acts but some Chinese residents in the United States were deported as being "subversives or anarchists . . . some were naturalized citizens who were 'denaturalized' beforehand" (158). In a landmark case in 1954 the Supreme Court upheld laws forbidding Chinese Americans to send money to relatives in China, even through international aid organizations. The narrator, in both *The Woman Warrior* and *China Men,* tells of relatives writing to beg her parents to send money to them in China because they are starving. In *The Woman Warrior* the narrator observes, "My mother sends money she earns working in the tomato fields to Hong Kong. The relatives there can send it on to the remaining aunts and their children" (205). However, the 1952 Immigration and Nationality Act finally provided that Chinese women could immigrate under the same conditions as men.

The immigration of Chinese women to the United States has been limited historically by two primary factors. One is the legislative prohibition. The other factor is the cultural constraint placed upon women by the

1910 photo of Sun Yat-sen, leader of the Chinese Nationalist Party, included in his U.S. Immigration and Naturalization Service case file. He played a role in overthrowing the Manchu dynasty a year later. Political changes in China shaped the experiences and attitudes of Kingston's characters.

---

patriarchal culture of pre-Revolutionary China. According to custom and tradition, only the men could be "Gold Mountain sojourners." Women were required to remain behind in their home villages to ensure that the men sent money to the extended families and that they would eventually return to settle permanently in their ancestral villages. As a consequence, in the late nineteenth century and early part of the twentieth century, even before the American legal prohibition against female Chinese immigration, there were extremely few Chinese women in the United States. Following the revision of the law in 1930 to allow more Chinese women to immigrate, few women actually did. When Brave Orchid traveled from China to join her husband in New York, she was one of the few women who were able to make the journey. In the chapter "Shaman," the narrator describes the ordeal of repeated questioning her mother endured while she was held at the immigration station at Ellis Island before she was finally permitted to enter the United States.

The difficulty of emigrating from China to the United States is dramatized in *The Woman Warrior* by Brave Orchid's doomed attempts to reconcile her sister, Moon Orchid, with her estranged husband. He has taken a second, Chinese American wife with whom he lives in Los Angeles while he financially supports Moon Orchid and their daughter who live in Hong Kong. Moon Orchid lives a life of comfort while she waits for her husband to send for her. After thirty years he still has not sent for her and so Brave Orchid intervenes. First, she arranges for her niece to come from Hong Kong to be married to a Chinese American, a man described by the narrator as "a rich and angry man with citizenship papers. . . . a tyrant" (128). Five years later, by virtue of her marriage to an American citizen, Moon Orchid's daughter is able to bring her mother to the United States. Once she has arrived in California, Moon Orchid naively mistakes the Stockton Chinatown where her sister and brother-in-law run their laundry for America. She remarks of Chinatown, "It certainly looks different to China. I'm glad to see the Americans talk like us" (136). The historical emergence of Chinese communities, or Chinatowns, provides an important dimension to *The Woman Warrior* and *China Men* both in terms of the settings of the narratives and the political interest in racial discrimination. Though the development of these communities was inhibited by anti-Chinese legislation, the hostility and racial exclusion experienced by Chinese Americans also contributed to the emergence of tight-knit ethnic neighborhoods. The Chinatown of Stockton that provides some of the setting for *The Woman Warrior* and *China Men* is not, as Kingston has emphasized, a single geographical location, like San Francisco's famous Chinatown. Kingston has remarked, "The Chinatown in San Francisco is seeable. It's defined. We know pretty much what it is. It makes us think that that's what we look for when we look for Chinatown in Stockton. But the Chinatown in Stockton looks nothing like the Chinatown in San Francisco."⁷ Rather, in Stockton the Chinese American community is unified by a strong sense of common traditions and history. Kingston's Chinatown is, therefore, not so much a collection of buildings as a community of people; the "overseas Chinese" Brave Orchid calls them (136). Kingston has described how San Francisco feels to a person from Stockton: "a trip from Stockton to San Francisco is a journey into foreign territory—urban, competitive, the people like Hong Kong city slickers, not at all like the people in the San Joaquin Valley, where villager is still neighborly to villager as in the Chinese countryside they remember, helping one another, 'not Chinese against Chinese like in the Big City'."⁸ Consequently, when reviewers of *The Woman Warrior* assumed mistakenly that the narrative was set in San Francisco, Kingston was annoyed.

The Chinese American community supports her parents emotionally but they criticize her for her inability to conform to traditional Chinese values. In *The Woman Warrior* she remarks, "Quite often the big loud women came shouting into the house, 'Now when you sell this one, I'd like to buy her to be my maid.' Then they laughed. They always said that about my sister, not me because I dropped dishes at them" (190). One of the immigrant Chinese women tells her, "You have what we call a pressed-duck voice" (192); she is already inhibited about speaking in either Chinese or English and in her insecurity she recognizes truth in the woman's words: "she was right: if you squeezed the duck hung up to dry in the east window, the sound that was my voice would come out of it" (192). Through these immigrant women and their families, in addition to her mother's "talk-story," Kingston becomes aware of the low value attached to women and girls in traditional Chinese culture. From them she learns of such practices as female slavery, female infanticide, concubinage, and arranged marriages. She also learns to fear the prospect that her parents may return to China where she will be subject to these misogynistic practices. Her fear is heightened by her awareness that in China her mother owned a girl slave and that in America her mother arranged the marriage of her niece, Moon Orchid's daughter. From this fear arises Kingston's analysis of the oppression of women in traditional Chinese culture but also in contemporary American society as well. Kingston observed, "Politically and socially . . . I look at myself as being very much a feminist. . . . In Chinese culture, people always talk about how girls are bad. When you hear that, right away it makes you radical like anything."⁹

The feminist movement of the mid twentieth century, commonly referred to as the "second wave" of American feminism, is reflected in this aspect of *The Woman Warrior*. The first wave of American feminism is referred to as the period leading up to, and following from, the Seneca Falls Convention in 1848. Margaret Fuller, Elizabeth Cady Stanton, Susan B. Anthony, and Charlotte Perkins Gilman were all influential feminists of this earlier period. The second wave of American feminism dates from the 1960s and was shaped by feminists such as Betty Friedan, Shulamith Firestone, Kate Millett, and Gloria Steinem. Kingston was a young student at the University of California, Berkeley—a hotbed of student unrest—at the time of feminism's reemergence. When she wrote *The Woman Warrior* in the 1970s, feminism had developed into a powerful political movement.

The second wave of American feminism that emerged in the 1960s focused upon women's exclusion from the public world of work, especially the professions such as law and medicine, and the confinement of women in the domestic world of the home. In *The Feminine Mystique* Friedan called for women to renew the struggle for women's rights, which had culminated in the vote for women in 1920. The National Organization for Women (NOW)—founded by Friedan in 1966—campaigned for state and federal provision of child care and the legalization of abortion. During the time when Kingston was working on *The Woman Warrior* and *China Men*, in the early 1970s, positive legislative change was under way: the Educational Amendments Act of 1972 made it mandatory that all colleges instigate affirmative-action programs in relation to admissions, hiring, and athletics; Congress approved the Equal Rights Amendment, and the landmark decision by the Supreme Court in *Roe* v *Wade* (1973) overruled state laws forbidding abortions during the first three months of pregnancy. At this time, feminists called for equal rights, reproductive rights, and economic justice for women. The election of the Kennedy administration in 1960 helped to initiate more social reforms, and the formation of NOW created a new civil-rights group capable of lobbying government to enact and enforce legislation against sexual discrimination. The options available to women were changing at this time and were transforming the way in which young women, especially, thought about the shape of their future lives.

In *The Woman Warrior* Kingston highlights the anxiety experienced by her young narrator at the prospect of being subject to a traditional, arranged marriage. School has held out to her the possibility of an extended education that will take her into the echelons of a professional life, and with it more freedom and autonomy. She confesses, "Do you know what the Teacher ghosts say about me? They tell me I'm smart, and I can win scholarships. I can get into colleges. I've already applied. I'm smart. I can do all kinds of things. I know how to get A's, and they say I could be a scientist or a mathematician if I want. I can make a living and take care of myself" (201). Self-determination, the freedom to choose her own future, also offers her respite from the specter of female slavery that haunts her. From the time she becomes aware that in China her mother owned a girl slave, she fears that if her parents should return to China they will sell her into slavery.

In both *The Woman Warrior* and *China Men* Kingston explores not just the dynamics of gender oppression, but the interplay of sexual and racial discrimination within the context of oppressive cultures. Kingston's political themes incorporate her feminism and her opposition to racism; so, in addition to the women's liberation movement, the Civil Rights movement contributes an important historical context to understanding these narratives. The Civil Rights movement began in the 1950s and is commonly dated from the Montgomery Bus Boycott of 1955. In Montgomery, Alabama, a black woman named Rosa Parks refused to give up her seat to a white man. Her act of passive refusal to respect an unjust, racist law became typical of the method used by civil-rights activists to expose and oppose racist laws and practices. In 1960, in Greensboro, North Carolina, a group of black college students staged a similar protest when they took places at a "whites only" lunch counter in Woolworth's and refused to leave or to move until they received service. The Student Nonviolent Coordinating Committee joined with the Southern Christian Leadership Conference, led by the Reverend Martin Luther King Jr., to unite the efforts of student activists with those of civil-rights protesters. They were joined by members of the National Association for the Advancement of Colored People (NAACP) and the Congress of Racial Equality (CORE). Congress passed the Civil Rights Act in 1964 and the Voting Rights Act the following year. These two acts of legislation ensured basic civil rights for members of all ethnic groups. These legislative reforms did not bring an end to racial tension, however, which reached a climax with riots in the black neighborhood of Watts in Los Angeles in 1965. The riots were motivated by anger over issues of inadequate public housing, unemployment, crime, and poverty, which, in the view of northern urban blacks, had been neglected by the civil-rights effort that focused on the plight of southern rural blacks.

In *The Woman Warrior*, the narrator expresses her support for the values of the Civil Rights movement. At the end of the chapter titled "White Tigers" she speculates how she could adopt elements of the mythical warrior woman's righteous anger to her own situation in contemporary America. So, when her boss in an art-supply house refers to a shade of yellow as "nigger yellow" she refuses to let the moment pass; she recalls, "'I don't like that word,' I had to say in my bad, small-person's voice that makes no impact" (48). This is the narrator's way of adopting for herself the nonviolent resistance of racism that was the strategy recommended by the leaders of the movement. Likewise, when she types invitations to an industry banquet, she asks her boss, "Did you know the restaurant you chose for the banquet is being picketed by CORE and the NAACP?" (48). When he laughs in her face and tells her that he chose the restaurant precisely because it was subject to protest by antiracist organizations such as CORE and the NAACP, she refuses to type the invitations and accepts the loss of her job that follows immediately. Passive noncooperation with the forces of racism and injustice was the recommended way of opposing rac-

ON FICTION AND NONFICTION

"You know, what I wish that people could appreciate, they could see that what I'm doing is riding that border between fiction and non fiction. You know, we have a land of fiction and there is a land of nonfiction; there's a border in the middle. Well, what I'm doing is making that border very wide, and I am taking into consideration I am writing about real people and these real people have powerful imaginations."

Maxine Hong Kingston

From Laura E. Skandera-Trombley, "A Conversation with Maxine Hong Kingston," in *Critical Essays on Maxine Hong Kingston*, edited by Skandera-Trombley (New York: Simon & Schuster/Macmillan, 1998), p. 35.

ism by those who shaped and led the Civil Rights movement, and Kingston reflects this strategy in her narrative.

The final chapter of *China Men* is titled "The Brother in Vietnam": the conflict in Vietnam provides an important context for both this book and *The Woman Warrior*, which was published two years after the fall of Saigon, an event that marked the end of U.S. involvement in the war. When President Kennedy came to office in 1960 there were 2,000 American military advisors in Vietnam. When he was assassinated in 1963, this number had increased to 16,000. President Johnson inherited his predecessor's commitment to preventing a Communist takeover of South Vietnam, and throughout the 1960s American involvement in the civil conflict in Vietnam escalated. In 1965 the President ordered a sustained bombing of North Vietnam intended to disrupt the supply route known as the "Ho Chi Minh Trail" that connected guerrillas in the South with North Vietnam via the neighboring country of Laos. The first American combat troops were sent to Vietnam in March 1965. By the end of that year there were 184,000 troops and by 1966 that number had escalated to 385,000. These troops supported the South Vietnamese army in their conflict with both Vietcong guerrillas in the south and the North Vietnamese army. The intention was to prevent the North Vietnamese and Vietcong from unifying Vietnam as a Communist state rather than to conquer the North. The turning point in the war came on 31 January 1968, the first day of the Vietnamese New Year, or "Tet," when the Communists launched a series of surprise attacks during what should have been a holiday truce. In response, the United States launched the "Tet Offensive" to win back the ground taken by the Vietcong. Though this was a major defeat for the Vietcong, the Tet Offensive was an even bigger defeat for the President as public opinion at home turned decisively against the war. President Johnson's popularity plummeted as the American media proclaimed the war unwinnable. In May 1968 negotiations with the North Vietnamese opened in Paris to seek a negotiated cease-fire.

When President Nixon came to power in 1968 his negotiators in Paris were demanding the withdrawal of North Vietnamese forces from the

Parade in New York City's Chinatown during World War II. In 1943 the U.S. government repealed the Chinese Exclusion Act, thereby easing restrictions on Chinese immigration to the United States.

south and the retention of the American-backed government of Nguyen Van Thieu. The North Vietnamese, however, sought the unification of Vietnam as a Communist state. To assuage public opinion opposed to American involvement in the war, Nixon reduced the number of American combat troops in Vietnam to 50,000 by 1973, while increasing training and the provision of equipment for the South Vietnamese. He also stepped up the air war on North Vietnam in an attempt to force the Communists to negotiate a cease-fire at the Paris talks. In Paris an agreement to end American involvement in the war was reached in January 1973; the North Vietnamese were permitted to maintain troops in the south and to seek the unification of Vietnam. On 29 March 1973 the last American combat troops left Vietnam. Two years later, in March 1975, North Vietnam launched a massive invasion of the south and the southern capital of Saigon fell to the Communists on 30 April 1975. Television images of desperate Vietnamese fighting to board the last American helicopters marked the end of a war that had cost America $150 billion, 57,000 American deaths, and had divided the country more bitterly than at any time since the Civil War.

THE WOMAN WARRIOR AND *CHINA MEN* THROUGH TIME

The Woman Warrior, and its companion book *China Men,* is widely acknowledged to have shifted the ground of American literature in the late twentieth century. Kingston redefined the nature of the autobiography as a literary genre capable of representing the experience of women and members of ethnic minority groups. Kingston acknowledges that *The Woman Warrior* and *China Men* prompted a flowering of Asian American writing, much of it by women. In an interview with Marilyn Chin in 1989, she observed: "Amy Tan published *The Joy Luck Club,* and Hisaye Yamamoto published *Seventeen Syllables;* Frank Chin has a collection of short stories, and I think maybe Ruth-Anne Lumm McKunn just came out with her book on Chinese families. Jessica Hagedorn's is in the spring, and Bharati Mukherjee's is in the fall. She won the National Book Critics Circle Award. Something great must be going on."[10]

The Woman Warrior is counted among the most widely taught contemporary American literary texts. In the introduction to their collection of Kingston's interviews, Paul Skenazy and Tera Martin comment, "It is estimated that her work is the most anthologized of any living American writer, and that she is read by more American college students than any other living author. . . . Students, particularly Asian American women, look to her as a model, find themselves in her tales, seek her out with sycophantic regularity. She has opened the way to a whole generation of Asian American writers who have found a national audience for the first time."[11]

The Woman Warrior and China Men are widely studied and have been the subject of various critical interpretations: early feminist approaches to these texts were later complemented by interpretations sensitive to the interplay of racial issues together with the issue of social class in the narratives. Analyses of the power relationships represented in *The Woman Warrior* follow the writings of the influential French philosopher Michel Foucault, and the deconstructionist or poststructuralist style of analysis inspired by Jacques Derrida has also been applied to *The Woman Warrior*. Psychoanalytic approaches, inspired by feminists such as Hélène Cixous and Freudians such as Jacques Lacan, have been used to elucidate further meanings in Kingston's narrative. The analytic techniques and particular concerns of a wide range of theoretical schools have been applied to *The Woman Warrior* and *China Men*. Because the narratives are multifaceted, critics with differing values and attitudes toward the interpretation of literary texts continue to find *The Woman Warrior* and *China Men* challenging and stimulating.

NOTES

1. Paul Skenazy and Tera Martin, introduction, *Conversations with Maxine Hong Kingston*, edited by Skenazy and Martin (Jackson: University Press of Mississippi, 1998), p. xxiv.

2. Wong, p. 3.

3. Maxine Hong Kingston, "Personal Statement," in *Approaches to Teaching Kingston's The Woman Warrior*, edited by Shirley Geok-lin Lim (New York: MLA, 1991), p. 24.

4. Wong, p. 12.

5. Marilyn Chin, "Writing the Other: A Conversation with Maxine Hong Kingston," in *Conversations with Maxine Hong Kingston*, pp. 93–94.

6. Ibid., p. 94.

7. Paul Skenazy, "Coming Home," in *Conversations with Maxine Hong Kingston*, p. 114.

8. Maxine Hong Kingston, "San Francisco's Chinatown: A View on the Other Side of Arnold Genthe's Camera," *American Heritage* (December 1978), p. 36.

9. Gary Kubota, "Maxine Hong Kingston: Something Comes From Outside Onto the Paper," *Hawaii Observer*, 28 July 1977, reprinted in *Conversations with Maxine Hong Kingston*, p. 3.

10. Marilyn Chin, "Writing the Other: A Conversation with Maxine Hong Kingston," *Poetry Flash*, 198 (September 1989), reprinted in *Conversations with Maxine Hong Kingston*, p. 98.

11. *Conversations with Maxine Hong Kingston*, p. vii.

ADAPTATIONS OF *THE WOMAN WARRIOR*

During the years following the publication of *The Woman Warrior* Kingston considered adapting her work either as a movie or as a play. She had offers to adapt *The Woman Warrior* as a movie but did not act on any of them because of what she felt was her naiveté in relation to the movie business. In a 1977 interview she remarked, "One thing I do know, however, is that I don't want any haoles [whites] with taped eyelids playing roles as Chinese."[1] Kingston has, however, expressed her satisfaction with the 1994 Berkeley Repertory Theatre production of *The Woman Warrior*. In an interview with Eric J. Schroeder, Kingston recalled that she worked on scripts for *The Woman Warrior*, but it took several years for a production to materialize. One delay was caused by a devastating fire at her home in Oakland, California, in 1991, one that destroyed a novel in progress. Kingston said, "Soon after *The Woman Warrior* was published, we began trying to write scripts, but it wasn't until right after the fire that the Berkeley Rep got it together to produce the play. I was involved with it; I talked to various people: the producer, the director, the playwright."[2]

Directed by Sharon Ott, then the artistic director of the Berkeley Repertory Theatre, *The Woman Warrior* was adapted for the stage by playwright Deborah Rogin. Composer Jon Jang created the musical score, one that blended Western and Chinese influences. Kingston was pleased with the production: "I am amazed at the richness and beauty of the play—the costumes hand sewn in China, the immense stage sets and glorious lights by Ming Cho Lee, the voices of the actors transmitting my stories mouth-to-ear, the fusion of Western and Chinese music, the kung fu acrobatics. Much of what I write came out of talk-story. I put talk-story into text. Now, the play returns text to talk-story, and children and non-readers can appreciate these myths and legends too."[3] The casting of the roles was also successful with nontraditional casting. She speculated, "a movie would try to make everybody look the same, like everybody in the family would have to look the same. But in the

Kingston at the opening of the Berkeley Repertory Theatre production of *The Woman Warrior*, 18 May 1994 (Photo courtesy of the Lia Chang Gallery)

ON THE STAGE ADAPTATION OF *THE WOMAN WARRIOR*

"We've had three workshops for a play or a movie of *The Woman Warrior*. During the casting there were no end of women who can do Moon Orchid, or any of the failed women. But it's really hard to find anybody to do Brave Orchid. I think this shows that in 1986 the feminine, bound-foot, dainty type is with us. But where is the peasant woman with the big feet who is fierce and strong and of the earth, and yet beautiful? There aren't any, there isn't anyone out there. It's very sad what's happening to us now. Why aren't there actresses to choose from to play the powerful woman?"

Maxine Hong Kingston

From Jody Hoy, "To Be Able to See the Tao," in *Conversations with Maxine Hong Kingston*, edited by Paul Skenazy and Tera Martin (Jackson: University Press of Mississippi, 1998), pp. 48–49.

play, it was really wonderful to have Vietnamese accents, Japanese American accents, Hawaiian accents, a Singaporean accent, and all the different Chinese accents."[4] Kingston applauded Rogin's adaptation of the narrative into dramatic form: "Her feat was to find an organizing principle for my complex, non-linear books. She has braided three strands together—myth, ancestral history, and the life of a young girl."[5]

After its debut, the Berkeley Repertory Theatre's production of *The Woman Warrior* was staged in Boston, Massachusetts, as the first show of the 1994–1995 season at the Huntington Theatre. In February of 1995 the production was staged by the Center Theatre Group in Los Angeles.

REVIEW

From William A. Henry III, "The Lady Becomes the Tiger," in *Time* (20 June 1994): 64.

There can be few more inherently untheatrical topics than a writer's struggle to find his or her individual voice. The journey is internal, the judgment that it is over is purely subjective, and the quest is not of obvious relevance to any onlooker. From *Look Homeward, Angel* to *Brighton Beach Memoirs,* plays on this topic have been talk, talk, talk. So it is startling and satisfying to see a 68-ft.-wide stage crowded with white tigers, monkey kings, acrobats, sword fighters and 18-ft.-tall spirits of wisdom gliding by serenely as California's Berkeley Repertory Theatre unfolds *The Woman Warrior,* a version of two visionary coming-of-age novels by Maxine Hong Kingston.

The artistic search Kingston describes is more complex than most: she is an ethnic Chinese in "white ghost" America, a protofeminist woman caught between two male-dominated cultures, a natural writer in English whose parents are literate only in Chinese. In addition to being captivated by folk mythology, she is, like most writers, in the grip of intense family mythology—about an aunt shamed to suicide by giving birth to a bastard, about uncles murdered by communists who then arrogantly urge her father, safely in America, to "donate" the dead men's lands. These stories clearly indicated to young Kingston that America was better than China. Yet in the everyday dealings of her parents with a world that they did not understand and that accorded them little dignity, the family found ample evidence that America was far worse. This contradiction, among all the others, drove the pubescent Kingston into mute inertia, symbolized on stage by the heroine's spending most of an act strapped into a bed dangling from the ceiling.

. . .

The spectacle is impressive but often slow and emotionally remote. In veering away from the kitchen-sink realism of most immigrant dramas, Rogin and Ott have made too much oblique. Despite program notes, many allusions to Chinese heritage will elude even spectators acquainted with Peking Opera, the crucial inspiration. To Ott, femaleness, not ethnicity, is at the heart of the story. "The relationships this girl has with her parents," she says, "are very specifically a daughter's relationships, in ways that transcend culture but are deeply linked to gender." Yet the show seems far more a piece of Orientalia than an exploration of a young girl's mind and dreams. What it needs is fewer warriors and more women.

NOTES

1. Gary Kubota, "Maxine Hong Kingston: Something Comes from Outside Onto the Paper," *Hawaii Observer,* 28 July 1977, reprinted in *Conversations with Maxine Hong Kingston,* edited by Paul Skenazy and Tera Martin (Jackson: University Press of Mississippi, 1998), p. 4.

2. Eric J. Schroeder, "As Truthful as Possible: An Interview with Maxine Hong Kingston," *Writing on the Edge,* 7 (Spring 1996), reprinted in *Conversations with Maxine Hong Kingston,* p. 224.

3. Neila C. Seshachari, "Reinventing Peace: Conversations with Tripmaster Maxine Hong Kingston," *Weber Studies,* 12 (Winter 1995), reprinted in *Conversations with Maxine Hong Kingston,* p. 214.

4. Schroeder, p. 224.

5. Seshachari, p. 214.

THE WOMAN WARRIOR AND CHINA MEN AS STUDIED

OTHER WORKS FREQUENTLY STUDIED WITH *THE WOMAN WARRIOR* AND *CHINA MEN*

SIMILAR BY GENRE

Generic studies of *The Woman Warrior* and *China Men* have centered upon Kingston's use of autobiographical form. Kingston's work is similar to that of other minority writers who write autobiographical narratives in order to assert the importance and significance of the lives of women of color who are otherwise rendered invisible and silent. These would include nineteenth-century slave autobiographies, such as Harriet Jacobs's *Incidents in the Life of a Slave Girl* (1861), as well as books that follow in the tradition of slave narratives, such as Toni Morrison's *Beloved* (1988) and Maya Angelou's sequence of autobiographical narratives, beginning with *I Know Why the Caged Bird Sings* (1969).

The Woman Warrior is not simply an autobiography; Kingston weaves together with her autobiographical threads the recollection of the myths her mother told her, the histories that formed the family's talk-story, and the fictions that she builds from ideas and events in her own life. The complex narrative texture that results from the interweaving of these stylistic threads belongs to a category of autobiographical writing known as the *kunstlerroman*, which is distinguished by its subject matter. The *kunstlerroman* describes the early life of someone born to be an artist, and the narrative is mostly concerned with representing his or her growing artistic ability. The *kunstlerroman* culminates in the protagonist's mature awareness of himself or herself as an artist.

One of the best-known contemporary works of this kind by an American woman of color is Sandra Cisneros's *The House on Mango Street* (1983). Like the five linked but self-contained stories that comprise *The Woman Warrior,* Cisneros creates vignettes that are self-contained and autonomous, yet they link together in an emotionally logical fashion and build to create a picture of life in the barrio, seen through the experiences

Maxine Hong Kingston

ON VIRGINIA WOOLF

"Reading Virginia Woolf's Orlando was an event ... it's all right to make your man turn into a woman, it's all right to have a century of time flow by here and a moment of time flow by there. She showed me various freedoms I could take in writing."

Maxine Hong Kingston

From Jody Hoy, "To Be Able to See the Tao," in *Conversations with Maxine Hong Kingston,* edited by Paul Skenazy and Tera Martin (Jackson: University of Mississippi Press, 1998), p. 65.

of Esperanza and her developing consciousness of herself as an artist. In *The House on Mango Street* Esperanza learns first what she does not want to be, and then learns what she has the potential to become. She is named for a great-grandmother who was dominated by her husband and spent her life sitting at her window looking out, thinking of all the things she might have been. The book's characters also include the neighbor Marin, who has been brought from Puerto Rico to babysit her young cousins and look for a husband; Minerva, who writes poetry but is trapped physically in an abusive marriage; Esperanza's mother, who speaks two languages and sings opera but is too scared to go downtown because she cannot speak English; and Sally, who marries to escape her violent father. There are also the *comadres,* the three sisters, who tell Esperanza that she must escape in order to come back for those who cannot find a way out themselves. They instruct her to always remember her origin: "A circle, understand? You will always be Esperanza. You will always be Mango Street. You can't erase what you know: You can't forget who you are."[1] Alicia, her older friend, repeats this lesson: If life on Mango Street is ever to improve then it will be because people like Esperanza have made it better. No one else will do it. As an artist, Esperanza discovers how she can make a difference to life on Mango Street: by telling the stories of the people who live there.

The house provides a controlling metaphor in *The House on Mango Street*. Esperanza's growing awareness of herself as an artist is tied to her need to discover a space of her own—a place to think her own thoughts and to write them down in an appropriate silence. Aunt Lupe and Minerva in *The House on Mango Street* seek in poetry both a refuge from their oppressive lives and an authentic kind of freedom that resolves rather than simply eludes the conflicts that characterize their experience of subjectivity. These women, however, have no space to call their own. Esperanza experiences the house in which she lives as a metaphor for her entire sense of self. In the first vignette, she describes the shame evoked by a nun's words: "You live *there*? The way she said it made me feel like nothing. *There.* I lived *there*" (9). From this humiliation comes a determination to live in a "real" house: "I knew then I had to have a house. A real house. One I could point to" (9). With this real house will come a firm and stable sense of being, in place of the nothingness evoked by the nun. Esperanza sees an image of herself reflected in the nun's face and in the nun's words; as a poet Esperanza is able to use words to construct both a means of escape and a means to return to the house on Mango Street.

Another Chicana writer who uses the form of the *kunstlerroman* is Denise Chávez. In *The Last of the Menu Girls* (1987) Chávez represents, like Cisneros and Kingston, through a sequence of interlinked stories, the development of her protagonist, young Rocío Esquibel, as she discovers her artistic destiny. Rocío, like the young narrator in *The Woman Warrior,* witnesses the lives of a series of women who represent the models of femininity that are available to her. Her mother, her aunts, and other female relatives, the women patients in the hospital where she takes a summer job distributing menus for the hospital caterers, the students in her drama class—all represent different life stories to Rocío as she struggles to find a way of living with the pressures placed upon her as a woman and a member of an ethnic minority. At the end of the narrative Rocío discovers that her identity and her destiny lie with her writing: "I tell her, Roque, just write one *Gone With the Wind*. That's all. Just one. You don't even have to go anywhere. Not down the street. Not even out of this house. There's stories, plenty of them all around."[2] The narrative up to this point in the book is about this street, this house, and these stories. In the same way, the entire narrative of *The Woman Warrior* fulfils the promise of the last story, that of Ts'ai Yen, whose poetry is able to mediate between two cultures: her own and that of the barbarians by whom she is held captive. In both cases, the *kunstlerroman* concludes by directing the reader's attention back to the narrative he or she has just finished reading, to recognize the story as the fulfilment of the artistic promise of its own protagonist.

SIMILAR BY LITERARY MOVEMENT

Preeminent among the Chinese American women writers named by Kingston as having an impact upon her work is Jade Snow Wong, whose autobiographical novel, *Fifth Chinese Daughter* (1945), represents the power of opportunity that is available to an oppressed Chinese woman in America. Wong wrote about the experience of a previous generation of Chinese American women. Kingston's narratives, which were written after the first impact of the Civil Rights movement and the women's liberation movement of the 1960s and 1970s, share this interest in the issue of opportunity, and equality of opportunity, in particular. In her 1979 essay on Kingston and Wong, Patricia Lin Blinde argues: "The popular view is that the Chinese are a hard-working, education-oriented and thrifty people is

ON JADE SNOW WONG

"I read all the things that children read, but Jade Snow Wong's *Fifth Chinese Daughter* was important to me. It was published during World War II and for the first time I saw a Chinese American character, and it was told from the point of view of a young girl. For the first time I could see a person somewhat like me in literature."

Maxine Hong Kingston

From Jody Hoy, "To Be Able to See the Tao," in *Conversations with Maxine Hong Kingston*, edited by Paul Skenazy and Tera Martin (Jackson: University of Mississippi Press, 1998), p. 62.

itself a framework that lends itself well to the Horatio Alger paradigm. Coupled with the belief that with hard work and sacrifice anyone (not least of all, a Chinese woman) can achieve success in America, the individual about whom the autobiography is being written is him/herself reduced to a type, i.e. endowed with character traits which ensure success."[3] In *Between Worlds: Women Writers of Chinese Ancestry* Amy Ling develops this view by arguing that Kingston's work then "is a much more personal text, written not as an exemplum for others but as a means of exorcising the personal ghosts that haunt the author."[4] If the two books are different in tone and attitude—the one restrained and polite, the other angry and rebellious—they are also different in form, as Ling explains: "*Fifth Chinese Daughter* is a sober, straightforward narrative delivered in chronological order, as though to tell this much were effort enough. *The Woman Warrior* is poetic, experimental, fragmented in narrative line, a virtuoso performance of imaginative power and verbal dexterity."[5] Wong and Kingston, however, are both American-born daughters of immigrant parents from southern China, who seek to bridge their dual inheritance and to reconcile the conflicting demands made upon them by China and America, by East and by West. They both have impressed upon them by their parents the sense that they are living only temporarily in America and one day they will return to China; they both find their parents' traditional beliefs and values embarrassing; they both attempt to reconcile conflicting self-images; and they both struggle with silence and the difficulty of articulation to realize an authentic sense of self.

Among contemporary Chinese American writers the author most frequently compared to Kingston is Amy Tan. Both writers explore the impact of racism and patriarchal oppression on Chinese American women, particularly in terms of the influence of these negative forces on feminine relationships. Her novel, *The Joy Luck Club,* deals with the relationships between mothers and daughters, alternating between the viewpoints of the two generations. The structure of the novel consists of juxtaposed narratives: in the first section the mothers tell their stories, in the second section the daughters tell theirs. The third section is also comprised of four stories, each told by one of the daughters, and the stories of the final section are narrated by each of the mothers. In Tan's *The Joy Luck Club* (1989), the character An-mei finds that her relationship with her mother is poisoned by her mother's low and shameful status as a concubine. According to Tan, her representation of this relationship is modeled on the relationship between Tan's mother and grandmother: "'My mother still feels that she can never be rid of the burden of her own experience and that of her mother, the widow of a scholar, who was 'raped by a man who wanted her as his concubine.' Dishonored, Tan's grandmother felt that she had no choice but to become his concubine. 'She was very unhappy but hoped to gain comforts to make things better for her children.' However, after 'she had a son and his second wife claimed that son as her own, she killed herself in 1926 by swallowing opium. My mother was nine years old when she saw her mother dying; she felt great shame to be the daughter of a concubine.'"[6] The patriarchal practice of concubinage, where a man can take multiple mistresses in addition to his legal wife, in this case destroys the lives of Tan's grandmother and mother as well. In this 1990 interview, Tan described how her mother "has for most of her life felt oppressed by unhappiness; she feels that 'everything is cumulative; that if the sequence begins wrong everything is wrong; only in the past few years has she felt that she can be happy.'"[7]

ON ASIAN AMERICAN AUTOBIOGRAPHIES

"There are a lot of Asian American autobiographies. To say they are not legitimate or there's something wrong with them, that has to do with ranking the genres. That somehow autobiography is a lower form, that one doesn't have to be an artist, that all you have to do is just live an interesting life and take notes. So to call something an autobiography politically is an attack on the work because that is the bottom."

Maxine Hong Kingston

From Laura E. Skandera-Trombley, "A Conversation with Maxine Hong Kingston," in *Critical Essays on Maxine Hong Kingston*, edited by Skandera-Trombley (New York: Simon & Schuster / Macmillan, 1998), p. 43.

Family stories such as these prevent characters such as Rose, An-mei's daughter, and Lena, in *The Joy Luck Club,* from acknowledging sexism in the United States. These women mistakenly believe that sexual oppression is a problem only for women in China. They are so concerned about combating racism in America that they do not see they are being exploited by their husbands. Both Lena and Rose have been conditioned by their upbringing to blame themselves and other women rather than men for the difficulties they encounter. Lena confesses her deep fear that she somehow does not deserve her husband, Harold, that one day he will realize his mistake and leave her. She reflects, "I think that feeling of fear never left me, that I would be caught someday, exposed as a sham of a woman. But recently, a friend of mine, Rose, who's in therapy now because her marriage has already fallen apart, told me those kinds of thoughts are commonplace in women like us."[8] Women such as Lena and Rose have been raised to mistrust themselves and to devalue themselves in relation to men. Eventually, however, they discover that their mothers know the reality of oppression because they have experienced the combined effects of racism and sexism. The false assumption that only racism operates in the United States traps Lena and Rose in their oppressive relationships.

Where sexual discrimination and oppression do not differ markedly between China and the United States, characters discover that the feminine world in which their mothers grew up is not significantly different to the American world of women. For example, Mrs. Jordan treats her daughter Rose just as a Chinese mother-in-law would; she is not interested in Rose for herself, she is only interested in her son's welfare. Gender roles within marriage are not qualitatively different between China and America. So the obedience demanded of a Chinese wife is not so different to the conformity demanded of a wife in America. The shared experiences as women create a bond between mothers and daughters that is symbolized by their physical resemblance. Lindo reports, "'You can see your character in your face,' I say to my daughter without thinking. 'You can see your future.'. . . These two faces, I think, so much the same! The same happiness, the same sadness, the same good fortune, the same faults" (292). In a variation of this image Tan suggests that the cross-cultural conflict that keeps the generations apart is symbolized by the two faces Lindo is able to adopt: her "American face . . . the face Americans think is Chinese, the one they cannot understand" (291) and her "Chinese face" (291). Even her daughter does not understand Lindo's "American face"; the issue of how to cross the bridge that separates the immigrant generation from the American-born generation is an important theme in both *The Joy Luck Club* and *The Woman Warrior*.

When her mother's friends, the "aunties" as she calls them, of the Joy Luck Club invite Jing-mei to take her dead mother's place at the mahjongg table and, more than that, to return to China to meet the sisters her mother had to leave behind, June slowly realizes why it is so important to the aunties that her mother's story should be told: "In me, they see their own daughters, just as ignorant, just as unmindful of all the truths and hopes they brought to America. . . . They see that joy and luck do not mean the same to their daughters, that to these closed American-born minds 'joy luck' is not a word, does not exist. They see daughters who will bear grandchildren born without any connecting hope passed from generation to generation" (31).

The issues of inheritance, tradition, and how to communicate across generational and cultural gaps emphasize the importance of lan-

Chinese American rally in New York City in 1992

guage and of cultural conventions. For example, Jing-mei mistakes the social conventions of the Joy Luck aunties. She believes that through politeness they are protesting at the suggestion she should leave the mah jong party, when in fact they are preparing to tell her about her sisters, whom they have located in China. Rose has Chinese words and concepts that she experiences but cannot be translated into English; she speculates, "Maybe they can't be easily translated because they refer to a sensation that only Chinese people have" (210). Waverly, who intends to spend her honeymoon in China, only knows Chinese baby talk; her mother reflects, "Pee-pee, choo-choo train, eat, close light sleep. How can she think she can blend in? Only her skin and hair are Chinese. Inside—she is all American-made" (289).

The working of historical change to separate families is seen in the fate of Jing-mei's sisters and the inability of her mother, Suyuan, to trace them. This underlines the importance of knowing the role of roots and ancestry in establishing personal identity. This situation also offers Tan the opportunity for a happy ending—an ending that is happy for Jing-mei because her family is complete: for her sisters because they discover their mother through their sister, and for their mother, Suyuan, because her wish is granted and her daughters are finally found. This happy ending, however, is qualified because Suyuan does not live to see the reunion of her family, so the experience of loss is firmly inscribed in the ending.

In Amy Tan's second novel, *The Kitchen God's Wife* (1991), the theme of storytelling, which is so important in *The Woman Warrior* and *China Men,* comes to the forefront. As in Kingston's narrative, storytelling is a way to pass knowledge, advice, and traditions down to daughters and to preserve ethnic culture. Stories can also be lies, however, like the romance novels Winnie, the main protagonist is given to read that are designed to educate women in their own subservience by perpetuating a false view of marriage and sexuality. Stories also teach women how to behave if they want to survive. Winnie recalls the advice given her by Old Aunt, "'Don't strike a flea on a tiger's head.' Don't settle one trouble only to make a bigger one."[9] Survival on these terms, however, ensures the survival of masculine abuses and the violent, demeaning treatment of women. Winnie comes to the realization that the struggle against patriarchy is a life or death struggle. Much of the action of the novel takes place against the backdrop of the Chinese resistance to Japanese military occupation. The war against Japan symbolizes the historical upheaval that shapes Winnie's life, but the war, or warfare, also symbolizes her relationship with her husband, one characterized by violent conflict. The war represents those forces that are outside the control of individuals but that still limit the possibilities of an individual's life.

As a young girl, Winnie begins life with her assumption that women are to blame for their own suffering (she blames herself and her mother-in-law rather than her husband, Wen Fu.) Gradually she discovers that culture works to oppress women through religion, the lack of education for women, and the stories women are told—about romance, lies about their bodies, and tales of what happens to bad wives. The discovery of her cousin Peanut, who has run away from her bad marriage, and Peanut's Communist friends makes Winnie realize that what she had assumed to be natural—the structures and institutions of patriarchal society—is in fact cultural and so can be changed. When she has made this realization, then she knows that she can escape. The central moment of realization for Winnie comes when she stops turning her anger inward, blaming herself and the women around her for her miserable condition, and instead places the blame with the woman-hating patriarchy that is the society in which she was living. Winnie thinks, "And perhaps it was wrong of me, to blame another woman for my own miseries. But that was how I was raised—never to criticize men or the society they ruled, or Confucius, that awful man who made that society. I could blame only other women who were more afraid than I" (257). In China, women are kept subordinate through intimidation, imprisonment, and physical violence but not through feminine inferiority. In America, more subtle techniques and cultural pressures produce the same result. This knowledge is ultimately Winnie's legacy to her daughter, the narrator of the novel, Pearl.

SIMILAR BY THEME

Among the most prominent writers who share Kingston's concern with the nature of race and gender oppression in contemporary America are the African American writers Alice Walker and Toni Morrison. Kingston herself has remarked upon the common strategy these writers use by claiming to break the silence surrounding events that their communities wish to keep secret. In an interview with Eric J. Schroeder, Kingston explained that by writing about her determination to speak out, "I could free myself and my voice to be able to tell the story."[10]

Walker has commented upon the affinity of the themes about which she writes in novels such as *The Color Purple* (1982) and the situation of Chinese women: "What interests me is how many of the things I've written about women certainly do, in China, look Chinese: the impact of poverty, forced sex and childbearing, domination as a race and a caste (before the Chinese Revolution); the struggle to affirm solidarity with women, as women, and the struggle to attain political, social, and economic equality with men."[11] The interconnectedness of race and gender oppression is Walker's major theme. *The Color Purple* offers a parable of change through the agency of poor black women and challenges the complicity of white feminism (past and present) with racism, while Walker also contests earlier representations of black women as powerless or repressive or hostile to black masculinity. Walker shows how dominant images of masculinity lead to oppression in black families where women suffer multiple repressions; until she escapes to Memphis, Celie, Walker's heroine, suffers as a consequence of her family roles. Walker creates emblematic characters in Celie, Shug, and Sophia, and she dramatizes their capacity to assess and affect social relations and to survive the exploitation of their bodies and minds by both the dominant Anglo-American society and by their own community.

Walker's engagement with racial politics influences the form of her narrative. The reader is required to share the novel's resistance of cultural imperialism by trying to understand the story within its particular racial context. A basic assumption of the text is that individuals are not all fundamentally the same, that racial and gender differences are fundamental and require separate understanding. Black women cannot be treated like white men or women; "equality" on those terms is unacceptable. The understanding of black women's condition is only possible within the context of black women's historical experience.

In *The Woman Warrior* Kingston exposes the experience of women in China and America, telling the stories that have been kept silent. In the same way, the record of black women's historical experience is corrected in *The Color Purple* when Walker takes issue with the view that black men suffered more under slavery and its aftermath. For example, the emasculation of black men dominates the popular imagination: white fears of black sexuality are symbolized by the castration that often accompanied lynching and other forms of racialized murder. Women were lynched, though infrequently; commonly, black women were deprived of their humanity, treated as livestock, and used for breeding purposes to provide children (often the children of their masters) for market. The systematic rape of black women under slavery leads to dehumanization and the death of the spirit, if not a physical death. Walker exposes the extent of female suffering under this regime, but in *The Color Purple* she distances her characters from violence and victimization by whites and instead focuses upon the ways in which women are oppressed by black men as well as by white men and women. Celie suffers twenty years of rape and beatings at the hands of her African American husband, but she controls her violent rage and reacts in subtle ways to avoid losing her humanity, brutalizing herself, and acting as is expected of a "nigger."

If the oppression of black women is related closely to the exploitation of their sexuality, then Walker uses sexuality as an avenue of liberation in *The Color Purple*. Incestuous rape is a motif in black women's writing, such as Toni Morrison's *The Bluest Eye* (1970), Gayl Jones's *Corregidora* (1975), and Maya Angelou's *I Know Why the Caged Bird Sings* (1969). This motif has its origins in the forced breeding of slave women who were raped by their white owners and who, in some cases, were the fathers of these women. Rape was used as an instrument of terror both on the plantation and as part of the enslavement process. Celie's experience is typical—she turns inward the guilt and pain, transforming them into masochistic self-loathing. Loss of pride and self-respect follows; these feelings of worthlessness are heightened for Celie, who believes that her children have been taken from her and killed. Through her friendship with Shug, Celie finds she is complete in herself; she is transformed from the object of male ridicule to the subject of female support. The dominant message emerges from the book: apart from men, women can find dignity, spiritual sustenance, and also sexual satisfaction.

In this context Walker refers to her commitment to "womanism" as opposed to feminism. A "womanist" loves women and women's culture; a womanist is concerned to assert women's identity and independence on their own terms; being a womanist involves "wanting to know more and in greater depth than is good for one"; a womanist represents women as complex undiminished human beings.[12] The women of *The Color Purple* are liberated through pride in their gender, their womanness. Celie's frailty and strength, her humility and pathos represent her as ordinary, representative of the mass of oppressed women, where Shug is strong, self-confident, and exemplary of what women can become—in her way, she is a warrior woman.

The Color Purple describes a dual quest for literacy and freedom; this quest structures both the subject and the structure of the narrative. The book also displays a pervasive distrust of language. Kingston does not trust the language of *The Woman Warrior* and *China Men* not to betray the people about whom she writes to the immigration authorities they fear. Walker mistrusts language because of the racial context within which it is read. This reticence about language is expressed as a distrust of the white reader who may be illiterate in black terms and who may then censor the text in the process of interpreting it, or otherwise misinterpret the text as the result of a white inability to read accurately the record of black experience. *The Color Purple* also responds to the possibility that white readers will not accept the truth of the story and the author's credentials to tell such a story. Walker has been attacked for representing all black men as brutal and violent; she has been criticized for her activism on behalf of sexually mutilated women when she herself has not been mutilated; and, historically, the writers of slave narratives were accused of inventing horrors that did not exist under slavery. The attack on the writer, especially the minority woman writer, who writes to expose the realities of life lived under a racist patriarchal regime is a common strategy to discredit not just the writer but the suffering of the oppressed people of whom she writes. Walker is acutely aware of this prejudice and takes steps to counter such allegations: the narrative is carefully crafted so that Celie tells her own story, in her own words, using her own dialect, and the presence of the writer is minimized throughout the telling of the story. In the postscript, Walker places herself in the position of medium in relation to her characters; she writes "I thank everybody in this book for coming."[13]

Toni Morrison's *The Bluest Eye* shares with *The Color Purple* and *The Woman Warrior* an interest in the intersection of race and gender oppression. Morrison explores the internalization of racist and misogy-

ON TONI MORRISON

"The way you get energy from the ancestors is you find out the truth about them. Some of her images—putting a gaga in a slave's mouth—that has to do with silence and voice and freedom. By writing that book she takes the gag out."

Maxine Hong Kingston

From Paul Skenazy, "Kingston at the University," in *Conversations with Maxine Hong Kingston,* edited by Paul Skenazy and Tera Martin (Jackson: University of Mississippi Press, 1998), p. 148.

---

nistic attitudes as a determining influence of white culture on black identity. She describes the social and psychological effects of marginalization on those black women whose culture is discredited. Morrison does this exploration by dealing with systems of value that depend upon the black woman as a negative standard of value. For example, in *The Bluest Eye,* the protagonist Pecola is represented as physically unattractive, and because of this unattractiveness the other girls can define their own prettiness by contrast with her ugliness. Those who come closest to a sense of personal wholeness or integrity are those who believe themselves to be in close proximity to the cultural center. Characters such as Pauline, Maureen, and Geraldine refer themselves not to dominant images of femininity but define themselves by contrast with one (Pecola), who fails to conform to these images. Geraldine denies her own blackness in order to maintain her social position; her lifestyle emulates the white middle-class model that is a key part of the racial ideal. Pecola represents to Geraldine the self she has rejected.

This psychological tactic of rejecting part of one's self forms the basis of Pecola's parents' marriage. Each represents what the other rejects, and so they find themselves locked into a dialectical relationship of love and hate. Pauline's self-contempt leads her to an overwhelming identification with the world portrayed in movies and the world of the white family for whom she works: "Power, praise, and luxury were hers in this household."[14] She confuses virtue with self-repression, servitude with obedience to God. Her husband, Cholly, measures Pauline's righteousness, and she measures his freedom. Cholly transforms his powerlessness into the kind of freedom that is a liberation from the moral restraints of the society that rejects him. The narrator comments, "the love of a free man is never safe. There is no gift for the beloved" (206). This kind of freedom from responsibility is utterly destructive. The rape of his daughter, Pecola, represents for Cholly a complex mix of freedom, love, protest, and power, as well as sorrow, bitterness, and regret.

This act of sexual violence represents the fate of black men in an emasculating society and the fate of black women in a world of patriarchal domination. So Cholly's formative adolescent experience with Darlene, in which "with a violence born of total helplessness" he is transformed into spectacle for the two white men (148), is juxtaposed in the narrator's telling of the story with the rape of his daughter where again he experiences "the hatred mixed up with tenderness" (163). Only the narrator, Claudia, and the three prostitutes discover any way to live in this atmosphere of pervasive black loathing. The prostitutes reject and exploit the values of polite society. They are pariahs, like Pecola, because they are the immoral extreme by which polite society defines itself. They claim a freedom that is similar to Cholly's, but they also retain some capacity for care, though it is limited. They live according to self-interest, a hatred of men, and a cynical exploitation of the society that rejects them. The prostitutes offer for sale the sexuality that is, in any case, commodified by their society. They offer an ironic counterpart to the images of female sexuality that are offered for sale by polite society.

Amy Tan

Claudia, in contrast, finds a basis for positive self-definition through knowledge; specifically, the analysis of the modes of interpretation that destroy black girls such as Pecola. By actively rejecting the myths of romantic love and physical beauty that victimize Pecola, Claudia tries to retain her sense of her own humanity—the humanity denied by these racially-motivated images. The novel describes Claudia's attempts to discover why Pecola is doomed: "*But since why is difficult to handle, one must take refuge in* how" (6, Morrison's italics). This question is refined in the course of the narrative and the answer is identified with "the Thing" that possesses Maureen Peal. "The *Thing* to fear was the *Thing* that made *her* beautiful, and not us" (74). Freedom for Claudia is found in her resistance of cultural myths, which she manages to do by resisting stereotypes and appropriating experience to her own authentic sense of self. Freedom, then, lies in creating the world as one sees it and not as one is told it is or should be.

Violence is represented as the consequence of the characters' violent repudiation of aspects of themselves that are identified with blackness. Pecola is treated violently by both her parents, but pale-skinned Maureen is treated gently by all who encounter her. Violence becomes the expression of a will to power that can express itself only through the physical domination of one who is weaker. Gloria Naylor, in her novel *The Women of Brewster Place* (1982), observes of one of her characters:

> Born with the appendages of power, circumcised by a guillotine, and baptised with the steam from a million nonreflective mirrors, these young men wouldn't be called upon to thrust a bayonet into an Asian farmer, target a torpedo, scatter their iron seed from a B-52 into the wound of the earth, point a finger to move a nation, or stick a pole into the moon—and they knew it. They only had that three-hundred-foot alley to serve them as stateroom, armored tank, and executioner's chamber. So Lorraine found herself, on her knees, surrounded by the most dangerous species in existence—human males with an erection to validate in a world that was only six feet wide.[15]

Masculine violence is a primary strategy for the assertion of masculinity and, in a racist culture that emasculates black men, this violence is directed against women, and black women in particular. Sexual violence becomes a strategy of intimidation that validates masculine gender identity by reasserting the male domination of women.

Both Naylor and Morrison use rape as an image of masculine gender identity. The crisis of rape precipitates Pecola into madness. She retreats into an insane pursuit of the conventional values of the white world. Her final victimization by Soaphead Church imprisons her in nineteenth-century colonial attitudes; he uses her obsessive desire for blue eyes in order to take revenge upon her blackness, and to use her delusions for his own self-interest. His act of moral and spiritual violence destroys Pecola's mind, just as Cholly's physical violence destroys her body. Throughout the narrative a distinction is sustained between the point of view of the narrator, Claudia, and the black adults. Only the children Claudia and Frieda hold out any hope for Pecola's child and for her future. Claudia clearly sees Pecola's fate—that in her madness she is incapable of self-knowledge—and so the consequences of Pecola's fate must be borne by the other characters: "It's too late. At least on the edge of my town, among the garbage and the sunflowers of my town, it's much, much too late" (206).

The blue eyes Pecola desires are symbolic of her desire for approval and physical beauty within a racist culture, but she never experiences a confirmation of self-worth. The lack of that confirmation leads to self-loathing. In the eyes of Mr Yacobowski, Pecola finds the "total absence of human recognition" (48); "she has seen it lurking in the eyes of all white people. So. The distaste must be for her, her blackness. . . . And it is the blackness that accounts for, that creates, the vacuum edged with distaste in white eyes" (49). Geraldine finds in Pecola's eyes a reflection of the brutal cultural reality she has embraced: "The end of the world lay in [those] eyes, and the beginning, and all the waste in between" (92). Pecola thinks of Geraldine and the self she has denied. The connection between self and world that is symbolized by eyes is then symbolically severed for Pecola, when she seeks to exchange her brown eyes for blue. She surrenders irrevocably any hope for her authentic relation with the world. So, in her final madness, she stares into mirrors and talks schizophrenically to her imaginary friend who is but a reflection of part of herself. She collapses inwardly, into her imaginary blue-eyed self. In *The Woman Warrior,* women who cannot deal with the pressures of sexual oppression and racial discrimination also retreat into madness, which the narrator describes as having only one story to tell and lacking the words with which to tell it. Maxine in *The Woman Warrior,* Claudia in *The Bluest Eye,* and Celie in *The Color Purple* struggle to find a voice with which to tell these stories and hence break the silence that perpetuates the injustice of racial and sexual oppression.

NOTES

1. Sandra Cisneros, *The House on Mango Street* (Houston: Arte Publico Press, 1983), p. 98. Subsequent parenthetical references in the text are to this edition.
2. Denise Chávez, *The Last of the Menu Girls* (Houston: Arte Publico Press, 1987), p. 190.
3. Patricia Lin Blinde, "The Icicle in the Desert: Perspective and Form in the Works of Two Chinese-American Women Writers," MELUS, 6 (1979), p. 59.
4. Amy Ling, *Between Worlds: Women Writers of Chinese Ancestry* (New York & Oxford: Pergamon Press, 1990), p. 120.
5. Ibid.
6. Katherine Henderson, "Amy Tan," in Mickey Pearlman and Katherine Usher Henderson, *Inter/View: Talks with America's Writing Women* (Lexington: University Press of Kentucky, 1990), p. 20.
7. Ibid.
8. Amy Tan, *The Joy Luck Club* (New York: Ballantine, 1989), p. 169. Subsequent parenthetical references in the text are to this edition.
9. Tan, *The Kitchen God's Wife* (New York: Putnam, 1991), p. 260. Subsequent parenthetical references in the text are to this edition.
10. Eric J. Schroeder, "As Truthful as Possible: An Interview with Maxine Hong Kingston," *Writing on the Edge,* 7. 2 (Spring 1996), reprinted in *Conversations with Maxine Hong Kingston,* p. 215.
11. Alice Walker, "A Thousand Words: A Writer's Pictures of China," (1985) in *Living by the Word: Selected Writings, 1973–1987* (London: Women's Press, 1988), p. 109.
12. Walker, *In Search of Our Mother's Gardens* (London: Women's Press, 1984), p. xi.
13. Alice Walker, *The Color Purple* (New York: Simon & Schuster, 1982), p. 296.
14. Toni Morrison, *The Bluest Eye* (New York: Penguin, 1970), p. 128. Subsequent parenthetical references in the text are to this edition.
15. Gloria Naylor, *The Women of Brewster Place* (New York: Penguin, 1980), pp. 169–170.

RESOURCES FOR STUDY OF
THE WOMAN WARRIOR AND *CHINA MEN*

Study Questions 145
Glossary of Terms in
    The Woman Warrior *and* China Men. 149
Unfamiliar Words or Terms in
    The Woman Warrior *and* China Men. 151
Historical Events, People, and Places in
    The Woman Warrior *and* China Men. 155
Selected Bibliography 157

STUDY QUESTIONS

1. Kingston has been criticized for her use of traditional Chinese myths; explain how her handling of myth is controversial.

2. In *The Woman Warrior,* Kingston refers to the practice of "talk-story." What does she mean by this, and in what ways can this narrative and *China Men* be described as "talk-story"?

3. One of the major themes of *The Woman Warrior* is the difficult acquisition of language; how does this theme relate to Kingston's own use of language to write the narratives of *The Woman Warrior* and *China Men?*

4. Evaluate the importance of the values of individualism versus those of community in *The Woman Warrior* and *China Men.*

5. Although *The Woman Warrior* has been received as a work of autobiography by many critics, others have argued that the role of fiction in the construction of the narrative places it in some other fictional genre. How would you describe the generic status of the text? How does it compare with the style of *China Men?*

6. Kingston has described her literary style in *The Woman Warrior* as "convoluted"; to what extent does Kingston's use of irony contribute to this convoluted style?

7. Describe Kingston's narrative point of view in *The Woman Warrior.* When and why does it shift away from the narrator?

8. *The Woman Warrior* is characterized by Kingston's juxtaposition of the historical with the contemporary and her creation of a non-chronological plot. What are the advantages to her as the author of this particular treatment of time in *The Woman Warrior* and *China Men?*

9. Compare and contrast the woman warrior Fa Mu Lan with the Western figure Joan of Arc.

10. In the "Shaman" chapter of *The Woman Warrior,* Brave Orchid possesses a quilt decorated with a tiny red triangle that is identical to the quilt Fa Mu Lan sews for her baby and similar to the quilt with which Brave Orchid covers her daughter. The same image is repeated in different contexts. Does Kingston use this technique elsewhere in the narrative? To what effect does she use this technique in *The Woman Warrior* and *China Men?*

11. Are all the men in *The Woman Warrior* and *China Men* represented as being fundamentally the same? Does Kingston create any positive representations of men? If so, on what terms could they be described as positive?

12. How is the image of the barbarian used in *The Woman Warrior?* How does the concept of barbarism compare with Kingston's use of the image of ghosts?

13. Compare Brave Orchid with her sister, Moon Orchid, and her sister-in-law, the No Name Woman.

14. Identify the similarities and differences between the young narrator and the following characters: No Name Woman, Fa Mu Lan, Brave Orchid, Moon Orchid, and the silent girl, Ts'ai Yen.

15. Compare the characterization of the narrator's father with the legendary character of Ch'ü Yüan. Can you find points of comparison between the No Name Woman of *The Woman Warrior* and Ch'ü Yüan of *China Men?*

16. Compare Kingston's representation of the mother-daughter relationship in *The Woman Warrior* with that found in other contemporary texts by Asian American women, such as Amy Tan's *The Joy Luck Club.*

17. Both Brave Orchid and her daughter are highly educated women; consider in what ways the theme of education relates to Kingston's treatment of race and gender in *The Woman Warrior* and *China Men.*

18. Kingston expresses her fear that as a daughter she is subject to the woman-hating attitudes of the China her parents left behind. How does she create a distinction between the systematic and cultural misogyny of the immigrant Chinese and the attitudes of her individual parents?

19. Why does Kingston describe the Chinese children as silent at the American school but loud at the Chinese school? How do these schools represent different aspects of her education?

20. Kingston has described some of the episodes in *The Woman Warrior* as raucously funny. Discuss her use of humor in the episodes that you find amusing.

21. How frequently does the figure of the silent character appear in *The Woman Warrior* and *China Men*? Can you relate this figure to the twin themes of keeping silence and breaking silence?

22. In what ways does Kingston attempt to reconcile Chinese and American cultural pressures within her developing sense of personal identity?

23. How does the theme of slavery relate to Kingston's concern with race and gender issues?

24. The title of *The Woman Warrior* could be interpreted as a recommendation of conflict and warfare as the means to resolve cultural differences. Do you find this a compelling explanation of the title?

25. How many instances of physical mutilation can you find in *The Woman Warrior* and *China Men*? What is the importance of this image?

26. Kingston expressed disappointment that the first reviewers of *The Woman Warrior* found the book exotic and "oriental" but failed to recognize its American qualities. How "American" do you find her books?

27. One of the most famous dictums of the women's movement of the 1960s and 1970s was "the personal is political." Is this concept useful in describing the political dimensions of *The Woman Warrior* and *China Men*?

28. How important is it to understand something of the history of China in the twentieth century in order to read *The Woman Warrior* and *China Men*?

29. Identify the various significances of Stockton, California, as a primary setting of *The Woman Warrior* and *China Men*.

30. How does the form of the feminine *kunstlerroman* differ from its masculine counterpart, such as James Joyce's *Portrait of the Artist as a Young Man*?

31. In *The Woman Warrior* the narrator expresses her desire to be remembered as having "conquered both North America and Asia." In what way can Kingston be seen as having achieved this as a writer?

GLOSSARY OF TERMS IN *THE WOMAN WARRIOR* AND *CHINA MEN*

Autobiography. The story of the life of an individual, told by the subject. An autobiography is assumed to be based upon fact, rather than invention, and to present a full account of the personal history of the subject. In contrast to autobiography, a **memoir** places emphasis upon the people the subject has known and the historical events witnessed.

Bildungsroman. A novel of development, telling the story of an individual's developing character from earliest childhood through various experiences to maturity. The narrative ends with the beginning of adult life and the recognition of the protagonist's role in the world.

Episodic narrative. A narrative that consists of a series of incidents or episodes. Each episode possesses its own unity or coherence and is loosely connected by a single narrative device, such as the protagonist or the narrator or a motif such as the journey or quest.

Epistolary novel. A novel in which the narrative is wholly represented by the exchange of letters written by one or more of the characters.

Feminism. A politically based movement concerned with the liberation of women from male oppression and feminine marginalization. Feminists are committed to reforming society, which is seen to be based upon the interests of men. Feminism seeks to expose the cultural practices and attitudes that create an imbalance of power and to transform those power relationships into relations of equality between men and women.

Genre. This French term refers to the types of literary forms, such as poetry, prose, and fiction, or the types of effects produced by those various forms, such as comedy, tragedy, romance, and lyric.

Imagery. The pictorial elements of a literary work or, more broadly, those elements that evoke a sensory perception in the reader. Imagery also refers to the figurative language used in a literary text, such as the metaphors and similes, to generate particular meanings and effects.

Juxtaposition. The close physical contrast or comparison between two elements in a narrative.

Kunstlerroman. A subtype of the bildungsroman that describes a kind of narrative which tells the story of a young artist's development to maturity, beginning with his or her earliest memories and ending with the realization of his or her artistic destiny.

Legend. A story about a human being involved in great adventures and feats of extraordinary courage or daring.

Misogyny. The term refers to the hatred of women or to a set of social and cultural practices that enforce the inferior position of women.

Myth. A story about supernatural beings, once believed to be true by a particular cultural group, which explained the operations of nature or the establishment of social customs and rituals.

Narrator. A character who tells the story. Narrators vary in their level of knowledge about the events and people in the story; they can tell only what they see or know. Third-person narratives are often told from a perspective that is omniscient, or knowledgeable about every aspect of the story, but they may be limited as well.

Patriarchy. A government by men. In a patriarchy, women are excluded from positions of influence and are kept in a position of powerlessness relative to men.

Plot. The structure of actions or sequence of events that comprise a narrative.

Point of view. The way in which a story is told; how the reader is introduced to characters and actions in the narrative.

Setting. The location and historical period within which the narrative action takes place.

Symbolism. A symbol is one thing used to refer to something else; usually, an object is used to refer to a concept, such as "the Cross" or "the Crown." A **simile** refers to an object said to be like (similar to) another object or concept; an **analogy** is an implied comparison; a **metaphor** places two elements together and creates an implicit correspondence between them; in a **synecdoche** one part of an object or complex concept represents the whole.

UNFAMILIAR WORDS OR TERMS IN *THE WOMAN WARRIOR* AND *CHINA MEN*

Abacus. A mathematical tool invented in China in the twelfth century, comprised of lines of ten beads threaded on a wire frame.

Almanac. An annual reference book listing astronomical data, such as lunar movements, weather data, and other items of information.

Ancestral tablets. Lists in which the names of the ancestors are recorded.

Anemia. A condition in which the blood is deficient in red blood cells, in hemoglobin, or in total volume.

Animalcules. Minute microscopic organisms.

Apprentice. Someone who is bonded to an experienced craftsman for a specific length of time in order to learn a craft or trade.

Atavism. The reappearance after several generations of some inherited characteristic.

Barons. The most powerful group of landowners, after the king or emperor, under feudal government.

Benevolent association. A community organization that protects its members and works to secure their economic and social welfare within the wider society.

Boa. A large snake that crushes or suffocates its prey; also, a long decorative neck scarf, usually made of feathers or fur.

Bride's price. Payment made by a groom to his bride's family.

Bunds. Low mud walls used to enclose rice paddies.

Burlap. A coarse fabric used to make sacks.

Camphoraceous. Smelling of camphor, a substance produced by the camphor tree, an evergreen native to eastern Asia, used to repel insects and moths.

Carp. Freshwater fish, often bred in ponds.

Concierge. A doorkeeper, or porter, usually in a hotel or apartment block, whose job it is to serve the guests.

Conscription. A system of compulsory military service.

Contracts. Labor contracts.

Cutworms. Larva that cut through plants as they feed on them.

Depilatory. An agent used in hair removal.

Dermatology. The study of the skin and skin diseases.

Dirigible. An airship.

Dowry. Property or money brought by a bride to her husband.

Faggots. Bundles of sticks.

Fatalism. A system of belief in which all events are seen as predetermined, where free will does not exist because personal choice is not possible.

Fiefdoms. Land held by lords or barons under the feudal system and operated as autonomous kingdoms.

Flay. Literally, to strip off the skin or hide; metaphorically, to criticize severely.

Flotage. Loose, discarded material floating in water.

Fontanel. A membrane-covered opening between cranial bones that have not completely fused.

Foot binding. The practice of binding young girls' feet so that the toes are folded downward and the arch cannot develop normally. This practice began during the T'ang dynasty (A.D. 618–906) and ended in 1911 with the establishment of a Republic in place of the imperial system of government; foot binding was practiced by the social elite to indicate the wealth of families that did not require their women to work.

Frenum. Kingston's word for the frenulum, the membrane that anchors the tongue to the bottom of the mouth.

Gall. Literally, bile obtained from an animal; figuratively, resentment, rancor, and bitterness.

Gaucheries. Rude or awkward expressions.

Geishas. A class of Japanese women who work within, or are indentured to, a geisha organization for the purpose of entertaining men.

Guru. A spiritual teacher or leader of a religious sect.

Gynecology. The branch of medicine that deals with the diseases and routine physical care of the reproductive system of women.

Ideograph. A drawn character or symbol that indicates the idea of an object without expressing the sounds of its name.

Infanticide. The murder of newborn or young children.

Jade tree. A domestic plant with fleshy succulent leaves.

Jasper. A semiprecious gem found in green, red, yellow, and brown varieties.

Kris. A dagger with a ridged blade in the shape of a serpent.

Lepers' socks. Socks worn by sufferers of leprosy, an infectious disease characterized by skin sores, to prevent the spreading of the disease.

Lichee. Litchi; a sweet pulpy fruit with a thin brown shell, from the lichee tree, which is indigenous to China.

Loquat tree. A small evergreen tree that bears edible fruit.

Maelstrom. Literally, a whirlwind or a violent storm; metaphorically, a confused emotional state.

Mallard. A common breed of wild duck.

Menses. Menstruation.

Metempsychosis. Reincarnation, or the belief that after the death of the body, the soul is reborn into a new living form that may be either human or animal.

Mien. Air or bearing expressing an attitude.

Moon cakes. Round pastries eaten during the full moon of the eighth month of the lunar calendar.

Nadir. Point of the heavens directly under the observer; opposite to zenith.

Nape. Back of the neck.

Night-soil buckets. Buckets used at night in lieu of going to the outdoor latrine.

Nock-whistles. Whistles carved with grooves.

Opthalmology. A branch of medicine specializing in the care and treatment of the eyes.

Origami. Japanese art of folding paper into representational shapes.

Palanquin. A sedan chair, often roofed and ornately decorated, conveyed by servants carrying the poles attached to the chair.

Pandanus fronds. Leaves of the pandanus tree, used to weave mats.

Peat dirt. Soil derived from peat.

Pediatrics. The branch of medicine concerned with the development, care, and diseases of infants and children.

Phoenix. A mythical bird that lives for five hundred years before setting itself on fire atop its funeral pyre. From the ashes there comes a new phoenix to live again. In Chinese custom, the phoenix has a special affinity with music.

Purple dromedaries. Dromedaries are single-humped camels; purple dromedaries are fictitious.

Red money. Money given in red envelopes as one of the customs of the Chinese New Year, a time when debts are paid, conflicts are resolved, and all preparations are made for a fresh start to the new year.

Rheumatism. Painful inflammation of the joints, often of the fingers.

Rictus. A gaping grimace.

Romany. Literally, gypsy; refers to the language used by gypsies and the gypsy homeland.

Runners. Long narrow lengths of fabric; runners made as carpet are used in hallways and those made of finer fabric are used as tablecloths.

Samurai. A caste of Japanese warriors that enforced imperial rule. The samurai were influential from the eleventh to the seventeenth centuries.

Sandalwood. A tree native to Asia; its fragrant wood is often used for carving.

Scythe. Tool with a long curved blade swung over the ground to cut or reap.

Sea swallow. A seabird, also known as a tern.

Seagram's 7. A brand of Canadian whiskey.

Self-immolation. To commit suicide by setting oneself on fire.

Shaolin. A form of martial arts emphasizing strength and speed, developed in northern China. Shaolin temples were places where the martial arts were taught and practiced.

Spirit money. Fake money burned by a dead person's family as a bribe to the gods so they will not harass the deceased's spirit.

Strafed. Bombarded with gunfire from low-flying aircraft.

Talisman. An object supposed to possess magic powers, especially the power to protect the bearer from evil or to bring good luck.

Taro leaves. Leaves of the taro plant, used to wrap food.

Tarry oil. Thick black oil derived from tar.

Teak. Evergreen tree, native to Southeast Asia, used in furniture making and shipbuilding.

Thorazine. An antipsychotic drug.

Tong ax. An ax carried to kill people who are opposed to the Chinese organized-crime syndicate known as the tong.

Totem. A natural object, especially an animal adopted as the emblem of a clan or individual.

Train trestle. A railway bridge.

Transmigration. To change shape by passing into a different body.

Tubercular handkerchiefs. Handkerchiefs used by sufferers of tuberculosis, an infectious bacterial disease of the lungs, to prevent the spread of the disease through coughing.

Tules. Plants that grow in swamps and marshes.

Varicose veins. Abnormally swollen veins, usually in the legs.

Were-person. Kingston's variation of the term "werewolf," a person who is transformed into a wolf at the full moon, but used here to indicate a ghost or malignant spirit.

Wetbacks. Offensive slang term for illegal immigrants, usually applied to Mexican immigrants though Kingston refers to illegal Chinese immigrants.

Whorls. Spirals.

Yellow croaker. A saltwater fish.

Yin and yang. Opposed, yet complementary, elements of Chinese philosophy; yang is the masculine element, aggressive, hot, dry, and bright; yin is the feminine element, receptive, passive, cool, moist, and dark.

Zenith. The highest point of the heavens, directly above the observer. Opposite to nadir.

HISTORICAL EVENTS, PEOPLE, AND PLACES IN *THE WOMAN WARRIOR* AND *CHINA MEN*

Bali. One of the islands of Indonesia.

Canton, Guangzhou. Capital of Kwangtung Province and the largest city in southern China.

Changchow. Or, Chanzhou, a city in eastern China.

Chen Luan-feng. A mythical figure who cut off the leg of Lei Kung, the thunder god.

Chiang Kai-shek (1887–1975). Leader of the Kuomintang, or Nationalist Party, which was defeated by the Communists after three years of civil war. He fled to the island of Formosa, later Taiwan, where the Republic of China was established in 1949.

Ch'in. The Ch'in Dynasty ruled China from 221 to 206 B.C. Kingston refers to the first emperor of Ch'in, Chao Cheng, who ruled from 247 to 206 B.C.

Chung-li Ch'uan. One of the Eight Sages (see below) who is represented as a fat, bearded, wine-drinking hermit.

Confucius (circa 551-478 B.C.). A traveling teacher and sage whose teachings are recorded by his disciples in the *Analects*.

CORE. Congress of Racial Equality, established in 1942 to advance the cause of racial equality.

Eight Sages. Or, the Eight Immortals, eight mythological figures who represent wisdom; although unrelated, they are depicted as a group.

Ellis Island. An island in the Hudson River near New York City where the primary U.S. immigration facility was located between 1892 and 1943.

Five Year Plan. The Communist economic-program, instituted in Soviet Russia, imposed by China's central government. The second Five Year Plan included the failed attempt, known as the Great Leap Forward, to reform agricultural communes.

Gobi Desert. The desert that extends from northern China into southeast Mongolia.

Han people. The dominant ethnic group of China; the term is derived from the Han Dynasty that ruled China from 202 B.C. to 220 A.D.

Hanchow. Or, Hangchow, a city southwest of Shanghai in Chekiang Province.

Hong Kong. Located on the southeast coast of Kwangtung Province; former British colony, returned to Chinese rule in 1997.

I Ching. Or, *The Book of Changes*. An ancient Confucian text of the twelfth century B.C. The hexagrams to which Kingston refers represent different ethical qualities.

Java. The most densely populated of the islands of Indonesia.

Joan of Arc (1412–1431). French girl inspired by the voices of the Catholic saints who regularly spoke to her, she led the French army to victory over the English at Orléans in 1429. She

155

was later captured by the English and burned at the stake as a heretic.

Korean War (1950–1953). The civil war fought between the Communist forces of the North, who were supported by the Soviet Union, and the Nationalists of the South, who were supported by the United States. The conflict ended with the division of the peninsula into North Korea and South Korea.

Kwangtung Province. Or, Guangdong Province; a region of southeast China.

Li T'ieh-kuai. One of the Eight Sages (see above) who is represented as an old man who doctors the poor with medicine carried in the gourd slung over his shoulder.

Long Wall. Otherwise known as the Great Wall of China; construction began in the third century A.D. as a defense against invaders from the North.

Malaya. Part of Malaysia; the peninsula region south of Thailand.

Mao Zedong (Chairman Mao), 1893–1976. Founder of the Chinese Communist Party in 1921 and the first chairman of the People's Republic of China (1949–1959). Until his death, Mao retained control of the Chinese Communist Party.

Middle Nation. A translation of the Chinese word for "China."

Mongols. The nomadic people of Mongolia, which is located to the north of China.

Mount Fuji. The highest mountain in Japan; a dormant volcano sacred to the Japanese.

NAACP. National Association for the Advancement of Colored People, established in 1909 to end segregation and racial discrimination.

Peiping (Beijing). Literally, "northern peace"; the present capital of China.

Shantung. Literally "Eastern Mountains," a northern coastal province of China.

Singapore. An island nation in Southeast Asia; a British colony from 1824 until 1965.

Southern Hsiung-nu. The nomadic people against whom the Great Wall of China was built. From the third century B.C. to the second century A.D. they repeatedly made raids into northern China from their territories in what is now Siberia and Mongolia.

Sun Yat-sen (1866–1925). Leader of the Chinese Kuomintang, the political party that overthrew the Manchu Dynasty in 1911, he was the first provisional president of the Republic of China, in 1911–1912, and later its ruler, from 1923 until his death.

Taiwan. Formerly the island of Formosa, located off the coast of China. In 1949 the Chinese Nationalists, led by Chiang Kai-shek, established the Republic of China in Taiwan.

SELECTED BIBLIOGRAPHY

PRIMARY SOURCES

BOOKS

China Men. New York: Knopf, 1980.

Hawai'i One Summer: 1978. San Francisco: Meadow Press, 1987.

Through the Black Curtain. Berkeley: Friends of the Bancroft Library/University of California, 1987.

Tripmaster Monkey: His Fake Book. New York: Knopf, 1989.

The Woman Warrior: Memoirs of a Girlhood among Ghosts. New York: Knopf, 1976.

ESSAYS

"The Coming Book." In *The Writer on Her Work,* edited by Janet Sternberg. New York: Norton, 1980.

"Cultural Misreadings by American Reviewers." In *Asian and Western Writers in Dialogue: New Cultural Identities,* edited by Guy Amirthanayagam. London: Macmillan, 1982.

"Exploring Old Myths in a Contemporary American Voice." *Humanities Discourse,* 2 (1988): 3–5.

"Finding a Voice." By Kingston. In *Language: Readings in Language and Culture,* edited by Virginia P. Clark, Paul A. Eschholz and Alfred F. Rosa. New York: St. Martin's Press, 1998.

"Forward." By Kingston and Thich Nhat Hanh. *Learning True Love: How I Learned and Practiced Social Change in Vietnam,* edited by Sister Chân Không. Berkeley: Parallax Press, 1993.

"How Are You? I Am Fine, Thank You. And You?" In *The State of the Language,* edited by Christopher Ricks and Leonard Michaels. Berkeley: University of California Press, 1980.

"Literature in a Scientific Age: Lorenz's *King Solomon's Ring.*" *English Journal,* 62 (January 1973): 30–32.

"The Novel's Next Step: From the Novel of the Americas to the Global Novel." In *The Novel in the Americas,* edited by Raymond Leslie Williams. Niwot: University Press of Colorado, 1992.

"Personal Statement." In *Approaches to Teaching Maxine Hong Kingston's* The Woman Warrior. Shirley Geok-lin Lim. New York: Modern Language Association, 1991.

"Postscript as Process." In *The Bedford Reader,* edited by X. J. Kennedy and Dorothy M. Kennedy. New York: St. Martin's Press, 1985.

"Precepts for the Twentieth Century." In *For a Future to be Possible: Commentaries on the Five Wonderful Precepts.* By Thich Nhat Hanh, Robert Aitken, and others. Berkeley: Parallax Press, 1993.

"Reservations about China." *Ms.* (October 1978): 67–68.

"San Francisco's China Town: A View from the Other Side of Arnold Genthe's Camera." *American Heritage,* 30 (December 1978): 36–47.

"Violence and Non-Violence in China, 1989." *Michigan Quarterly Review* (Winter 1990): 62.

"A Writer's Notebook from the Far East," *Ms.* (January 1983), pp. 85–86.

SECONDARY SOURCES

INTERVIEWS

Skenazy, Paul and Tera Martin, eds. *Conversations with Maxine Hong Kingston.* Jackson: University Press of Mississippi, 1998. Brings together sixteen interviews, with an introduction by the editors and a chronology of Kingston's life and career.

Thompson, Phyllis Hoge. "This Is the Story I Heard: A Conversation with Maxine Hong Kingston and Earll Kingston." *Biography,* 6 (Winter 1983): 1–12.

BASIC REFERENCE WORKS

Lim, Shirley Geok-lin, ed. *Approaches to Teaching Kingston's* The Woman Warrior. New York: Modern Language Association, 1991. A collection of essays with a pedagogical bias; useful discussions of Kingston's formal experimentation, her use of traditional Chinese sources, and ways of approaching the text in the classroom.

Madsen, Deborah L. *Maxine Hong Kingston.* Gale Study Guides to Great Literature: Literary Masterpieces, volume 9. Detroit: Gale/Manly, 2000.

Simmons, Diane. *Maxine Hong Kingston.* New York: Twayne, 1999. A comprehensive account of Kingston's work to date. Simmons includes an extensive biographical essay and a brief interview with Kingston as well as close textual analyses of *The Woman Warrior, China Men,* and *Tripmaster Monkey.* She devotes two extensive chapters to discussion of *The Woman Warrior.*

Wong, Sau-ling Cynthia, ed., *Maxine Hong Kingston's* The Woman Warrior: *A Casebook.* New York & Oxford: Oxford University Press, 1999. A useful collection representing the characteristic approaches to the text, the issues discussed, and the historical development of criticism of the text.

ASIAN AMERICAN LITERATURE

Hune, Shirley, and others, eds. *Asian Americans: Comparative and Global Perspectives.* Pullman: Washington State University Press, 1991.

Lim, Shirley Geok-lin, and Amy Ling, eds. *Reading the Literatures of Asian America.* Philadelphia: Temple University Press, 1992.

Ling, Amy. *Between Worlds: Women Writers of Chinese Ancestry.* New York & Oxford: Pergamon Press, 1990.

Ling. "Chinamerican Women Writers: Four Forerunners of Maxine Hong Kingston." In *Gender/Body/Knowledge: Feminist Reconstructions of Being and Knowing,* edited by Alison Jaggar and Susan Bordo. New Brunswick, N.J.: Rutgers University Press, 1989).

Ling. "Chinese American Women Writers: The Tradition Behind Maxine Hong Kingston." In *Redefining American Literary History,* edited by A. LaVonne Brown Ruoff and Jerry W. Ward. New York: Modern Language Association, 1990.

CRITICAL STUDIES

Blinde, Patricia Lin. "The Icicle in the Desert: Perspective and Form in the Works of Two Chinese-American Women Writers." *MELUS,* 6, no. 3 (1979): 51–71. Discussion of the autobiographical work of Kingston and Jade Snow Wong.

Buss, Helen M. "Memoir with an Attitude: One Reader Reads *The Woman Warrior: Memoirs of a Girlhood among Ghosts.*" *A-B: Auto-Biography Studies*, 12 (Fall 1997): 203–224.

Castillo, Debra A. "The Daily Shape of Horses: Denise Chávez and Maxine Hong Kingston." *Dispositio*, 16, no. 4 (1991): 29–43.

Cheung, King-Kok. *Articulate Silences: Hisaye Yamamoto, Maxine Hong Kingston, Joy Kogawa*. Ithaca: Cornell University Press, 1993. Places Kingston within the context of significant Asian American women writers.

Cheung. "'Don't Tell': Imposed Silences in *The Color Purple* and *The Woman Warrior.*" *PMLA*, 103 (March 1988): 162–174.

Cheung. "Self-Fulfilling Visions in *The Woman Warrior* and *Thousand Pieces of Gold.*" *Biography*, 13 (Spring 1990): 143–153.

Cheung. "*The Woman Warrior* versus *The Chinaman Pacific*: Must a Chinese American Critic Choose between Feminism and Heroism?" In *Conflicts in Feminism*, edited by Marianne Hirsch and Evelyn Fox Keller. New York: Routledge, 1990.

Chun, Gloria. "The High Note of the Barbarian Reed Pipe: Maxine Hong Kingston." *Journal of Ethnic Studies*, 19 (Fall 1991): 85–94.

Dasenbrock, Reed Way. "Intelligibility and Meaningfulness in Multicultural Literature in English." *PMLA*, 102 (January 1987): 10–19.

Donaldson, Mara E. "Woman as Hero in Margaret Atwood's *Surfacing* and Maxine Hong Kingston's *The Woman Warrior.*" In *Heroines of Popular Culture*, edited by Pat Browne. Bowling Green, Ohio: Bowling Green State University Popular Press, 1987.

Eakin, Paul John. *Fictions in Autobiography: Studies in the Art of Self-Invention*. Princeton: Princeton University Press, 1985. Includes a relatively early discussion of Kingston's innovative use of the autobiographical form within a generic context.

Fong, Bobby. "Maxine Hong Kingston's Autobiographical Strategy in *The Woman Warrior.*" *Biography*, 12 (Spring 1989): 116–126.

Friedman, Susan Stanford. "Women's Autobiographical Selves: Theory and Practice." In *The Private Self: Theory and Practice of Women's Autobiographical Writings*, edited by Shari Benstock. Chapel Hill: University of North Carolina Press, 1988.

Frye, Joanne S. "*The Woman Warrior*: Claiming Narrative Power, Re-creating Female Selfhood." In *Faith of a (Woman) Writer*, edited by Alice Kessler Harris and William McBrien. Westport, Conn.: Greenwood Press, 1988.

Henke, Suzette A. "Women's Life-Writing and the Minority Voice: Maya Angelou, Maxine Hong Kingston, and Alice Walker." In *Traditions, Voices, and Dreams: The American Novel Since the 1960s*, edited by Melvin J. Friedman and Ben Siegel. Newark: University of Delaware Press, 1995.

Hunt, Linda. "'I Could Not Figure Out What Was My Village': Gender vs. Ethnicity in Maxine Hong Kingston's *The Woman Warrior.*" *MELUS*, 12 (Fall 1985): 5–12. A discussion of the interplay between racial and gender issues.

Juhasz, Suzanne. "Maxine Hong Kingston: Narrative Technique and Female Identity." In *Contemporary American Women Writers: Narrative Strategies*, edited by Catherine Rainwater and William J. Scheick. Lexington: University Press of Kentucky, 1985. Analysis of Kingston's narrative technique in *The Woman Warrior* by comparison with *China Men*.

Krauss, Karoline. "Identity as a Textual Event: *The Woman Warrior* by Maxine

Hong Kingston." *Utah Foreign Language Review,* 2 (1992–1993): 147–158.

Lappas, Catherine. "'The Way I Heard It Was . . .': Myth, Memory, and Autobiography in *Storyteller* and *The Woman Warrior,*" *CEA Critic,* 57 (Fall 1994): 57–67. A comparative discussion of Kingston and the Native American writer Leslie Marmon Silko.

Lee, Rachel. "Claiming Land, Claiming Voice, Claiming Canon: Institutionalized Challenges in Kingston's *China Men* and *The Woman Warrior.*" In *Reviewing Asian America: Locating Diversity,* edited by Wendy L. Ng and others. Pullman: Washington State University Press, 1995.

Lee, Robert A. "Ethnic Renaissance: Rudolfo Anaya, Louise Erdrich, and Maxine Hong Kingston." In *The New American Writing: Essays on American Literature Since 1970,* edited by Graham Clarke. New York: St. Martin's Press, 1990.

Li, David Leiwei. "The Naming of a Chinese American 'I': Cross-Cultural Sign/ifications in *The Woman Warrior.*" *Criticism,* 30 (Fall 1988): 497–515.

Lidoff, Joan. "Autobiography in a Different Voice: Maxine Hong Kingston's *The Woman Warrior.*" *A-B: Auto-Biography Studies,* 3 (Fall 1987): 29–35.

Ling, Amy. "Thematic Threads in Maxine Hong Kingston's *The Woman Warrior.*" *Tamkang Review,* 14 (Autumn 1983–Summer 1984): 155–164.

Madsen, Deborah L. "(Dis)Figuration: The Body as Icon in the Writings of Maxine Hong Kingston." *Yearbook of English Studies,* 24 (1994): 237–250.

Melchior, Bonnie. "A Marginal 'I': The Autobiographical Self Deconstructed in Maxine Hong Kingston's *The Woman Warrior.*" *Biography,* 17 (Summer 1994): 281–295.

Miller, Margaret. "Threads of Identity in Maxine Hong Kingston's *Woman Warrior.*" *Biography,* 6 (Winter 1983): 13–33.

Mitchell, Carol. "'Talking Story' in *The Woman Warrior:* An Analysis of the Use of Folklore." *Kentucky Folklore Record,* 27 (January–June 1981): 5–12.

Morante, Linda. "From Silence to Song: The Triumph of Maxine Hong Kingston." *Frontiers,* 9, no. 2 (1987): 78–82.

Nishime, LeiLana. "Engendering Genre: Gender and Nationalism in *China Men* and *The Woman Warrior,*" *MELUS,* 20 (Spring 1995): 67–82.

Ordonez, Elizabeth J. "Narrative Texts by Ethnic Women: Rereading the Past, Reshaping the Future." *MELUS,* 9 (Winter 1982): 19–28.

Outka, Paul. "Publish or Perish: Food, Hunger, and Self-Construction in Maxine Hong Kingston's *The Woman Warrior.*" *Contemporary Literature,* 38 (Fall 1997): 447–482.

Rabine, Leslie W. "No Lost Paradise: Social Gender and Symbolic Gender in the Writings of Maxine Hong Kingston." *Signs,* 12 (Spring 1987): 471–492. Rabine uses French feminist theory to distinguish between gender as a system of social relations and gender as an effect of discourse and applies these ideas to Kingston's representation of gender.

Rolf, Robert. "On Maxine Hong Kingston and *The Woman Warrior.*" *Kyushu American Literature,* 23 (May 1982): 1–10.

Rose, Shirley K. "Metaphors and Myths of Cross-Cultural Literacy: Autobiographical Narratives by Maxine Hong Kingston, Richard Rodriguez, and Malcolm X." *MELUS,* 14 (Spring 1987): 3–15.

Sato, Gayle K. Fujita. "Ghosts as Chinese-American Constructs in Maxine Hong Kingston's *The Woman Warrior.*" In *Haunting the House of Fiction: Feminist Perspectives on Ghost Stories by American Women,* edited by

Lynette Carpenter and Wendy K. Kolmar. Knoxville: University of Tennessee Press, 1991.

Schueller, Malini. "Questioning Race and Gender Definitions: Dialogic Subversions in *The Woman Warrior*." *Criticism*, 31 (Fall 1989): 421–437.

Wang, Veronica. "Reality and Fantasy: The Chinese-American Woman's Quest for Identity." *MELUS*, 12 (Fall 1985): 23–31.

Wong, Sau-ling Cynthia. "Necessity and Extravagance in Maxine Hong Kingston's *The Woman Warrior:* Art and the Ethnic Experience." *MELUS*, 15 (Spring 1988): 4–26.

INDEX

A

"The Adventures of Lo Bun Sun" (Kingston) 16
"Alaska China Men" (Kingston) 16
Alger, Horatio 130
"The American Father" (Kingston) 13, 16
American Literary History 89
Angelou, Maya 126, 136
Anthony, Susan B. 115
Apana, Chang 82
"At the Western Palace" (Kingston) 1, 3, 10–11, 23, 41, 58
"Autobiography as Guided Chinatown Tour? Maxine Hong Kingston's *The Woman Warrior* and the Chinese American Autobiographical Controversy" (Wong) 72, 84
"Autobiography in a Different Voice: *The Woman Warrior* and the Question of Genre" (Lidoff) 74

B

Beloved (Morrison) 126
Bergland, Betty Ann 90
Berkeley Repertory Theatre 122–124
Between Worlds: Women Writers of Chinese Ancestry (Ling) 130
Biggers, Earl Derr 82
Blake, William 85
Blinde, Patricia Lin 129
The Bluest Eye (Morrison) 68, 136–138, 141
Bone (Ng) 61, 63–65
"The Brother in Vietnam" (Kingston) 13, 17, 58, 118
Burlingame Treaty of 1868 111
Butler, Judith 93

C

Cavendish, Margaret 69
Chan, Jeffery Paul 73, 84–85
Charke, Charlotte 69
Chávez, Denise 129
Chiang Kai-shek 109
Chin, Frank 72–73, 81–82, 91, 120
Chin, Marilyn 107, 120
China Men (Kingston)
    character profiles 24–27
    plot summary 12–17
    themes 47–68
"*China Men*: Maxine Hong Kingston and the American Canon" (Li) 89
The Chinaman Pacific and Frisco R. R. Co.: Eight Stories (Chin) 82
Chinese Exclusion Act of 1882 112
Chung Wah Chinese School 19
Cisneros, Sandra 83–84, 126, 129
Civil Rights Act of 1964 117
Cixous, Hélène 121
The Color Purple (Walker) 68, 135–137, 141
Compromise Formations: Current Directions in Psychoanalytic Criticism 87
Confucius 134
Contemporary American Women Writers 78
Conversations with Maxine Hong Kingston 3, 12, 17, 39, 41, 44, 52, 54, 71, 73, 92, 109, 124, 128, 130, 138
Corregidora (Jones) 136
Critical Essays on Maxine Hong Kingston 118, 131
Critique: Studies in Contemporary Fiction 95
"Cultural Mis-readings by American Reviewers" (Kingston) 75, 77

D

Defoe, Daniel 17
Derrida, Jacques 121

E

"Eighteen Stanzas for a Barbarian Reed Pipe" (Kingston) 24
"Engendering Genre: Gender and Nationalism in *China Men* and *The Woman Warrior*" (Nishime) 92–93
Et l'une ne bouge pas sans l'autre (Irigaray) 84
Evans, Martha Noel 88

F

"The Father from China" (Kingston) 12–14
The Feminine Mystique (Friedan) 53–54, 116
Fifth Chinese Daughter (Wong) 129–130
"Filiality and Women's Autobiographical Storytelling" (Smith) 79–81
Firestone, Shulamith 115
Foucault, Michel 121
Freud, Sigmund 97
Friedan, Betty 53–55, 57, 115–116
Fuller, Margaret 115

G

Genthe, Arnold 48
"The Ghostmate" (Kingston) 14
Gilman, Charlotte Perkins 115
"The Grandfather of the Sierra Nevada Mountains" (Kingston) 12, 15, 111
"Great Grandfather of the Sandalwood Mountains" (Kingston) 40
"The Great Grandfather of the Sandalwood Mountains" (Kingston) 12, 15

H

Hagedorn, Jessica 120
Hawaii Observer 39

Henderson, Katherine 66
Henry, William A., III 124
Hoge Thompson, Phyllis 40–42, 44
Hong, Tom 18, 30, 109
Hong, Ying Lan Chew 18–20, 110
hooks, bell 92
Horton, Karen 39
The House on Mango Street (Cisneros) 126, 128–129
"The Hundred-Year-Old Man" (Kingston) 17
Hwang, David Henry 81–82

I

I Know Why the Caged Bird Sings (Angelou) 126, 136
"Immigration and Diaspora" (Lim) 94
Immigration and Nationality Act of 1952 112
In the American Grain (Williams) 89
Incidents in the Life of a Slave Girl (Jacobs) 126
An Interethnic Companion to Asian American Literature 94
"Introduction to Jacques Lacan's Lecture: The Neurotic's Individual Myth" (Evans) 88
Irigaray, Luce 84, 97
Islas, Arturo 37, 42

J

Jacobs, Harriet 126
Jang, Jon 122
Johnson, Lyndon B. 118
Jones, Gayl 136
The Joy Luck Club (Tan) 65–67, 95–96, 120, 131–132
Juhasz, Suzanne 78, 96

K

Kempe, Margery 69
Kennedy, John F. 116, 118
King, Martin Luther, Jr. 117
Kingston, Maxine Hong
    biographical information 18–21

on Asian American autobiographies 131
on biography 44
on *China Men* 3
on creativity 41
on exclusion 109
on fiction and nonfiction 118
on ghosts 52
on her critics 72–73, 75, 77
on Jade Snow Wong 130
on memory 54
on myth 92
on narrative style 71
on the Lo Bun Sun episode in *China Men* 17
on the origin of *China Men* 39
on the reception of her work by contemporary Chinese writers 107
on the relationship between *The Woman Warrior* and *China Men* 12
on the stage adaption of *The Woman Warrior* 122–124
on Toni Morrison 138
on Virginia Woolf 128
writing techniques 37–45
"Kingston's Handling of Traditional Chinese Sources" (Wong) 95
"Kingston's *The Woman Warrior*: The Object of Autobiographical Relations" (Miller) 87–89
Kissinger, Henry 110
The Kitchen God's Wife (Tan) 65, 67, 95, 134
Kubota, Gary 39, 45

L

Lacan, Jacques 88, 121
"The Lady Becomes the Tiger" (Henry) 124
The Last of the Menu Girls (Chávez) 129
"The Laws" (Kingston) 16, 33, 111–112
Lee, Ming Cho 122
Leonard, John 37, 39
"The Li Sao: An Elegy" (Kingston) 17
Li, David Leiwei 89
Lidoff, Joan 74–75
Lim, Shirley Geok-lin 89, 94, 107
Ling, Amy 130
Look Homeward, Angel (Wolfe) 124

M

M. Butterfly (Hwang) 81
Madame Butterfly (Puccini) 81
Mahler, Margaret 87
"The Making of More Americans" (Kingston) 13, 16
Malcolm X 75
Malloy, Michael T. 77
Mao Zedong 109–110
Martin, Tera 120
Martineau, Harriet 69
"Maxine Hong Kingston: Narrative Technique and Female Identity" (Juhasz) 78–79
Maxine Hong Kingston's The Woman Warrior: A Casebook 80, 82, 84
McKunn, Ruth-Anne Lumm 120
McMahon, Alan 77
MELUS 79, 84, 92, 94
"Metaphors and Myths of Cross-Cultural Literacy: Autobiographical Narratives by Maxine Hong Kingston, Richard Rodriguez and Malcolm X" (Rose) 75
Miller, Elise 87, 98
Millett, Kate 115
Morante, Linda 103
Morrison, Toni 68, 126, 135–140
"The Most Popular Book in China" (Chin) 82
Mukherjee, Bharati 120
Mulan 24
Multicultural Autobiography: American Lives 84

N

National Observer 77
National Organization for Women (NOW) 57, 116
Nationality Act of 1870 111
Naylor, Gloria 140
"Necessity and Extravagance in Maxine Hong Kingston's *The Woman Warrior*: Art and the Ethnic Experience" (Wong) 84–87, 101
New West 78
New York Review of Books 92
New York Times 37
New York Times Book Review 41
Ng, Fae Myenne 61, 64
Nishime, LeiLani 92

Nixon, Richard M. 110, 118, 120
"No Lost Paradise: Social Gender and Symbolic Gender in the Writings of Maxine Hong Kingston" (Rabine) 83–84, 99
"No Name Woman" (Kingston) 1, 3–5, 22, 50–51, 70, 79, 88–89, 101, 104

O

"On Discovery" (Kingston) 13
"On Fathers" (Kingston) 13
"On Listening" (Kingston) 17
"On Mortality" (Kingston) 15
"On Mortality Again" (Kingston) 15
Orlando (Woolf) 128
Ott, Sharon 122, 125

P

Parks, Rosa 117
"Personal Statement" (Kingston) 107
Pfaff, Timothy 45
"Photography and the Status of Truth in Maxine Hong Kingston's *China Men*" (Zackodnik) 94
A Poetics of Women's Autobiography: Marginality and the Fictions of Self-Representation (Smith) 69, 79–80
Puccini, Giancomo 81

R

Rabine, Leslie W. 82–83, 97, 99, 105
Rabinowitz, Paula 40
"Reality and Fantasy: The Chinese-American Woman's Quest for Identity" (Wang) 79
Redefining American Literary History 89
"Representing Ethnicity in Autobiography" (Bergland) 90–92
"Reservations About China" (Kingston) 83
Robinson Crusoe (Defoe) 17
Rodriguez, Richard 75
Roe v Wade 116
Rogin, Deborah 122, 124–125
Rose, Shirley K. 75

S

Schroeder, Eric J. 68, 122, 135
"The Semiotics of China Narratives in the Contexts of Kingston and Tan" (Yuan) 95–96
Seventeen Syllables (Yamamoto) 120
"Shaman" (Kingston) 1, 8–10, 22, 113
Signs 83
Skenazy, Paul 18, 120
Smith, Sidonie 69, 71–72, 75, 79–80, 96
"A Song for a Barbarian Reed Pipe" (Kingston) 1, 3, 10–12, 42, 70
Stanton, Elizabeth Cady 115
Steinem, Gloria 115
Stockton, California 17–20, 39, 76–78, 114
Sun Yat-sen 47, 109, 113

T

Tan, Amy 61, 65–67, 95, 120, 130–134, 139
Thieu, Nguyen Van 120
"This is Not an Autobiography" (Chin) 73
Time 107
Tong, Benjamin 73, 84–85
"Twelve Asian American Writers: In Search of Self-Definition" (Lim) 89–90

U

University of California, Berkeley 115
"The Unmanly Warrior" (Chin) 81–82, 91

V

Vietnam War 58, 60, 118, 120
Voting Rights Act of 1965 117

W

Walker, Alice 68, 135–137
Wang, Veronica 79
War Bride Act of 1946 112
"White Tigers" (Kingston) 1, 5–8, 24, 41, 110, 117

"The Wild Man of the Green Swamp" (Kingston) 16
Williams, William Carlos 89
The Woman Warrior: A Memoir of a Girlhood Among Ghosts (Kingston)
    character profiles 21–24
    plot summary 1–12
    stage adaption 122–125
    themes 47–68
The Women of Brewster Place (Naylor) 140
Wong, Jade Snow 129–130
Wong, Sau-ling Cynthia 72–74, 84, 91, 95, 101, 104, 107
Woolf, Virginia 128

Y

Yalom, Marilyn 37, 42
Yamamoto, Hisaye 120
Yearbook of English Studies 90
Yezierska, Anzia 83–84
Yuan Shih-k'ai 109
Yuan, Yuan 95

Z

Zackodnik, Teresa C. 94